THREE-
MARTINI
AFTERNOONS
AT
THE RITZ

THREE-MARTINI AFTERNOONS AT THE RITZ

◆

The Rebellion of
Sylvia Plath & Anne Sexton

GAIL CROWTHER

G

GALLERY BOOKS

NEW YORK   LONDON   TORONTO   SYDNEY   NEW DELHI

G

Gallery Books
An Imprint of Simon & Schuster, Inc.
1230 Avenue of the Americas
New York, NY 10020

This Gallery Books trade paperback edition January 2022

GALLERY BOOKS and colophon are registered
trademarks of Simon & Schuster, Inc.

For information about special discounts for bulk purchases,
please contact Simon & Schuster Special Sales at 1-866-506-1949
or business@simonandschuster.com.

The Simon & Schuster Speakers Bureau can bring authors
to your live event. For more information or to book an event, contact
the Simon & Schuster Speakers Bureau at 1-866-248-3049
or visit our website at www.simonspeakers.com.

Interior design by Michelle Marchese

Manufactured in the United States of America

1   3   5   7   9   10   8   6   4   2

Library of Congress Cataloging-in-Publication Data
is available for the hardcover.

ISBN 978-1-9821-3839-4
ISBN 978-1-9821-3842-4 (pbk)
ISBN 978-1-9821-3843-1 (ebook)

For my parents and my sister

Contents

Kicking at the
Door of Fame

In 1950s America, women were not supposed to be ambitious.
When Sylvia Plath graduated from Smith College in 1955,
her commencement speaker, Adlai Stevenson, praised the female
graduates and pronounced the purpose of their education was
so they could be entertaining and well-informed wives when
their husbands returned home from work. The postwar ideals
of domesticity, the nuclear family, and the white middle-class
woman who stayed at home dominated American thought until
the mid-1960s. For those with enough privilege, a woman's place
was ensuring that a strong family unit would mean a strong,
united society. Women were respected for not pursuing their own
careers or ambitions. So, they had a lot to look forward to then.

Six years after graduation, when she was writing *The Bell Jar*,
Plath satirized this viewpoint with the memorable lines: "What

a man is is an arrow into the future, and what a woman is is the place the arrow shoots off from."[1] But subversively, Plath's narrator, the sassy and wry Esther Greenwood, declared, "The trouble was, I hated the idea of serving men in any way."[2] Far from planning to be a well-informed and interesting wife, Plath's protagonist wanted an ambitious and varied future on her own terms. She rejected gendered double standards in all their forms, declaring that if men could do what they wanted and have sex with whom they wanted, so could she. One can only imagine how men must have withered beneath her gaze. Upon her first glimpse of male genitalia, Esther Greenwood pondered, "The only thing I could think of was turkey neck and turkey gizzards and I felt very depressed."[3] (Hetero)sexual liberation had its drawbacks.

In 1959, when Anne Sexton won a fellowship to study poetry under the greatly respected American poet Theodore Roethke, she wrote sarcastically to her poet friend Carolyn Kizer that he probably wouldn't like her work and she'd be left sobbing in her "cave of womanhood." More seriously, though, Sexton described the frustration of "kicking at the door of fame that men run and own and won't give us the password for."[4]

But in 1950s America, Sylvia Plath and Anne Sexton met for the first time. Both were emerging poets, and both were hugely ambitious women in a cultural moment that did not know how to deal with ambitious women. They realized that to pursue their desire to be writers would require determination, energy, and resilience. Operating in a male-dominated discipline was not easy, and their rebellion against the status quo seethed just below the surface.

Curiously, Plath and Sexton both grew up in Wellesley, a suburb of Boston, but never met during their teenage years. When their paths did finally cross, Plath was twenty-six and Sexton was thirty. Their meeting was dramatic and literary, in a writing workshop at Boston University run by the well-known poet Robert Lowell. Throughout the spring of 1959, on a Tuesday afternoon between 2 and 4 p.m., Plath and Sexton shared the same seminar space, room 222 at 236 Bay State Road. This room still exists today: tiny, with creaking wooden floors, a book-lined wall, and three airy windows offering a glimpse of the Charles River. It is a space that seems too small to have housed the personalities of Lowell, Sexton, and Plath. Sexton described it as "a dismal room the shape of a shoe box. It was a bleak spot, as if it had been forgotten for years, like the spinning room in Sleeping Beauty's castle."[5] The two women spent hours reading their poems, listening to about eighteen other students, and taking advice from Lowell about what they were working on. The atmosphere was mostly awkward silences, slight terror at having their poems chosen for discussion, and equal terror at having them ignored. Poet Kathleen Spivack, who attended these classes as an undergraduate student, wrote, "The experience of being there was nerve-racking."[6] Lowell dominated with one question he repeated again and again, "But what does the poem really *mean*?" Often long, uncomfortable silences would follow, and students would make embarrassed eye contact with each other or shift nervously in their seats. Sometimes, for Sexton, the silences would get too much "so I act like a bitch . . . [H]e will be dissecting some great poem and will say 'Why is this line so good. What makes it good?' and there is total silence. Everyone afraid to speak. And finally, because I can stand it no longer, I speak up saying, 'I don't think it's so good at all. You would never allow us sloppy language like that.'"[7] Students also observed Lowell's moods and manic depression with some alarm, noticing how during certain seminars he simply seemed, in Sexton's words, "so gracefully insane." Insomuch as he was a brilliant poet-critic, he could be distracted and vague, and would become increasingly obsessed with the same point during his manic phases. He could lash out at students if they said the wrong thing or irritated him. One April afternoon, he was so agitated that they became convinced he was about to throw himself out the window. In fact, immediately after the class, he was admitted to McLean Hospital on the outskirts of Boston, where Plath had already been a patient and Sexton would eventually become one.

Although during these sessions Plath and Sexton tentatively circled each other, Lowell finally paired them up. Perhaps he saw a similarity that neither woman could see. Perhaps he saw thematic connections in their work. Or maybe it was just chance. Whatever it was, the two women were then connected and forced to work together, and from this point on their friendship took a different turn. Plath had a grudging respect for Sexton and was ambivalent in her praise. Her journal notes that Lowell had "set me up with Ann [*sic*] Sexton, an honor, I suppose. Well about time. She has very good things, and they get better, though there is a lot of loose stuff."[8] Sexton, on the other hand, was keen to indicate that *she* was the trailblazer whom Plath, and other poets, followed: "She heard, and George Starbuck heard, that I was auditing a class at Boston University given by Robert Lowell. They kind of followed me in . . ."[9] What Sexton's casual claim overlooks was her insecurity and fear at asking to be admitted. Her exchange of letters with Robert Lowell reveal a nervous, apologetic-sounding Sexton admitting that she is not a graduate, has not been to college, and has been writing for only a year. Included with the letter are manuscripts of "The Musicians," "Consorting with Angels," "Man and Wife," and "Mother and Jack and the Rain." Lowell responded warmly, assuring Sexton that of course she qualified for the course and that he had read her poems with admiration and envy. An elated Sexton replied, saying she planned to frame his letter and would require no further praise from anyone for "possibly a month."[10]

As with all small literary circles there was competition and jealousy among the same people applying for the same prizes, fellowships, and publishing opportunities. Literary life in the cobbled streets of the Beacon Hill area of Boston brimmed with poets: Plath, Sexton, Lowell, Starbuck, Ted Hughes, Adrienne Rich, and W. S. Merwin. Plath immediately felt direct competition and rivalry over awards such as the Yale Series of Younger Poets prize, an award she coveted (but much to her fury finally went to George Starbuck).

Students who audited Lowell's class recalled the polar differences between Sexton and Plath, who each in her own way created an atmosphere of awe. Sexton was often late, all breezy and open, jangling with jewelry, wearing brightly printed dresses and glamorous hairstyles, and chain-smoking. According to Spivack, Sexton was a soft presence in the class, observing keenly with her green eyes behind cigarette smoke. She used her shoe as an ashtray. Her late entrances were dramatic as she stood in the doorway, dropping books and papers and cigarette stubs, while the men in the class jumped to their feet and found her a seat. Her hands shook when she read her poems aloud.

Plath on the other hand was mostly silent and often turned up early. Spivack would find her already seated at the table when she arrived, astonishingly still and perfectly composed. Her pencil would be poised over a notebook, or she would be reading and paying no attention to the comings and goings, the chair scrapings and nervous coughing. Occasionally Spivack found Plath a little restless and preoccupied, pleasant but noncommittal, with an intent, unnerving stare. In contrast to Sexton's appearance, Plath wore her hair pulled severely into a bun and owned a range of sensible buttoned-up shirts and cardigans. Her camel hair coat would either be carefully folded over the back of her chair or wrapped around her shoulders. She mostly took the seat at the foot of the table, directly opposite Lowell, and was the only student there who was not out-intellectualized by him. None of his obscure references were obscure to Plath; she was impeccably educated. When she did speak it was often to make a devastating comment about somebody else's work, though she could be equally brilliant at analyzing structure, rhythms, and scanning. Most students were afraid of her. While outwardly Plath seemed self-contained and critical, those sharing the room with her could not have known the doubt, agony, and longing she was pouring into her journals: "I have a vision of the poems I would write, but do not. When will they come?"[11] she asked plaintively in March 1959.

At this early stage in their writing careers, both Sexton and Plath were married, seemingly living the conventional lifestyle expected of white, middle-class, heterosexual American women lucky enough to have a certain level of privilege. Sexton's husband, Alfred Muller Sexton II, known as Kayo, worked in her family's business selling wool samples. Plath's husband, Ted Hughes, was an increasingly well-known poet whose success at that stage easily eclipsed Plath's. But running alongside this surface acceptance of the dutiful housewife was an underlying rejection of suffocating gender roles and expectations. Plath mostly vented these frustrations in her journals, complaining about herself, her husband, her writer's block, and her fury at rejections and failed applications. Sexton took lovers, and in the spring of 1959 she began an affair with her classmate George Starbuck. He, too, was an emerging poet and a junior editor at the publishing house Houghton Mifflin. The poet-editor Peter Davison recalls Starbuck being "all knees and elbows, tall as a crane with great shadows under his eyes, and a slow melancholy, throw-away manner of speaking . . ."[12] This affair developed under the watchful and disapproving eye of Plath, who decided the best way to deal with it was to turn it into a story: "Here is horror. And all the details."[13]

The affair was almost certainly sparked by the after-class drinking that Plath, Sexton, and Starbuck started soon after encountering one another. Following the seminar, the three of them would pile into the front seat of Sexton's old Ford Saloon and drive through Boston to the Ritz-Carlton on the edge of the Public Garden. Here, Sexton would pull into a loading-only zone, yelling at bemused hotel workers, "It's okay, because we are only going to get loaded!"[14] Then Starbuck would hold out his arms and Plath and Sexton would take one each and drink, in Sexton's words, "three or four or two martinis"[15] in the lounge bar of the hotel. Sexton recalled the hushed quiet, plush, dark-red carpeting, leather chairs, and white-coated waiters serving the best of Boston. The three young poets hoped they might be mistaken for Hollywood types with their books, poems, and fiery conversations.

The two women must have realized at this point the many ways in which they were linked and the sensibilities they shared. Poised at the magnificent door of the Ritz, it is tempting to look back through a ghostly history to imagine the conversations that must have taken place over martinis and free potato chips. Both women were demonstrative and enthusiastic talkers, becoming relaxed and louder as they drank more alcohol. If, as Sexton claimed, the conversations were fiery, they must have been talking about things that mattered to them. What might those topics have been? We get tantalizing glimpses and memories, details here and there from journals and letters. Although they came from very different economic backgrounds, both women had overbearing and emotionally demanding mothers. From a young age, both were ambitious in a subversive gendered way, thinking and acting in a manner that was regarded as unusual for women at that time. Neither accepted the double standards regarding sexual pleasure, relationships, marriage, children, and careers. They could only cope with domestic and social expectations if they gave priority to their own time and ambitions. Women were not supposed to even think this in 1950s America, nor were they supposed to leave their husbands waiting for them at home while they went out to drink martinis with friends and lovers in the middle of the afternoon.

Family, poetry, husbands, sex, and Boston gossip in general were all fascinating topics. But Plath and Sexton shared an experience that overshadowed all other conversations that took place at the Ritz bar: they had both survived suicide attempts and mental illness. "We talked death with burned-up intensity,"[16] said Sexton. Yes, they knew, in Sexton's phrasing, that it was "sick," but they felt death made them more real. Plath had survived a suicide attempt six years earlier when, at age twenty, she hid away in a crawl space of the family home and took a large quantity of sleeping pills. Although this was a determined effort to die, Plath took too many pills and vomited them back up. She gradually came to consciousness two days later with a nasty gash under her right eye where she had repeatedly banged her head on the concrete ground. Sexton had survived numerous suicide attempts, all overdoses, some more serious than others.

These death conversations were treated as scandalous gossip, swapping stories in loving detail under the mostly silent gaze of George Starbuck. "It is a wonder we didn't depress George with our egocentricity,"[17] wrote Sexton. Both women were seeing therapists, and Sexton was completely open about this. Her daughter Linda observed that her mother had no sense of privacy, so if death and suicide were on the table, it seems likely therapy would be too. After their afternoon drinking at the Ritz, they would weave through the streets of Boston to the Waldorf Cafeteria on Tremont Street for a seventy-cent dinner and then Sexton would drive to an evening appointment with her psychiatrist in the city. Plath was in weekly therapy sessions with Dr. Ruth Beuscher, who had treated her immediately following her suicide attempt in 1953. Sexton recalled during these death-suicide talks that they would fix their eyes intently on each other, soaking up the gossip and the details while devouring dish after dish of free potato chips. Aware that this was unusual, that people could not understand the fascination, Sexton was always asked "Why, why?" She tried to answer in her poem "Wanting to Die." "But suicides have a special language. / Like carpenters they want to know *which tools*. / They never ask *why build*."[18]

Which tools, she said, was the fascination.

These strange conversations formed the basis of their brief but intense friendship, a friendship based on rivalry, respect, and admiration. Now, years later, the poets are long gone from the Ritz, and the martinis consumed. But the aftermath of those conversations ripple uneasily through time and space. This is partly because both poets trouble what society and culture does to women. Their voices disrupt dominant ideals as their poems tear apart unfaithful men, gender expectations, the difficulties of marriage, how it feels to be a mother, a woman, a woman who menstruates, suffers miscarriages, who enjoys masturbation and sex. On those springtime Boston afternoons during their confessional drinking, Plath and Sexton were more radical than they realized. They began to pave the way for the rest of us. For although Sexton felt as though they were kicking at the door of fame waiting for men to share the password, in the end, the two poets kicked the door down anyway, no password needed, and found their own fame, on their own terms. We, at this later point in time, are lucky to see what is on the other side of that door.

THREE-
MARTINI
AFTERNOONS
AT
THE RITZ

CHAPTER ONE

Rebels

I think I would like to call myself "The girl who wanted to be God."

—Sylvia Plath[1]

I'm going to aim high. And why not.

—Anne Sexton[2]

There are two items in the Plath and Sexton archives that evoke a sense of social rebellion. Their address books.

Plath's is a green snakeskin-patterned pocket-sized book filled mostly with her immaculate handwriting, notes, and annotations. The front cover has the word ADDRESSES on it in embossed gold lettering. The black ink is shiny in places, almost wet looking. Sexton's is a loose-leafed vibrant red folder that still retains an odd odor. When the archive storage box is opened, it exudes a faint smell of musty nicotine. The plastic cover is sticky to the touch. The front page has a vague imprint of the word TELEPHONE engraved around the bottom of a square plinth holding a picture of what looks to be a once-gold telephone. This item was left on the top of Sexton's filing cabinet by her desk at the time of her death.

Although occasionally Ted Hughes had added the odd address or phone number in Plath's book, this very much feels like her own possession. The front page has, written in Plath's hand, "Mr. & Mrs. Edward J. Hughes," but the contacts are mostly her own and added neatly by her. Sexton's address book looks more family-based, with names written in by her children; a more chaotic, shared, practical item. The appearance of the two books somehow manages to reflect the appearance and personalities of the two women, one neat and self-contained, the other wilder and more flamboyant. But what the two books do have in common is the merging of the domestic with the professional. Alongside names of cleaning companies and dishwasher appliances are the editors' addresses at the *New Yorker*, the *Atlantic Monthly*, and publishers such as Faber and Faber, Heinemann, and Houghton Mifflin. Other poet friends, such as Adrienne Rich, Elizabeth Bishop, Marianne Moore, Robert Lowell, T. S. Eliot, Stephen Spender, and Theodore Roethke, are also included.

Leafing through Plath's address book gives a sense of the range of people and businesses she was engaged with. One page contains contact details for a babysitting service that she perhaps employed so she could go to Faber events where she drank champagne with Eliot, Spender, and Louis MacNeice. The Better Buying Service,[3] which she used to purchase a variety of rugs and carpets for Court Green, her Devon home, is listed alongside contact details for the Royal Literary Fund, the *Bookseller*,[4] and the BBC. T. S. Eliot himself shares a page with the South Western Electricity Board. Random House and the *Chelsea Review* are listed on the same page as the fabulously named Mrs. Reckless (who appears to work at a North London clinic). Memorial trusts, journals, booksellers, publishers, and national newspapers are listed in alphabetical order with a beekeeper, a midwife, home help, and Mrs. Vigors, the Kentish Town cleaner whom Plath suspected was stealing from her.

Like Plath, Sexton's address book was important to her, so important that she wrote a poem about it called "Telephone," beginning with a clear, accurate description: "Take a red book called TELEPHONE, / Size eight by four. There it sits. / My red book, name, address and number. / These are all people that I somehow own."[5]

While the poem then muses upon all the "dear dead names" that "won't erase" from the book, what we can see in Sexton's list of contacts is how closely family, therapists, psychiatric hospitals, suicide hotlines, and pharmacies sit side by side with journals, editors, poetry prize committees, and university contacts. Sexton also lists some impressive poet friends: Elizabeth Bishop, Carolyn Kizer, Adrienne Rich, Maxine Kumin, and W. D. Snodgrass. As her poem suggests, Sexton has tried to erase some names from the book, which is a swirl of strike-throughs, different-colored ink, stains, smears, and smudges. Her eldest daughter, Linda, recalls that this address book was her mother's Bible, which she carried everywhere, even in the car. At home it was always kept close at hand, and poignantly the book shows how "its decreasing legibility in recent years mirrored her decline."[6] As with Plath's address book, Sexton's showed the range of people she was dealing with and the almost double life of housewife-poet, or, as she put it, "I do not live a poet's life. I look and act like a housewife" until the point when a poem has to be written and then, she writes, "I am a lousy cook, a lousy wife, a lousy mother, because I am too busy wrestling with the poem to remember that I am a normal (?) American housewife."[7]

The tension of these two areas running alongside each other, the housewife-mother and the professional poet, was one that both women felt throughout their careers. But it was a position that was frowned upon at the time. Women were expected to sacrifice their careers to ensure a stable home. In fact, in more affluent homes, if women chose to work when the paycheck was not needed, they were regarded as selfish for putting their own needs before those of the family. Marriage and children were part of the national agenda and regarded as one feature that made America superior. Operating within the Cold War agenda, stay-at-home mothers were contrasted favorably with mothers in communist Russia who worked in dismal factories and left their children in cold day-care centers. American wives could be well-groomed, focusing on orderly homes and tending to all their children's needs.[8] As a result of this propaganda, by the 1950s marriage rates were at an all-time high, and women were getting married younger.

Despite the power of this message, neither Plath nor Sexton could fully accept this cultural norm. In 1962, in a candid letter to the sculptor Leonard Baskin, Plath admitted that she was only able to cope with being a wife and mother and all the domestic chores that came with it because she could also write, "which is my life blood & makes it possible for me to be domestic & motherly, which latter is my nature some of the time, & only when I have the other consolations & reprieves."[9] Sexton, too, records on numerous occasions the tension of being a woman as both poet and mother and how she felt displaced among other suburban housewives of the time. And yet neither could, at first, fully reject the societal expectations that formed part of their upbringing. Neither was there really a precedent yet that would support their breaking away from such domestic ideals. That would come too late for Plath, who died just months before the advent of second-wave feminism, a movement that surprisingly did not sweep Sexton up to the extent one might expect.

What Plath and Sexton did try to achieve was a subversive rebellion that increasingly became an open rebellion as they found their voices and their platforms from which to speak. If in 1950s America women of a certain class were supposed to sacrifice their own careers for those of their husbands, Plath and Sexton were having none of it. Both became increasingly outspoken in their poetry, prose, interviews, and correspondence while somehow balancing this against staying fairly conventional in their home lives. Marian Foster, a Devon neighbor, recalls how Plath insisted on going to the Sunday church services in town even though she despised them. When Foster asked her why she persisted, Plath admitted that she was concerned about what people would think if she didn't attend. Yet Plath's poems at that time are markedly hostile to religion, and her 1962 short story "Mothers" does little to disguise the local vicar whom Plath exposes as misogynistic and hypocritical. In a letter to her mother she was even more open about the "ghastly sermons" and the rector for whom she was full of "scorn."[10] Yet she still planned to have her children christened there. This rebellion and conformity ran in uneasy conjunction, often bumping into each other. In September 1962, when Plath invited the Fosters to her home for genteel afternoon tea and homemade cakes, they had no idea that that morning she had been furiously writing her infamous *Ariel* poems.[11]

Sexton was slightly more daring than Plath in her rejection of conventional ideals and domestic chores. She sometimes tried to bake cakes with the children, but they often went wrong. Kayo, her husband, did most of the cooking. She employed a cleaner and someone to do the laundry. While Sexton occasionally expressed some guilt about this seeming domestic aberration from the expected norm, she also had the courage to stand by her belief that she deserved the time to write and would take it and use it.

What Plath and Sexton established was a position that would last for the rest of their lives and afterlives—that of women who refuse to be silent. Their voices were not just asserting some louder version of the oppressed female experience; their voices were confrontational and started to open up a space for women to express anger, disgust, frustration, and dissatisfaction. Rage became legitimized. They also began writing about the female body in a way that caused genuine shock and revulsion among male editors and critics. Plath's poems, such as "Lady Lazarus," "Daddy," "The Applicant," and "Fever 103°," were regarded as dangerously extreme. Sexton's poems, such as "The Abortion," "Menstruation at Forty," and "The Ballad of the Lonely Masturbator," sent some male critics into apoplectic rage—rage and criticism that Sexton then took on and replied back to in her poems, which presumably left the critics even more paralyzed with fury.

The result was that Plath and Sexton were, and still are, regarded as both troubling and troublesome figures in society. Their work is subjected to the kind of misogynistic critique rarely heaped on other writers. And this gendered attitude filters down to their readers too. Young women are told they'll "grow out" of reading Plath, that they lack any critical faculties, merely worship at the shrine of a suicide death goddess, and so on. They become objects of humor, no longer proper or serious readers, but rather devotees. Goths and emos who wear black with a death fixation. Plath scholar Janet Badia spends a whole book exploring the ways in which female readers of Plath (and Sexton) are denigrated and used to denigrate the authors themselves, arguing, "Plath's popularity with women readers is all the evidence that is needed to make a case for the *lack* of brilliance in her work."[12] The poet-critic John Holmes actually referred to Sexton as evil and warned her best friend Maxine Kumin to stay away from her. In 1977, reviewing *Anne Sexton: A Self-Portrait in Letters*, Susan Wood declared that the letters have a built-in readership: "those, who since her suicide in 1974 have perversely worshiped her, as they do Sylvia Plath, as some sort of Sacrificial Priestess of Madness and Art . . . these suicide cultists seem to be predominantly female . . ."[13] In the 1990s Plath's poems were discussed as being too dangerous for the British 'A' level English Literature syllabus for fear they would encourage young readers to kill themselves. Plath and Sexton are portrayed as crazy, suicidal women, an attitude that impressively manages to sweep up sexism and stigma toward mental illness and suicide in one powerful ball of dismissal. Plath's suicide is often treated as a lighthearted joke. In popular culture, characters in film or on television are always the troubled and anguished characters if they are seen reading Plath or Sexton. It's all doom, gloom, and misery with a snide swipe at women who apparently take themselves too seriously by reading this stuff. In recent years a fashion magazine used Plath as its inspiration for a clothing photo shoot featuring an oven right in the center of the spread. On social media, people post photographs of themselves attending costume parties dressed as Plath with cardboard ovens on their head. This trivialization of suicide further attempts to belittle and downgrade the power of Plath's and Sexton's voices. But despite the attempts to ridicule, these two women refuse to be silent. And, if anything, their voices are becoming louder.

Although both died young, Plath and Sexton have never really gone away. This presence is around in a number of ways. Their books remain in print, and their poems anthologized, ensuring their disruptive voices are still heard. Power is also retained in the full and impressive archives that exist holding their work, personal effects, documents, and correspondence. For those lucky enough to visit, never do they feel more present than when one handles a poetry manuscript, or their typewriters, or some personal effect like a pair of glasses or a dress. These items still contain traces, as though Plath and Sexton have just briefly left the room and will be coming back shortly. Their realness is contained in things and objects. Often Plath's letters or manuscripts have a brown, wrinkled coffee cup stain. Sexton's are full of cigarette holes where dropped ash has burned right through the paper. Both women have locks of their hair held in their archives. Hair that retains its vitality; shiny and fresh, as if cut yesterday. Sexton's lock of baby hair, dating from 1932, is wrapped in cream tissue paper, bound neatly with a pale pink ribbon curved perfectly into an *S*. The hair removed from a teenage Plath is long, thick, and dense, held together with an elastic band, and curled inside a cardboard box. What this realia achieves is to humanize the women. We see their foibles, their doodles on manuscripts, the traces of what they were eating, drinking, or smoking. We understand their physical dimensions, the color and texture of their hair. They are not these removed or romanticized doomed women writers of an imaginary goddess cult. They were, and remain, relatable women, if extraordinarily gifted poets.

Why are Plath and Sexton regarded as so troublesome? During their lives and in the decade or two afterward, the subject material they used was new ground, and for many, shocking. They started to draw on their own life experiences and then linked these to bigger, more universal themes, a true precursor to the feminist "personal is political" mantra that would follow years later. Sexton opened this up first, having read and been utterly changed forever by "Heart's Needle," a poem by W. D. Snodgrass about the loss of his daughter following his divorce. In a 1962 interview, Plath name-checks Sexton as a forerunner in introducing previously taboo subjects into poetry: "I think particularly the poetess Anne Sexton, who writes about her experiences as a mother, as a mother who has had a nervous breakdown, is an extremely emotional and feeling young woman and her poems are wonderfully craftsmanlike poems and yet they have a kind of emotional and psychological depth which I think is something perhaps quite new, quite exciting."[14] Having read *All My Pretty Ones*, Sexton's second collection, Plath was left stunned by the poems. In particular she rated "The Black Art," of which the opening lines are "A woman who writes feels too much, / those trances and portents!"[15] But the collection also contained poems about abortion, a failed love affair, the death of Sexton's parents, and scrutiny of the female body.

It is important to balance this rebellion against the areas where Plath and Sexton did *not* venture. They absolutely took on the male-dominated discipline they wanted to succeed in, but they took it on as white middle-class women. When Betty Friedan published *The Feminine Mystique* in 1963 she was criticized for focusing on liberating those women who were entitled enough to take the escape routes she was offering. This involved having a certain level of social, cultural, and economic privilege. Both Plath and Sexton were comfortable employing women from lower social classes to do their housework in order to find time to write. And while both Plath and Sexton would be appalled to think they could ever be regarded as racist, some of their language and observations, in particular about Black people, leave a lot to be desired.[16] Nobody battling for change can be expected to take on every single aspect of social injustice, but it is equally important to have conversations about crucial areas that get overlooked. Plath and Sexton operated in the social space they inhabited and tackled the injustices they saw there, and if that meant shocking (male) editors by sending them poems about menstrual blood and orgasms, then so be it.

These topics did not go down well with some of the reading public back in the 1950s. Today it is much easier for women poets to publish work about menstruation, masturbation, sexual pleasure, and hating their parents because of the work that Plath and Sexton put into breaking these taboos. But, even today, women's books get less of a chance of being reviewed if they write about topics that are not deemed "feminine" enough.[17]

This gendered view of what is deemed "acceptable" was woefully evident back in 1959 when Robert Lowell's work on madness and psychiatric hospitals was described by reviewers as brave and serious. John Thompson in the *Kenyon Review* wrote, "[F]or these poems, the question of propriety no longer exists. They have made a conquest; what they have won is a major expansion of the territory of poetry."[18] In contrast, with the publication of her first book, Sexton already began to get the type of reception that would dog her career. James Dickey opened his *Poetry* review with the words "Anne Sexton's poems so obviously come out of deep, painful sections of the author's life that one's literary opinions scarcely seem to matter; one feels tempted to drop them furtively into the nearest ashcan, rather than be caught with them in the presence of so much naked suffering."[19] Sexton was stunned by this review and carried a copy of it around with her for the rest of her life.

These seeds of open sexism still exist today. When men write about their personal experience they are referred to as brilliant, sensitive essayists, as seen by the critical reception of Karl Ove Knausgaard, David Foster Wallace, and Jonathan Franzen, for instance. Indeed, after the publication of his third novel, *The Corrections*, *Time* magazine awarded Franzen the title of Great American Novelist. In contrast, when women such as Elizabeth Wurtzel or Susanna Kaysen write about their life experiences, their critical reception focuses on them as being hysterical, confessional, and overemotional. Research into book reviews in the *New York Times* showed that this contrast can happen even when men and women are writing about the *same topic*. If men write about family, it is seen as intellectual critique; if women write about family it is dismissed as domestic soap opera and drama. There is much less value attached to female experience and less value attached to the literature that deals with it. Women are still less likely to be published in top-tier literary outlets or have their work reviewed, especially by male reviewers.[20]

In a revealing article exploring this persistent sexism, novelist John Boyne exposed the tendency of male novelists to pronounce their own brilliance while boasting about never reading work by women writers. He quotes the Nobel laureate V. S. Naipaul, who declared that he doesn't read or teach novels by women because no woman writer can ever be his equal. This is due to a woman's tendency toward "sentimentality" and that a woman is "not a complete master of a house, so that comes over in her writing."[21] In 2017, the writer Anne Enright gave a speech pointing out that books by men are read and reviewed by both genders, but books by women are less likely to be reviewed by male critics, as if it is somehow beneath their dignity. She concluded that literary editors regard novels by male writers as expressing universal concerns, whereas novels by women are seen as much narrower in scope and less able to capture the cerebral male brain.[22] Today we can expose this sexism, research it, and offer solidarity and resistance. But back then it must have been bewildering for Sexton and Plath to find themselves so publicly vilified and humiliated.

Plath certainly on some level understood these challenges, which is perhaps why, when she wrote to Sexton praising *All My Pretty Ones*, she described the collection as "womanly in the greatest sense, and so blessedly underlire." She was also convinced, correctly as it happens, that Sexton would one day win a Pulitzer Prize.[23]

Because Plath did not live long enough to see her new style of poems published in a collection, she was not even aware of the stir they were creating when she submitted them to journals and newspapers. Although she had the full support of Al Alvarez, poetry editor of the *Observer*, other publications recoiled from what they saw as her extreme shift in subject matter—anger, rage, searing attacks on men, mental suffering, and descriptions of menstruation.[24] Like Sexton's reception, these were not seen as appropriate topics for a woman to be writing about. Karl Miller, editor of the *New Statesman*, told Alvarez that she must be mentally ill to be writing in this way. After the posthumous publication of *Ariel*, critics such as Stephen Spender and Harold Bloom used words like *shrill* and *hysterical* to describe Plath's poetic voice. Spender went even further, comparing Plath unfavorably to the poet Wilfred Owen, who claimed that all a poet can do is "warn." According to Spender, the nature of Plath's warning is very different: "Being a woman, her warning is more shrill, penetrating, visionary than Owen's. . . . With Sylvia Plath, her femininity is that her hysteria comes completely out of herself, and yet seems about all of us."[25] He goes on to make comparisons with a witches' brew. These words were deliberately gendered, as they are today. If women complain, they are told to calm down. If women are angry, it is seen as irrational (or hormonal), and if women are upset, it is because they are too sensitive. Then, as now, there is little room for women to openly express a full range of emotions without some ulterior motive being attached to them or without women somehow being regarded as unreasonable and excessively emotional.

Alongside the sexism of these representations is the stigma attached to women and mental illness. The disparity between Lowell's bravery and Plath's and Sexton's so-called inappropriate sickness is astonishing. The fact that Plath and Sexton were writing from a female point of view appeared to enrage male critics, who somehow wanted to control it. In a letter John Holmes wrote to Sexton in 1959 he advised her to never publish the *Bedlam* poems. She should, he suggested, write them all out until she was "emptied" and then put them away for five years and see what she thought of them then. The poems were, in his opinion, selfish and shortsighted, and if she carried down the route of only writing about her mental illness and hospital stays, then she would eventually have nothing else to write about. The selfishness lay in the poems forcing the reader to listen and giving nothing back to them other than the spectacle of Sexton's own suffering. Holmes continued with his advice that the poems would not only haunt and hurt Sexton for the rest of her life, but, in a really manipulative turn, he claimed they would do the same to her children. Mother-shaming is a classic historical and contemporary piece of social control over women. Nothing is designed to hurt more than to suggest a woman is a bad mother. When Lowell wrote about his mental suffering, there was no hint that this made him a bad father. Such selfishness on the part of Sexton, Holmes concludes, is a dangerous misuse of her writing gifts. Again, he asserts, do not publish the *Bedlam* poems.[26] Sexton's response to this showed her absolute bravery in the face of a more well-known poet and critic attacking her early work (after all, Sexton had only been writing for one year at this point). Rather than nurse her hurt in private, she took the criticism, turned it around, and exposed it in a poem, even name-checking Holmes in "For John, Who Begs Me Not To Enquire Further." And in a further brilliant move, Sexton included the poem in *To Bedlam and Part Way Back*. She defended the validity of her experiences, that there was indeed "something worth learning / in that narrow diary of my mind" and that ultimately what links us all is experience of one kind or another: "At first it was private. / Then it was more than myself; / it was you, or your house / or your kitchen."[27]

This rebellion and absolute refusal to stay quiet, the determination to validate her own experiences as worthy poetic topics, was a battle that continued for Sexton throughout her life. And it is one that has paved the way and opened up space for women today to validate their own experiences as being worth something, and worth listening to. In 2016 Katie Goh argued just this when she acknowledged that the sort of confessionalism that came out of the twentieth century made it easier for twenty-first-century artists facing similar struggles, and in some cases even more underrepresentation, to make their voices heard. She cites Beyoncé as emerging from this personal/political landscape as the singer explores topics such as her husband's infidelity, her feminism, female sexuality, motherhood, and the Black Lives Matter movement.[28] Beyoncé is also a woman who has been able to take complete control of her creative career.

Plath, sadly, was not alive long enough to protect her last work. At the time of her death she left a manuscript of *Ariel* on her desk ready for publication, and had already moved on to what she described as a new batch of poems, those that were written in early 1963.[29] Although she was separated from Ted Hughes, they had not yet divorced so she died intestate, meaning Hughes retained full control over her estate and copyright. When he read the poems in *Ariel,* by his own admission he was horrified by the content of some and consequently made the decision to fiddle with Plath's manuscript in order to remove some of the more "personally aggressive" poems.[30] These poems were the ones dealing with unfaithful men and failed marriages. He also admitted he would have removed more if the odd one had not already been accepted for publication elsewhere. "Daddy," for example, which Plath recorded for the British Council, has a narrator who lays into her parasitic husband: "If I've killed one man, I've killed two— / The vampire who said he was you."[31] Hughes then altered the trajectory of *Ariel* by including Plath's final 1963 poems, the ones she had described as being something quite different. Unfortunately, by protecting himself Hughes portrayed Plath in a way that still blights our reading and understanding of her. His version of *Ariel* ends with a slow descent into suicide and the dead body of a woman with her children. Plath's *Ariel,* as she pointed out, began with the word *Love* and then took the reader on a journey through a series of emotions and challenges, sufferings and grief, and gallows humor, but ultimately ending on a note of hope, the last line being "The bees are flying. They taste the spring."[32]

Hughes then made the extraordinary decision to place Plath's estate under the control of his sister, Olwyn, who notoriously disliked her estranged sister-in-law. Suddenly in charge of who could and could not access or publish Plath's work, Olwyn Hughes is on record in interviews and correspondence as referring to Plath as "a complete bitch."[33] She dismissed

Plath's work as a few poems in magazines and regarded her as straight poison, a mixed-up, self-important, crazy American. Biographers throughout the 1970s, '80s, and '90s encountered obstruction and a wall of silence. In an interesting contrast, when Anne Sexton died, her daughter Linda, who was now literary executor of the estate, observed what was happening with the Plath estate and took it as an example of how not to represent her mother. While the Hugheses were criticized for suppression, Linda herself would enter controversy over the coming years for releasing what was regarded by some as too much (in particular her mother's therapy tapes).

What became established, even during Sexton's lifetime, was the idea that some women who wrote openly about mental illness or suicide attempts and time spent in psychiatric hospitals were somehow selfish, showy, and overly dramatic. And worse, that this "craziness" really devalued their work.

Plath did not get to defend herself. *Ariel* in its altered form was not published until 1965, two years after her death. Sexton admirably spoke up on her behalf, describing the poems as eating time, and in a letter to the writer Susan Fromberg Schaeffer claimed that Plath "wrote the best hate poems of her time. To me she was seemingly less depressed than angry, but who can figure it. She is already a myth."[34] Sexton was somewhat in awe.

The decision by Plath and Sexton to challenge certain domestic norms, legitimize their anger, and show how male-dominated societies and relationships actually made women "crazy" left them vulnerable to attack by the very people they were criticizing. They did not flinch and they refused to stay silent. Linda Gray Sexton recalls that in white middle-class America, "normal" was "nearly everywhere I looked in my neighborhood of the early 1960s": the women who sold pies at church socials, who ran the PTA, who wore housedresses, and "squirreled away 'pin money'" instead of earning their own. "'Normal' were the women who bore in silence the obtuseness of their husbands rather than provoking full-scale war by arguing."[35] Plath and Sexton were not these women, however ambivalent they felt about it.

Not only did they start arguments, they refused to back down once they had done so. When Plath's 1962 poems were being rejected from journals and magazines, she defiantly wrote to her mother, "I am up at 5 writing the best poems of my life. They will make my name."[36] And when her mother questioned the content of some of her writing, Plath replied boldly, "Don't talk to me about the world needing cheerful stuff! What the person out of Belsen—physical or psychological—wants is nobody saying the birdies still go tweet-tweet, but the full knowledge that somebody else has been there and knows the worst, just what it is like."[37] Whatever was thrown at them, Plath and Sexton took it and hung on to their self-belief, though of course we cannot really know what it took for them to do that.

Part of the problem was summed up by one of their contemporaries, Adrienne Rich, who observed that "I have a sense that women didn't talk to each other much in the fifties—not about their secret emptinesses, their frustrations . . . There was little support for the idea that another woman poet could be a source of strength or mutual engagement."[38] This description perfectly explains how the friendship unfolded between Plath and Sexton.

The sense of competition was certainly there in the early days. If the two women talked publicly about death and suicide over Ritz martinis, in private there were tensions pulling them apart. Sexton and Starbuck's affair created a strain between the three poets, with Plath feeling somehow implicated—"where is responsibility to lie?"[39] she asks her journal in May. Sexton said Plath should never have left her and Starbuck alone in his room on Pinckney Street following drinks at the Ritz. From Plath's point of view the whole affair was tawdry, and she wrote bitingly, "I left, yet felt like a brown-winged moth around a rather meager candle flame, drawn. That is over."[40]

However, there were more far-reaching effects of the affair in Plath's eyes that created professional jealousy and rage and highlighted Rich's observation that women just didn't support each other enough. In his editorial position at Houghton Mifflin, Starbuck had some influence over the acceptance of certain poetry manuscripts. Plath, who had been working hard on putting a collection together, was planning to submit it that May but realized that "A.S. is there ahead of me with her lover G.S. . . . [I] felt our triple-martini afternoons at the Ritz breaking up."[41] Less than three weeks later, she was furious to discover Sexton was drinking champagne to celebrate two acceptances—her poetry collection at Houghton Mifflin and an essay in the *Christian Science Monitor*, a publication Plath had appeared in for years. "But who's to criticize a more successful copycat,"[42] Plath seethed, admitting she was unable to work because of her green-eyed fury. If this wasn't bad enough, Plath's last hope was that she would win the Yale Series of Younger Poets prize that year, so when less than a month later she discovered that this had been awarded to George Starbuck, she was lying awake at 3 a.m. "feeling again the top of my head would come off."[43]

Running alongside this jealousy, however, was respect and admiration. As Plath cast a critical eye over her own poems, calling them too forced and rhetorical, she reflected that she could do with taking a leaf from Sexton's book, admiring her honesty and relaxed turn of phrase. It is easy to forget that Plath and Sexton were operating pre–second-wave feminism. Had there been a platform and consciousness for female solidarity, perhaps their relationship might have developed differently. Sexton was mostly dismissive of Plath's work during 1959, admitting that she felt many of her poems missed the point and were essentially derivative. She saw nothing great in Plath at that time. Spivack herself felt that Plath did not get the recognition she deserved from Lowell, who was "more dazzled by Anne, his other female visitors, and most of all, by his own poetic prowess."[44] Yet there were hints of solidarity, particularly in the workshop when Lowell was at his most obtuse. One poem Plath read in class, "Sow," was presented by Lowell as "almost perfect" while simultaneously claiming that there was really not much to say about it. Spivack recalls the class sat in silence after the reading, waiting. Everyone still and awkward. Plath did not move. Sexton started fidgeting but then realized her bracelets were jangling so she stopped moving too. Lowell asked if anyone wanted to say anything about the poem. Everyone was too intimidated. Another long silence ensued. Then Lowell dismissed the poem, saying he was sure it would be published, and began reading a Randall Jarrell poem instead.[45] The class felt that Plath had been damned with faint praise. Sexton, in a moment of true comradeship, smiled supportively at Plath across the table and the class continued.

The friendship between Plath and Sexton really warmed up once they were living in different countries, as though geographical distance reduced their sense of rivalry. In late 1959 Plath moved back to England, while Sexton stayed in the Boston suburbs. The two women never saw each other again, though they stayed in touch writing infrequent letters and sharing copies of their books. Plath told Sexton about giving birth to a daughter and then a son. She wrote about moving from London to Devon, where she started keeping bees and growing potatoes. Sexton's letters to Plath are not held in any archive, so it is impossible to know the contents, though we can glean from Plath's responses that they were long and full of scandalous gossip. After reading them, Plath would pin them above her writing desk.

In an August 21,1962, letter Plath heaped praise on Sexton for her new collection, *All My Pretty Ones*, saying the poems left her "stunned" and that the book was "womanly in the greatest sense."[46] Pulling out of a more formal style of writing, Plath had just about completed her collection that would eventually be published as *Ariel*, the poems that, with some prescience, she believed would make her name. English literature, she felt, was caught in a straitjacket, and it was really only the voices coming out of America tackling subjects like madness and nervous breakdowns that excited her—the emotional and psychological depth offered by such poems.

This transatlantic support and encouragement was heartening to see, and when Plath was asked to edit a supplementary pamphlet called *American Poetry Now* for the *Critical Quarterly*, she chose to include two of Sexton's poems, "Kind Sir: These Woods" and "Some Foreign Letters," alongside other lesser-known women writers of the time. Plath's opportunity to create female friendships in literary circles was problematic, though, and this was connected to being married to a famous poet. She was often regarded as "Mrs. Hughes"; people had no idea she was Sylvia Plath.[47] Sexton fared much better in this regard. This may have been because she wasn't half of a famous writing couple, but also because she lived longer, through the early years of second-wave feminism, and was fortunate to be awarded a fellowship that was ahead of its time. In 1961 Sexton became part of a movement at Radcliffe College called "the Equivalents," where female writers and artists exchanged ideas and inspiration.[48] In November 1960, the Radcliffe Institute for Independent Study announced a fellowship program aimed at supporting marginalized women in American society—mostly mothers, those who were having to give up their dreams because they could not manage being a housewife and mother as well as being creative. Established by Radcliffe's president, Mary Ingraham Bunting, it consisted of a stipend of up to $3,000, because as Maggie Doherty describes in her book *The Equivalents*, Bunting realized that "you couldn't simply tell women to work hard and keep studying if the world didn't give them the tools and resources to do so."[49] Despite nearly two hundred applications, with only twenty-four awards available, Sexton found herself being granted a fellowship alongside poet Maxine Kumin, painter Barbara Swan, sculptor Marianna Pineda, and writer Tillie Olsen. This was an early cultural moment that, as Virginia Woolf understood even earlier, recognized women not only needed financial independence to succeed but a space of their own in which to work. This was a rare, practical application of such beliefs.

But back in the 1950s this sort of platform was not yet widely available. The conversations between Rich and Plath were few but telling. Plath wanted to know if it was possible to be a poet and mother. Rich warned her to think carefully about it. "What I wanted to tell her," wrote Rich, "was 'Don't try,' because I was in such despondency: I'd just had my third child, I was thirty, and I felt that in many ways my life was over, that I would never write again."[50]

Rich may have been surprised to know that Plath, who up to that point appeared fairly unremarkable to her Boston contemporaries, had already figured out that living up to conventional gender expectations would destroy her ambition, possibly her life. Even at eighteen years old, Plath wrote in her journal: "I am jealous of men—a dangerous and subtle envy which can corrode, I imagine, any relationship. It is an envy born of the desire to be active and doing, not passive and listening. I envy the man his physical freedom to lead a double life—his career, and his sexual and family life. I can pretend to forget my envy; no matter, it is there, insidious, malignant, latent."[51]

It is this underlying sense of injustice that Plath tapped into during the last months of her life. Sexton had already used hers and Rich had noticed and envied her ability to realize anger in her poetry. The subject matters Plath and Sexton began to write about included men (critically) but excluded them (experientially). Pregnancy, childbirth, miscarriage, abortion, and menstruation were not only taboo subjects but locked men out of knowing exactly how they felt. These were experiences men would never be able to have, and here were strong female voices suddenly explaining exactly how they felt. Men, for once, were not the experts; they simply could not know. In response, many male critics wrote the poems off as inappropriate, crass, and self-absorbed. And if perhaps one might hope things have changed today, sadly this is not the case. Books by women stand more of a chance of getting reviewed if they deal with topics such as romance, gender, and family, and if they are fictional. As scholar Judith Scholes points out, "We have an idea that men writing about factual information is going to be more valid or more legitimate than a woman's take," whereas "the kinds of topics that are being reviewed and the choices that are being made for the reviewing of books is maybe in line with stereotypical feminine or feminized topics."[52]

Because Plath and Sexton stood their ground, today it may not seem so shocking for a woman to write about pregnancy or the challenges of motherhood, but in the 1950s and '60s it was.

To understand the cultural position of women, one only has to look at popular advertisements of the time and the assumptions and messages they conveyed. First of all, it appeared that all women were white, middle-class, and heterosexual. And they were, in effect, pretty useless. They needed to stay in the domestic realm, but often they were useless there, too, and needed their husbands to buy them some kind of technology to make them better wives. "The [Kenwood] Chef does everything but cook—that's what wives are for!" Alcoa Aluminum bottle caps are so easy to use, "You mean a woman can open it?" Van Heusen ties, complete with important-looking faux crests and coats of arms, would apparently depict "It's a man's world," in which a wife would deliver her husband breakfast in bed on her knees while he sat there looking pleased with himself, wearing a tie. Other taglines were "Can she cook?," "Women don't leave the kitchen!," and "Keep her where she belongs" (apparently on the floor looking at his shoes) while simultaneously warning women not to neglect their stockings, their complexions, and their red hands (hardly surprisingly given the obsession with women needing to wax their kitchen floors daily). Sometimes the message was directed at men: "Christmas morning she'll be happier with a Hoover," "Successful marriages start in the kitchen!," and "So the harder a wife works, the cuter she looks!" Adverts aimed personally at women were very much about control and respectability: make sure you stay in good shape for your man, don't get acne, wear the right bra, and in a more daring advert for sanitary protection, "The tampon that's right *even for single girls*" (my emphasis).

Many of these dominant ideals were absorbed and rejected by Plath and Sexton. On October 11, 1962, Plath wrote a poem called "The Applicant" in which an ideal marriage candidate is wheeled out for consideration: "A living doll, everywhere you look. / It can sew, it can cook, / It can talk, talk, talk."[53] Dripping with sarcasm and rage, Plath's narrator tears apart the exploitative assumption that women exist for the sole purpose of pleasing men. In "Housewife" Sexton explores the expectation that a woman will be tied to the home, spending much of the day on her knees cleaning, and concludes that this is a generational expectation—"A woman *is* her mother."[54] When the conventional chores and ideals are abided by there is a certain gritted-teeth, grudging approach, as with Plath's speaker in "A Birthday Present" who cooks in her kitchen, "[m]easuring the flour, cutting off the surplus, / Adhering to rules, to rules, to rules."[55]

Nobody can exist in a cultural vacuum or truly exist outside their historical moment. Plath and Sexton were no exception. The ideological messages had of course hit their mark, not only through popular culture but also through upbringing, education, and family expectations. To resist such overwhelming influences requires an immense amount of emotional energy and rebellion. Neither does such a voice of resistance have to be a complete, perfectly thought-out one. That Plath and Sexton felt the ambiguity of conforming to certain ideals but rejecting others is not surprising. In the 1950s there was little opportunity for shared female experience where frustrations and dissatisfactions could be normalized. Today we have the Women's March and places where women can share office space; there are safe women-only workshops and less-formal feminist grassroots groups. These are events and places where women can communicate, campaign, share experiences, and normalize the female voice. There are more opportunities for women to listen to and support each other, and to take to the streets, because they are no longer willing to put up with any more sexist garbage. Reflecting back, Adrienne Rich recalled that in the 1950s to own up to such sentiments of needing support created feelings of failure as a woman, a mother, and a poet. Fear is not often acknowledged, but it did lie very close to the surface, especially for Plath. She constantly worried that she would never be completely free to be a fully rounded, creative person if she had to mold herself to be somebody else's wife or mother. Would domesticity choke the life out of her? But equally she worried that if she were able to become accomplished, was that also destructive? "Why did Virginia Woolf commit suicide? Or Sara Teasdale—or the other brilliant women—neurotic? Was their writing sublimation (oh horrible word) of deep, basic desires? If only I knew. If only I knew how high I could set my goals, my requirements for my life!"[56] Although Sexton appeared less agonized about this on paper than Plath, she nevertheless repeated on numerous occasions that she felt like a fraud, hiding out in her suburban home, surrounded by people who simply did not understand her or what she was trying to do: "I wish there were more women around me who did *something*!"[57]

In the 1950s, just as Plath and Sexton were beginning to find their voices, they could not have known how rebellious they would end up being. They could not know they were about to become two of the most prominent voices in twentieth-century poetry, disrupting and troubling the social landscape decades after their deaths. It is difficult to read Plath as a young woman so worried about her future: "Will I be a secretary—a self-rationalizing, uninspired housewife, secretly jealous of my husband's ability to grow intellectually & professionally while I am impeded—will I submerge my embarrassing desires & aspirations, refuse to face myself, and go either mad or become neurotic?"[58]

Thankfully, no.

CHAPTER TWO

Early Days

I don't believe that the meek will inherit the earth:
The meek get ignored and trampled.

—Sylvia Plath[1]

I'm a terrible breaker of barriers.

—Anne Sexton[2]

Rebels don't simply spring out of the ether. They have a history, a background, and a childhood that ferments their dissatisfaction and defiance. Plath and Sexton were no exception, though to look at their upbringings they do seem the most unlikely pair of rebels. They were born within four years of each other into standard conformity; Sexton first, on November 9, 1928, in Newton, Massachusetts, and Plath on October 27, 1932, in Boston. Their backgrounds, however, were remarkably different.

Sexton came from a fairly privileged family with parents who were described as "characters out of a Scott Fitzgerald novel, children of the Roaring Twenties: good-looking, well-to-do, party-loving, and self-indulgent."[3] Her father, Ralph Churchill Harvey, was born into a prosperous, self-made family, with his father a successful banker and Ralph opening his own wool business by his late twenties. Her mother, Mary Gray Staples, was the cherished, only child of a wealthy family and raised in luxury. Although she had writerly ambitions herself, in 1922 while in her junior year at Wellesley College she met and eloped with Ralph Harvey, in effect ending her academic and writing careers. They had three daughters born close together: Jane (1923), Blanche (1925), and finally Anne (1928). Though near in age, the sisters did not form close bonds with one another. With parents who mostly put their own interests first, the daughters were in competition for attention. Jane became her father's favorite, Blanche was regarded as the smart one, and Anne, the baby of the family, was often seen as too loud, too messy, and too demanding.

The Harvey family would spend long summer vacations on Squirrel Island, off the coast of Maine, in two large houses called Dingley Dell and the Aerie. Here, surrounded by trees and the sea, the family would sail and swim. Sexton captured the feel of these seaside holidays in one of her early poems, "Kind Sir: These Woods," writing, "Kind Sir: This is an old game / that we played when we were eight and ten. / Sometimes on The Island, in down Maine."[4]

On the island the children had their own miniature bathrooms, and a small theater with a raised stage, footlights, and a curtain. Sexton would take over this theater for the vacation and entertain the family with her productions and acting. She was regarded as a born performer. The houses were big enough for staff and nursemaids. The adults indulged in parties, games, drinking, and speedboat antics. The summer would see a gathering of family generations: Ralph, Mary Gray, maternal grandparents, and, most important for young Anne, her great-aunt Anna Ladd Dingley, otherwise known as "Nana." This woman would become the most important influence in Sexton's younger years and her greatest source of warmth, love, and affection. In 1974, several months before her death, in an interview with writer Elaine Showalter, Sexton recalled, "My mother was very destructive. The only person who was very constructive in my life was my great-aunt, and of course she went mad when I was thirteen. It was probably the trauma of my life that I never got over."[5] Nana was around to be a loving presence until Sexton was thirteen, but in the years that followed, Anna Ladd Dingley would suffer from a mental breakdown and be institutionalized. Although she was briefly allowed home for visits, she ended her days in a mental hospital, distracted and uncomprehending. When she died, Sexton never recovered from this loss: "Nana's death was a great blow to me . . . it was the most shattering thing I went through."[6]

When Mary Gray was not being elusive and emotionally detached, she was seemingly being intrusive, subjecting her youngest daughter to physical examinations, inspecting any bowel movements, and administering enemas. Sexton drew these elements of her childhood together, revealing her mother's attitude toward physical contact between women. "My mother never touched me in my life, except to examine me. So I had bad experiences. But I wondered with this that every summer there was Nana, and she would rub my back for hours. My mother said, women don't touch women like that. And I wondered why I didn't become a lesbian."[7] During her therapy sessions later in life, Sexton reflected back on her feelings of guilt about the erotic pleasure she felt from this physical contact with Nana. The back rubs could last for hours and often Nana would use perfumed talcum powder. The nature of this contact also went beyond an age-appropriate stage, with Sexton and Nana still engaging in cuddling in bed and back rubs after Sexton had entered adolescence.[8] Her therapist, Dr. Orne, believed the relationship had been constricting and infantilizing. This confusion of barriers, both physical and sexual, would unfortunately play a part in Sexton's own life when she became a mother. Though Sexton would have fond memories of these summers on Squirrel Island, mostly "she remembered her own childhood as a time scarred with emotional pain."[9]

The family may have been wealthy and certainly they lived in comfort in a large house at 81 Garden Road in Wellesley, but Ralph and Mary Gray both drank heavily and partied. They would go out almost every night, leaving their daughters at home, or throw huge parties where the children were wheeled out for display. The three daughters were expected to be immaculate, to meet their father's high standards of appearance and dress. A standard so high, he insisted that even his underwear be ironed. If family friends came for dinner, the children were hauled downstairs and expected to perform. In later years Sexton recalled a comment that her oldest sister, Jane, had made about the contrived nature of their existence: "Nobody ever dropped in on our family. If they did, Father ran upstairs: he had to get ready for the performance."[10] Alcohol consumption, though, brought unpredictable moods and behavior. Ralph Harvey could lash out with cruel comments, and once he sent his youngest daughter away from the dinner table because her teenage acne disgusted him (a jibe that stayed with Sexton for the rest of her life). Mary Gray didn't need alcohol to be unpredictable. Years after her death, Jane commented, "[Y]ou never knew, with Mother, when she was going to be horrible or nice. The minute you thought you knew where you were, she'd turn on you."[11]

The daughters, desperate for their parents' attention, had to invent ways to try to be noticed, often leaving notes or drawings under their mother's pillow for when she got home from nights out. Affection was rare and elusive, but much sought after. Sexton seemed to deal with this by engaging in attention-seeking behavior. She would create dramatic plays, casting herself in every starring role. She would leap from room to room, dress hems unraveling, hair untidy, constantly ignoring adult authority. All her friends were expected to be devoted and subservient to her will. On one occasion, she kidnapped a more docile companion, locked her in the bedroom closet overnight, and only released her when a distraught mother called looking for her lost child. A friendship had to be all or nothing, an attitude Sexton carried throughout most of her life.

If we can see the beginnings of rebellious behavior in Sexton's younger years, there was not a hint of it in Plath's.

Rarely naughty, rarely stepping out of line, and in her earliest letters verging on goody-two-shoes, Plath appeared to be
the model child. Her background lacked the wealth and privilege of Sexton's and instead reflected the difficulties of having
first- and second-generation immigrant parents. Otto Emil
Plath immigrated to America in 1900, at age sixteen, from
Grabow in Germany (then in the Polish Corridor), ostensibly
to take up studies in the Lutheran ministry. After moving in
with his grandparents in Wisconsin, he spent a year taking
classes learning to speak English. Following this, he enrolled
in the Missouri Synod to begin a career in the ministry. Unfortunately for Otto, within six months he realized that he was
an atheist and decided he needed to leave the path he was on
and take up teaching instead. Alas, his grandparents did not
share his opinion, and not only disinherited him but struck his
name from the family Bible and never spoke to him again. In
the years that followed, Otto would become a teacher and an
expert on bumblebees, but he was never really able to leave
his German background behind. During the First World War,
he was interviewed by the FBI for suspected pro-German ten-
dencies (though they concluded that there was no evidence of
disloyalty to the United States).

In 1929, while teaching at Boston University, Otto Plath
encountered one of his postgraduate students, Aurelia Frances Schober. Her parents had moved to America from Austria,
and Aurelia had been born in Boston, Massachusetts, in 1906.
She was twenty-one years younger than Otto. After forming
a friendship and growing increasingly close, they were mar-

ried in January 1932 and wished to start a family immediately. Their firstborn, Sylvia, arrived nine months later. Their second child, Warren, two and a half years after that.

Life in the Plath household was dictated by Otto, who insisted that his younger wife give up her teaching job to stay at home and look after the children (and him). Aurelia Plath did not argue and recalled, "I was totally imbued with the desire to be a good wife and mother."[12] This involved domestic chores, helping her husband with his work, acting as secretary, and making sure the children stayed out of his way while he was working. At one stage in their small Jamaica Plain apartment, Otto took over the dining room table for a year working on a project called "Insect Societies." On the one evening a week when he was teaching late, Aurelia would invite her friends over for dinner, but not before she had drawn a plan of his books and papers so that she could replace everything in the exact same order before he returned home. She rapidly developed realistic expectations about her husband: "At the end of my first year of marriage, I realized that if I wanted a peaceful home—and I did—I would simply have to become more submissive, although it was not my nature to be so."[13] Within four years of marriage, the Plaths had moved to a larger house in Winthrop, by the sea, which gave them more space for their growing family and for Otto to finally have his own study.

Otto Plath ruled all aspects of his home life. He insisted on shopping for food, having free time to work, and from 1937 onward, when his health started to deteriorate, restricting the time he spent with his children. They would be brought downstairs by their mother for thirty minutes each evening when they would perform for their father, either singing songs, reciting poems, or listing the scientific names of insects. One of his colleagues, Professor Leland H. Taylor, described Otto as "the most dedicated and bitter misogynist I have known . . . He repeated his friendly warning that all women are evil to me time and time again."[14] But by 1938, Otto was becoming increasingly ill and seemed happy to lean more and more on his apparently evil wife. He self-diagnosed lung cancer and refused to see a doctor. By 1940, he suffered from insomnia, thirst, and leg cramps. In August, after stubbing his toe on a bedroom bureau, he was disturbed to see his foot turning black. Finally visiting the family doctor, he was diagnosed with diabetes mellitus. Having ignored it for so long, the condition, which would have been treatable, had become life-threatening, and despite efforts to save his life, Otto developed gangrene in his left leg. Not even an amputation could save him, and he died on November 5, 1940. Plath was eight years old when she lost her father.

This loss was a grief that Plath struggled to recover from even as an adult, but as a child it impacted greatly on the rest of her formative years. Suddenly she had only one parent, and money became tight. She witnessed what she would later call her mother "sacrificing" her life for her children. Plath both loved and hated her for this. It seemed to develop a need in Plath to please. The family left their house in Winthrop, as did her maternal grandparents, and they all moved into the same house in Wellesley. In rather blunt language shortly before she died, Plath described this move as being the end of her childhood and the end of her happiness: "My father died, we moved inland. Whereon those nine first years of my life sealed themselves off like a ship in a bottle—beautiful, inaccessible, obsolete, a fine, white flying myth."[15]

In the new setup Plath had even more family members to show how good and resourceful she could be. Letters home from summer camp show a young Plath explaining in great detail how much milk she had drunk (lots), how often she had been to the toilet (sometimes not enough), how well she had performed her activities, and how often she had been told her pictures/poems/stories were *the best*. As with Sexton, Plath's bodily functions were put under strict surveillance by her mother, who seemed anxious over and, frankly, obsessed with her daughter's bowel movements. A day without going to the toilet was regarded by Aurelia Plath as constipation and Plath was subjected to soap suppositories.[16]

Thinking about Plath's and Sexton's upbringings can shed a different light on how some of their later behavior was viewed. Rather than pathologizing Sexton's need for attention, or Plath's desire to be perfect at everything, an alternative reading would be that this was learned behavior. Not neurosis, not part of a mental illness, but actually a pattern that was established for them as children that they carried into their adult lives. Sexton's need to be noticed, whether in her life or her work, is often presented as some form of pathological, selfish attention seeking, like an innate form of mental illness. But looking at certain features of her childhood and the level of emotional neglect from her parents, her need to feel as though she was "somebody" makes sense. Plath's overachieving, her need to be the best poet, the best mother, the best wife, becomes understandable when you look at how hard she had to work to get anything at all. Her years spent at summer camp, her education, all came at the expense of her mother working long hours and giving her life over to her children. Plath knew this and she was both grateful and resentful at having to be so grateful. Equally, growing up with a German father in 1930s America was not easy. Plath was taunted for having a "spy" as a father. It is hardly surprising that she kept her head down, worked hard, and conformed. Of course, that doesn't mean that this learned behavior was not ultimately destructive for either woman, but it does depathologize the idea that they were afflicted with some negative innate hardwiring. It shows how much of their behavior was a response to life experiences and environmental stimuli, rather than neurotic irrationality.

One prominent feature of their upbringings that Plath and Sexton shared, and later spent many years discussing in therapy, was difficult relationships with their mothers. Mary Gray Staples and Aurelia Plath both shared failed literary ambitions. Mary Gray came from a family of journalists, editors, and publishers, and her father had high hopes of her following in the family footsteps. However, because she met and married Ralph Harvey while she was still at college, she made the decision to leave and become a full-time wife and mother. This, in effect, brought an end to her literary aspirations. When her youngest daughter began writing poems at school and in college, it created tension and jealousy. Bizarrely, Mary Gray accused Sexton of plagiarism and sent a sheaf of her work to a professor in New York to get an expert opinion as to whether the poems were original or not. He concluded that indeed they most likely were and showed much promise, but this suspicion led to all writing ceasing immediately. In fact, a devastated and humiliated Sexton never wrote another poem until ten years later when she was in her late twenties and at the suggestion of her therapist, Dr. Martin Orne. "The bitterness and sense of defeat she experienced at her mother's accusation never quite left her," observed her daughter Linda.[17] Sexton saw her mother's behavior as a direct result of her need to remain the star of the show; it crushed her and effectively silenced her voice for a whole decade. Ralph Harvey often told his daughters that they would never be as brilliant as their mother, and the regular boast was that Mary Gray had received the highest IQ score Wellesley College had ever recorded. "You are creative," Ralph Harvey told Sexton, "but she is brilliant."[18] This tension and jealousy persisted, and in the mid-1950s, when Sexton decided to take up writing in earnest, she appealed to her mother for financial help. In particular, Sexton wanted to go to college to learn more about the craft of writing poems and to fill any gaps in her knowledge of literature and language. Mary Gray's response was scathing: "No, why should I? . . . You could never do the work. You have no idea of how hard it would be."[19] Instead she urged Sexton to get a "proper" job, but tellingly, in response to her daughter's desire to write professionally, Mary Gray immediately started writing more poems herself.

This sense of competition accurately summed up Sexton's relationship with her mother. Years after Mary Gray's death Sexton admitted to her own daughter, "Even if I say my mother was mean, I still love her and anyhow she wasn't *that* mean. I exaggerate everything I fear."[20] Perhaps this fear was the risk of maternal rejection or disapproval. What is significant is that Mary Gray appears as a dominant presence in Sexton's poems, most notably after she died.

The death of a parent is a monumental life moment and Sexton lost both of hers within months of each other. Mary Gray died first, in March 1959 from breast cancer.[21] Since she believed cancer was brought on by stress, she accused Sexton of causing her sickness because of the trauma of her suicide attempts. Prior to her death Mary Gray had taken the manuscript of "The Double Image" from Sexton's desk and read it. This long poem, included in Sexton's first collection, looks at mother-daughter relationships and includes the lines "On the first of September she looked at me / and said I gave her cancer. / They carved her sweet hills out / and still I couldn't answer."[22]

This poem was one that Sexton brought to the Robert Lowell workshop and was made to read it aloud in its entirety by Lowell himself in March 1959. There is a cruelty about his insistence. Publicly reading a poem like this within days of her mother's death must have been, to put it mildly, difficult—not least because Sexton visited her dying mother each day and stayed with her until the end. Five years later she described how "I remember well being right beside my mother as she died, and trying to help her, to stay there, right there, so she wouldn't have to walk the barrier alone . . . to go as far as I could into that dumb country . . . I wanted to hold her hand, as one holds a child's hand, to take her across, to say 'It's all right. I'm here. Don't be afraid.'"[23] The poignant twist to Sexton wanting to be with her mother at the moment of death was reflected in her suicide, when she chose to die wrapped in her mother's fur coat, keeping a part of her close even during her own final moments.[24]

Plath would certainly have heard Sexton read "The Double Image," and they would have discussed it during class and most likely afterward over martinis at the Ritz. Plath even retained a mimeographed typescript of the poem in her papers. It seems inconceivable that Sexton would not mention that her mother had just died. It seems unlikely Plath and Sexton would not talk about their mother-daughter relationships. Although we do not know for sure which poems Plath read during the workshop, a poem written contemporaneously was "Electra on Azalea Path," about the death of a father, and a daughter in competition with a mother: "O pardon the one who knocks for pardon at / Your gate, father—your hound-bitch, daughter, friend. / It was my love that did us both to death."[25]

This sense of competition, as well as the push-pull of love-hate, is a tension that Plath would have well understood. The relationship with her own mother was equally as confusing, consisting of dependency, resentfulness, the need for approval, and ultimately a horror of ending up in the same situation as a single parent. Whether she was at college, on vacation, or living entirely in another country, Plath wrote compulsively to her mother. Sometimes twice a day. Ted Hughes noticed that no experience seemed to have any meaning to Plath until she had told her mother about it and had it validated by her. Many of her letters seem defensive and show a need to justify every dollar spent, every decision made, while simultaneously assuring Aurelia that everything in life was going wonderfully well. This exchange is now somewhat one-sided, since Plath threw many of her mother's letters into a fire during the summer of 1962, much to the dismay of Aurelia, who had literary ambitions that their correspondence might one day be published.

Part of Plath's ability to deal with her mother, whom she found somewhat suffocating and needy, was written into her work, or discussed in her therapy sessions with Ruth Beuscher. Observers noticed that Aurelia Plath could be overemotional and was often breathy and close to tears when she spoke to her daughter.[26] One of Plath's friends, Marcia Brown Stern, was amazed that Plath's mother wrote her letters every single day while Plath was at Smith College, outlining every thought she had, every errand she ran, what she bought at the store, asking for intimate details of Plath's college life and needing to be informed about everything her daughter did, said, or was thinking.[27] Plath felt as though her mother was parasitic, living her life through her children because "she gave herself to her children, and now by God they can give themselves back to her."[28] After the Plath family moved from Winthrop to Wellesley, the new house was small and a consequence of this was that Plath had to share a bedroom with her mother right up until she left for college. This meant very little privacy for Plath in her teenage years and into her twenties. Perhaps unwittingly in *Letters Home*, Aurelia described how she voyeuristically lived through her daughter, waiting for her to come home from dates and dances: "Ah, then she'd picture the evening for me, and I'd taste her enjoyment as if it had been my own."[29] More disturbingly, Aurelia also appeared to interfere in her daughter's emerging sexuality, finding out details of what her daughter had been up to and with whom—and even discussed intimate details of when and how her daughter orgasmed.[30]

As an adult, in a December 1958 therapy session, Plath suddenly felt reborn, like a new person, when her therapist said one sentence to her. This sentence, Plath claimed, was better than shock treatment: "I give you permission to hate your mother."[31] Psychologically, this unleashed Plath to explore years of resentment toward Aurelia, resentment mixed with a grudging compassion: "I don't imagine time will make me love her. I can pity her: she's had a lousy life; she doesn't know she's a walking vampire. But that is only pity. Not love."[32]

If on some level Plath really saw her mother as a walking vampire, she nevertheless needed her. There is no doubt that Aurelia Plath loved both her children deeply and Plath was secure with that knowledge. Unlike Sexton, who had to fight for her mother's attention, Plath battled to free herself from Aurelia's watchful eye. If this contrast was ever discussed in those conversations at the Ritz, the irony would almost certainly appeal to Plath's and Sexton's senses of humor. Perhaps they even suggested exchanging mothers, so Plath could be left alone and Sexton could get the maternal attention she so desperately craved. Both women, though, were dependent on their mothers, however differently it expressed itself. Just like Sexton, who chose to die wearing her mother's fur coat, when Plath died she, too, kept her mother close. Her purse contained a family photograph taken in 1955 showing Plath and her brother, Warren, which presumably she had been carrying around with her until the day she died. Aurelia had turned this photograph into a Christmas card and sent it to her daughter in England with a message ending "We all miss you terribly, Darling, but we are happy for you and with you at the same time."[33]

Plath's ambiguity toward conformity can certainly be traced back to her upbringing and maternal relationship. While on the one hand she wanted to break free, be creative, be different, live more recklessly, she was equally bombarded by culture, by her family, to get a steady job, marry well, be careful with money, and most importantly always consider "What would the neighbors say?" This was a powerful mix of manipulative control, and the fury this created was mostly poured out in Plath's journals. She ultimately refused to get a "good" job. In fact, to the horror of her mother, she turned quite a few down. She refused to take the safe option and refused to marry someone who would offer her financial security. While Plath felt able to almost boast about this rebellion ("I have done practically everything she said I couldn't do and be happy at the same time and here I am, almost happy"),[34] she nevertheless was keen to present herself as the perfect cook, wife, and homemaker. As much as Plath defied certain social expectations, there were some that were just too dominant to fully reject.

Oddly, Aurelia Plath, an intelligent and perceptive woman, was unable to see the type of pressure she put her daughter under. She could regard Plath as an overachiever who often took on too much to the point of nervous exhaustion without considering her own role in this. Instead she seemed to regard their relationship as something a little more inexplicable: "Between Sylvia and me there existed—as between my own mother and me—a sort of psychic osmosis which, at times, was very wonderful and comforting; at other times an unwelcome invasion of privacy."[35] Yet Aurelia Plath was often invasive on a practical level, and toward the end of her daughter's life, in 1962, actually snooped and interfered, which created difficulties for Plath in the small Devon town where she lived. Aurelia got neighbors to spy on her daughter and report back. But worse, she broke Plath's confidence and told the local doctor about Plath's breakdown and suicide attempt when she was twenty. From then on Plath claimed that she was treated in the town as a former "mental case."

As with Sexton, much of Plath's behavior, written off as neurotic or irrational, makes more sense when regarded through the lens of family relationships in a particular cultural and historical moment. These were the very real pressures facing women during the 1950s and '60s, and these pressures became much more pernicious when the decision was taken to reject them. "I could have had money and men with steady jobs. But they were dull, or sick, or vain, or spoiled. They made me gag in the long run . . . It's a hell of a responsibility to be yourself,"[36] Plath wrote. But defying social conventions carried consequences. As if preempting the sort of pathological way Plath would be viewed in the future, her therapist Ruth Beuscher made clear that there was a difference between dissatisfaction with oneself and anger and depression. Plath realized that the pressures from her mother and society in general stopped her from being who she wanted to be, and this made her angry. As long as she vented this anger, then fine. The problems came with repression; it was this that could cause depression. But when it came down to it, Plath just simply took a blunt, realistic view: "I do not seem to be able to live up to them [her mother and mother-like figures]. Because I don't want to."[37]

Another breeding ground for oppression and rebellion came from the school and college system. Plath and Sexton had very different experiences and certainly took contrasting views on the value of education. Although they were only four years apart, and both attended Wellesley High School—Plath started the autumn after Sexton graduated—they did not appear to know each other, or even know of each other. In later years Sexton seemed fairly relieved about this: "I met Sylvia later . . . and if she had known me in Wellesley I'm sure she would not have spoken to me."[38] Sexton claimed that by third grade her parents were told to give up on her, as she would never learn anything. By fifth grade her teachers were suggesting she needed psychiatric treatment.[39] It's interesting to see what was going on that would prompt such an extreme response from her school. Report cards show that Sexton was often regarded as too talkative, didn't listen, and sometimes her work was completed without thought. "Correction was occasionally required," and she was seen to lack efficient direction in her work. Her effort was graded as poor and sometimes her absences were noted (she was a notorious truant). By tenth grade her worst evaluation was for Typing I, somewhat ironic since that's what Sexton ended up doing every day of her life. After the first semester she consistently scored a P (poor) for effort and ended the year with an overall grade of D for her typewriter skills.[40]

Sexton's main aim in life during these years was, rather glamorously, to learn how to become a seductress. In 1945, she was sent for her senior year to Rogers Hall, a boarding school in Lowell. But here Sexton smoked in the bathroom, skipped lessons, disappeared from campus without permission, and spent most of her time composing love letters to an increasingly large coterie of lovestruck young men. She dominated dance assemblies wearing red satin dresses, and female school friends reported miserably that they were left standing as all the boys flocked to Sexton like moths to a flame. At this stage, Sexton didn't place much value on the merits of education. She described herself as laughing her way through exams and paying little attention in class, the end result being a lifelong inability to spell correctly.

From Rogers Hall she was sent to a finishing school, Garland Junior College on Commonwealth Avenue, in Boston. Here wealthy girls were supposed to learn how to cook and maintain a well-supervised household. Sexton claimed the only thing she learned was how to make a fantastic white sauce. This may well have been because she was rarely there. Despite some concern for her apparently wayward behavior, her parents thought at this stage it would be a good idea to buy Sexton a shiny black convertible, the result being she missed even more lessons as she whizzed about the city, chauffeuring a variety of boyfriends to bars, dances, and the theater. She was, in her own words, "a flunk-out in any schooling."[41] In her copy of *The Basic Cookbook*, alongside notations on different recipes, she practiced writing her signature, Mrs. Dick Bowker, Dick being a boy she considered marrying.[42]

This judgment of her behavior by teachers shows a rigid view of what young women in the 1940s were supposed to be like. Although Sexton's grades were not dazzling, neither were they terrible. Her crime seemed to be that, in her teenage years, she did not really respect what education had to offer. As a consequence, authoritative figures tried to control her, to no avail. They had no idea they were dealing with a future Pulitzer Prize winner.

As Sexton got older and started to think about writing again, she realized that she probably needed to catch up with reading and applied herself to this task diligently. The result was fascinating. Because she had not really paid attention in school, any interpretations of classic novels and poetry were her own. Her poet friend Maxine Kumin noted that "she was grim about her lost years, her lack of a college degree; she read omnivorously and quite innocently whatever came to hand and enticed her, forming her own independent, quirky, and incisive judgments."[43] Through being a rebel at school, Sexton became a rebel in her thoughts, never conventional, always engaged.

What is perhaps underplayed in Sexton's life is that despite her rejection of formal schooling, she not only later self-educated, but became a professor at Boston University and created innovative and radical teaching ideas for her own curriculum. It was almost as if she understood how boring and restrictive traditional education could be and she wanted to give her students something different.[44] "We want to find out what they feel in *their* literature and not impose *ours.*"[45] Her students adored her and she in turn adored most of them, writing in 1967 that she even liked the challenging ones: "I'd like to stamp on the fresh ones just twice and then pick them up and hug them."[46] Julie Kane, who was in Sexton's last class at Boston University, in 1974, remembered Sexton as strikingly beautiful. She would enter the teaching room, kick off her shoes, and start cackling, making raunchy jokes about poems and madness. One day after the workshop Sexton offered to take all her students out for drinks, but arriving at the faculty bar, they found it closed and full of workmen. Kane readied herself to flirt with the workmen to try and talk them around, but to her amazement Sexton had already turned on her full charisma. Immediately, the students were allowed in a corner of the bar, where Sexton produced from her bag a supply of airline mini-bottles of vodka. Within minutes, the dazzled workmen started waiting on her, bringing fresh glasses of cold water when they were unable to meet Sexton's request for ice in her drink.[47] Her unconventional approach to education, both her own and her responsibility for others', was refreshing and proof that messing about as a teenager didn't necessarily ruin your life chances.

Plath's education was the polar opposite of Sexton's. She was a diligent straight-A student, eager to succeed, anxious if she felt her grades might drop. Her school days appeared to be an exhausting and unrelenting whirl of study, reading, writing poems and articles, piano lessons, viola lessons, summer camp, crafts, sports, and drawing. She was also aware that as a girl she needed to be careful about revealing herself to be too intelligent, otherwise her popularity would wane. In 1947, when she was defeated for the first time by a boy in a spelling bee, she claimed it was probably better for a boy to be ahead of a girl. This was a sentiment that thankfully would not last. Neither was it a sentiment she displayed toward her brother, who was subjected to her teasing and older-sister superiority. "This morning I told Warren that he was 'ostentatiously, obnoxiously superfluous,' and he hadn't the slightest idea of what I meant,"[48] she boasted at age fourteen. Although the siblings adored each other, Plath was not above getting Warren into trouble, sometimes kicking him under the dinner table to make him cry, then feigning innocence and claiming he was just a crybaby, *unlike her.*

Plath pushed herself, often to unrealistic standards, and there always appeared to be an underlying air of anxiety that she had to do her best. This perfectionism never left her; perhaps it is even what made her into the writer she became. Yet the sense of pressure must have been crippling. Even at seventeen years old she was writing, "Never, never, never will I reach the perfection I long for with all of my soul—my paintings, my poems, my stories—all poor, poor reflections . . . for I have been too thoroughly conditioned to the conventional surroundings of this community . . ."[49] This observation shows that already dissent and dissatisfaction was brewing in Plath. What she was surrounded by was not enough, and she felt that the suffocating air of the suburbs would lead to her intellectual death. Furthermore, the expected path her life would take risked killing off her creativity for good. She was drawn to boys who liked literature, but if she started dating them, it all went wrong when she won a prize for her writing or had a poem published. Boys did not like brainy girls, claimed Plath, nor did they like to be outshone by her. The problem was, intellectually, Plath could pretty much outshine anyone, so most of her time seemed to be spent negotiating her own creative life against her social life in which her light needed to be dimmed. The thought of having to do this forever understandably distressed her: "I am afraid of getting older. I am afraid of getting married. Spare me from cooking three meals a day—spare me from the relentless cage of routine and rote. I want to be free. . . ."[50] Reading her early journals creates a jittery sense of unease. Nobody could live up to the standards she persistently set herself. What a shame that she did not know Sexton at this time and couldn't go whizzing around Boston in a convertible, forgetting about her studies for a day. Even her high school principal, Samuel Graves, in recommending her for college, wrote in his reference letter, "May college mean some 'fun' for her as well as intellectual accomplishments."[51]

As well as excelling at study and forging a social life, Plath was also working hard at other aspects of school life. Like Sexton, she began to take an interest in publishing in school journals and newspapers. However, unlike Sexton, she wanted a full role in the production and creation of these publications. In June 1949 she became co-editor of the school newspaper, *The Bradford*, and from this point on she began to be published regularly in other publications, such as *Student Life*, the *Christian Science Monitor*, and *Seventeen*. It was also during these years, at age sixteen, that she decided to tackle a professor, Irwin Edman, at Columbia University after reading an article he wrote in the *Atlantic Monthly*. Titled "A Reasonable Life in a Mad World," he argued that modern "man" should rely on his ability to reason in order for society to progress. Having read this in English class, Plath, along with her friend Jeanne Woods, decided Edman needed to be taken to task. They wrote to him, chastising him for failing to take into account that in order to live fully each person needed to embrace the universe's spiritual element and should aim to look outside themselves for guidance. Edman did reply but was obviously not impressed at being challenged by two sixteen-year-old girls. Rather than fully engage with them, he suggested they wait until they got to college to think things through in more depth.

When Plath did get to college, one feels she might have dismantled Edman rather easily. Entering Smith College in 1950, Plath not only escaped what she regarded as the stifling suburbs of Boston but was introduced to new academic disciplines and work routines. As in high school, Plath excelled, and she began writing articles for local newspapers, becoming the press board correspondent for Smith College. Over the next three years she also began to publish and win some serious prizes for her work, effectively becoming a professional writer in major US publications. Her short story "Sunday at the Mintons" was awarded first place in the 1952 *Mademoiselle* short fiction contest. The following year she won the guest editor competition offered by *Mademoiselle* with the prospect of spending a month in New York City working for the magazine. This experience, in June 1953, would become immortalized in *The Bell Jar*. She also started dating, though some girls in her shared house still felt she spent too much time in her room, typing. Plath's journal notes the sly digs, which she accepts silently from her housemates: "'We'd rather flunk school and be sociable than stick in our rooms all the time.'"[52] These quips left her quivering with anxiety and feeling sickened. The idea that she was a disappointment to anyone seemed to be her greatest fear. And although at this time Sexton claimed Plath wouldn't have liked her, one does feel that Plath would have benefited from Sexton as a friend, as someone whose sass would have quipped back on her behalf.

From Smith, Plath won a Fulbright scholarship and crossed the Atlantic in 1955 to study at Cambridge University. There she was faced with the bone-numbing cold of the English fens, but also a male-female ratio of ten men to every woman. Whether it was because she had already proved herself at Smith or whether it was because she was farther away from home, Plath did appear to relax. Although she still worked hard studying and writing, she spent time exploring London and the areas around Cambridge. She lived with other international students in Whitstead, a large white house on the edge of the gardens at Newnham College. Plath's room was in the attic, with a sloping ceiling and a view across the treetops and the house roofs. She decorated her room with bright throws, cushions, and extravagant coffee-table books. In the small fireplace was a gas heater that needed to be fed shillings to keep the cold at bay. Plath wore two pairs of socks and sweaters but still felt the cold and damp seep through. On a regular basis she hosted tea and sherry get-togethers, took part in local amateur dramatic productions, and published poems in the university magazine. Despite making full use of the male-female ratio for her dating life, less than a year after arriving in England she met and married Ted Hughes. Once she had finished her studies they planned their return to America, where she had lined up a teaching job back at Smith.

In many ways she was fulfilling what was expected of her. Her teaching post began in 1957 and she started researching the possibility of studying for a PhD. She had a good, steady, well-paid job with a creative husband who was also teaching for half a year at nearby University of Massachusetts, Amherst. Unlike Sexton, however, Plath was not a natural teacher. She did not like it or enjoy it and many of her students were terrified of her. She was strict; sometimes she made them cry. What they did not and could not realize was that Plath was terrified herself. She was only twenty-five and returning to her old college making, in only a two-year gap, the sudden switch from student to lecturer. All the teachers she had previously idolized now became her colleagues, and she rapidly became disillusioned with most.

At the start of the semester she recorded in her journal feeling "the sick, soul-annihilating flux of fear in my blood switching its current to defiant fight."[53] She lasted one year.

What these early years show is that Plath and Sexton began to rebel at different ages, in different ways. Sexton, perhaps because she had the privilege of a secure financial upbringing, was more able to openly and comfortably reject the social advantages that were offered to her. For a spirited schoolgirl in the 1930s and '40s it is disturbing that her rejection of educational norms was regarded as a pathological disorder requiring psychiatric treatment. Girls who didn't do as they were told were regarded as a problem. Plath, from a one-parent family, who only got to college on scholarships, had to work harder, had to prove herself. There was no open rebellion, and the need to repress her feelings of dissatisfaction caused pain, anguish, and uncertainty: "There will come a time when I must face myself at last. Even now I dread the big choices that loom up in my life—what college? What career? I am afraid. I feel uncertain. What is best for me? What do I want? I do not know."[54] This repression seethed just below the surface, occasionally breaking through in her journals, but never really in her life or her poems. This would come later, when it seemed as though over twenty years of internal rage finally found its outlet, and nothing was ever quite the same again.

CHAPTER THREE

Sex

One thing about sex. I hate comfortable rituals.

—Sylvia Plath[1]

You see, I can explain sex in a minute, but death—
I can't explain.

—Anne Sexton[2]

Sylvia Plath and Anne Sexton both enjoyed sex immensely. They had hearty sexual appetites and throughout their lives had numerous lovers. Both were refreshingly unapologetic about this at a time when sexual double standards were about as bad as they could be. While the postwar years in America laid out restrictive ideas about gender roles and marriage, sex, too, fell under the watchful eye of cultural ideals as something to be controlled and contained. In fact, sex was only regarded as something that happened for women within the context of marriage, and even then, in order to really be sex, it had to be penetrative intercourse. There was little space in this narrative to consider the sexual life of single people, gay or lesbian sex, or indeed any kind of sexual activity that fell outside of this expected norm. But even worse, any sexual activity that was deemed deviant was regarded as a national threat. In the Cold War era, it was essential that Americans stayed strong and stable for the protection of the free world. Uncontrolled sexual behavior was seen to lead to a moral decline that would sap the nation's strength. From the government and medical professionals, to films, novels, and the mass media, "post-war popular culture served up a range of crude and subtle narratives that depicted a populace threatened and weakened by sexually dangerous women and men."[3] Of course, the most dangerous men were gay men, and the most dangerous women were essentially those who didn't have straight sex within marriage. Straight white men were given the most leeway to act out any "natural" impulses. This double standard infuriated Plath as a seventeen-year-old: "I have too much conscience injected in me to break customs . . . I can only lean enviously against the boundary and hate, hate, hate the boys who can dispel sexual hunger freely . . . The whole thing sickens me."[4] Often she would leave dates feeling unfulfilled and "soggy [with] desire."[5] Sexton was less racked with guilt, and as a teenager entered into the world of boys and dating with admirable enthusiasm, determined to entice as many men as possible (and to get rid of them equally as quickly). As teenagers both Plath and Sexton left a string of young men lovelorn and brokenhearted. Their loving and dumping possibly brought about some of the worst poetry ever written by these rejected beaus.

Like most young women, Plath's and Sexton's curiosity about sex began in their teenage years as they reflected on, and worried about, their own desirability. Even as an adult, Sexton claimed, "There's nothing that makes a woman feel worse than to be not desired. I would rather never enjoy sex, truthfully, taking all my pleasure and throw it out the window, than to feel not wanted."[6] They were aware that social worth and popularity depended on somehow managing the fine line between being desirable but not getting a "reputation." Having absorbed the socially conservative views toward sex, they then had to decide to what extent they would conform or rebel. While there is no doubt that sexual constraint was the dominant ideal, it would be inaccurate to say that there were no emerging discourses to compete with this view. In 1948, Alfred Kinsey published *Sexual Behavior in the Human Male* and followed this up in 1953 with *Sexual Behavior in the Human Female.* These controversial studies suggested that sexual behavior in America was nowhere near as conventional as previously thought. Kinsey offered statistics for homosexual sex and desire, bisexuality, female extramarital sex, sadomasochism, and biting. Between them, Plath and Sexton indulged in many of these activities at some point in their lives.

But as teenagers, they remained conventional. Sexton liked to attract boys, but then appeared to get bored with them quite quickly. They were dismissed efficiently and with candor. An exchange of letters between sixteen-year-old Sexton and a slightly older boyfriend who called himself "Torgy" reveal a typical pattern. Having met on a cattle ranch out West, they embarked on a summer romance, after which Sexton returned to Massachusetts. With unfortunate timing for Torgy, he sent a letter full of yearning, declaring his love, and claiming that he could never be happy until they were together forever. He ended with the words that probably came to haunt him: "I'll be living for the day that I get a letter from you."[7] Her letter was already on the way, and likely crossed with his in the post, containing the expressions "upon thinking it over, I wouldn't marry you even if you had $100,000,000," and "[c]halk it off to experience, Torgie [*sic*]."[8] Furiously, he replied with one of the best displays of nonchalant masculinity, as if he hadn't just previously sent his undying love. Apparently, he only allowed himself to fall in love with Sexton because she was nice "as far as kids go" but as a "kid" she knows nothing. Furthermore, he feels lucky he'll never have to see her again and she really needs to know that "you're going to have to get up pretty early to think faster than Torgy." Anne took a bright red crayon and scribbled POOEY across his first letter.

Sexton's scrapbooks are also full of love declarations from boys, usually in the form of dreadful poetry. Two outstanding ones (and by *outstanding* read *bad*) are overblown ballads using faux Old English. In "Anne," the subject of the poem is apparently as free as the lark that climbs on high, singing its glory to the sky. This is followed by references to youth and the lovely buds of May, which is rhymed with *Nay!* to declare Anne's bones will be singed by eternity. However, this has nothing on "Maid of Wellesley," a plaintive cry of farewell: "Maid of Wellesley ere we part / Give, oh, give me back my heart." There are four long stanzas, each more forlorn than the last, until the final lines lament how his love is unceasing and his woe is great. Sexton carefully pasted these poems into her scrapbook with an accompanying photo of each author. It is hard to know, with her sense of humor, whether she was flattered or found them funny.[9]

Plath's teenage dating life was equally as active. In fact, her journals open with the drama of her first kiss, which took place in a barn at Lookout Farm. Plath and her brother were working there at a summer job picking strawberries and planting spinach. Ilo, an older resident worker, took her up to his room at the top of the barn to show her his sketches (really). After looking at a portrait and demonstrating his skill with the lead in his pencil, Ilo grabbed Plath and kissed her. Feeling both thrilled and mortified, Plath wrote, "No one ever kissed me that way before, and I stood there, flooded with longing, electric, shivering."[10] This moment created a sexual yearning in Plath that for many years remained unfulfilled. It also introduced her to the teasing and moral judgments made if a young woman gave in to her desires: "[T]omorrow I have to face the whole damn farm . . . If only he hadn't kissed me. I'll have to lie and say he didn't. But they know. They all know. And what am I against so many . . . ?"[11]

While it seemed possible for both Plath and Sexton to experiment sexually, they were only willing to go so far. Although friends claimed that Sexton was still a virgin when she married at nineteen, this was not the case. One of Sexton's early boyfriends, Dick Bowker, boasted that he had taken her virginity while she was so drunk on Singapore slings, she had no memory of the occasion. She also had sex with Kayo prior to their marriage, resulting in a pregnancy scare that somewhat hastened their desire to elope.[12] Plath's main, understandable concern, too, was a real fear of pregnancy, along with the stigma of social judgment: "I cannot gratify myself promiscuously and retain the respect and support of society (which is my pet devil)—and because I am a woman: ergo: one root of envy for male freedom."[13] In 1949 Plath dated over twenty boys, which seemed to involve playing a lot of tennis, watching movies, kissing in back seats, and agonizing over how far she should go sexually. One of her dates, John Hodges, ended their relationship because according to him she had forced the issue of sex. Plath's dating technique possibly needed some refinement at this point. For her first date with John, she took him to a local playground on a dreary, rainy day and proceeded to tell him all about its history. "I've run out of conversation," he said.[14]

There were, however, a couple of serious relationships for Plath and Sexton before marriage. For Sexton this was with Jack McCarthy, a contemporary who was a favorite with her family. Considering they were only fifteen, their courtship seemed impossibly glamorous: trips to New York to go all-night clubbing, visits to bars and dances, drinking Singapore slings, and smoking. McCarthy was a victim of Sexton's practical joking, though, and recalled an incident that, far from funny, disturbed him deeply. One evening they had agreed to meet to go tobogganing on a steep hill behind her home. When he arrived, he could not see Sexton, but eventually after searching was able to make out her lifeless body at the bottom of the slope. He ran down the hill and found her unconscious and bleeding from the head. Terrified, he carried her back to the house only to discover that the "blood" was Mercurochrome and that she had been faking her death. She was pleased with this joke, McCarthy less so.[15] Although they continued to see each other, and agreed to marry within five years, once Sexton was sent to Rogers Hall they drifted apart as Sexton began a variety of new romantic entanglements.

Plath's two serious premarriage relationships that had a lasting effect were with Richard (Dick) Norton and Richard Sassoon.[16] These men were significant to Plath in different ways and for different reasons: Sassoon, because Plath regarded him as her sexual teacher; Norton, because he appeared to crystallize everything that Plath ultimately hated about men. As a consequence, Norton found himself fictionalized and immortalized as Buddy Willard in *The Bell Jar*.

The relationship had started promisingly. In 1951, during her first year at Smith, Plath had a crush on Norton, who was the son of her mother's friend. The two families were delighted with the match and Plath was pleased to be dating someone who attended Yale and was training to become a doctor. This gave her kudos with her Smith housemates, who teased her for staying in her room too much. Norton had an unusual line in dating, though. One day he'd take Plath to watch him carve up a cadaver or view a baby being born, the next he'd be cycling round to her house to show off a fascinating specimen of moss he'd found.

There were two moments in the relationship that sparked rage in Plath. The first was a conversation in which she was told that Norton expected her to stay "pure" until they married. When she asked him if he would be doing the same, he admitted that he had already had a dalliance with a waitress on Cape Cod. The sexual double standard left Plath furious. She not only snitched on him to her mother (possibly hoping this would make it back to his mother, who was an advocate for virginity in both men and women), but she let the situation brew in her mind. In 1958 she considered turning his hypocrisy into a short story, about a virgin girl dating a doctor who doesn't flinch at watching babies being born or a cadaver being cut up: "What she flinches at is his affair with a waitress. She hates him for it. Jealous. Sees no reason for being a virgin herself."[17] Three years later, the episode made it into *The Bell Jar*, where Norton, as Buddy Willard, drops his trousers, takes off his washable underpants, and leaves Esther Greenwood distinctly underwhelmed by his turkey neck and turkey gizzards. This started Plath's sexual rebellion, which she expressed via her narrator: "I couldn't stand the idea of a woman having to have a single pure life and a man being able to have a double life, one pure and one not."[18]

The second significant incident for Plath was in late 1952, when Dick decided that doctors could be poets too. As if competing with Plath, he started to explain to her (a published poet since age eight) exactly what a poem was, "a piece of dust," and then, when diagnosed with TB and stuck in a sanatorium in the Adirondacks, began to write and publish poetry himself.[19]

Plath was seriously unimpressed, so much so that, on a visit, she hurled herself down the mountainside while skiing and broke her leg, ensuring a speedy escape home from the clinic. In her journal she confides, "I saw Dick, went to Saranac with him, and broke my leg skiing. I decided again that I could never live with him ever."[20] By this stage she was becoming increasingly disillusioned with Norton, and although the relationship staggered on for a couple more years with both dating other people, in 1954 she met, in her eyes, a much more interesting character: Richard Sassoon.

Sassoon was a nineteen-year-old Paris-born British subject related to the poet Siegfried Sassoon, and a young man with sophisticated taste in wine, music, art, and literature. Plath found him small and sickly looking but equally strangely sexually appealing. In a letter to her mother, she described him as thin, slender, and not as tall as her: "He's a very intuitive weird sinuous little guy whose eyes are black and shadowed so he looks as though he were an absinthe addict . . ."[21] They began dating and saw each other most weekends, occasionally taking trips to New York. It was during this summer that Plath became more sexually liberated, certainly from the fear of pregnancy, having had a diaphragm fitted at the suggestion of her therapist, Ruth Beuscher. Faced with the hypocrisy of gendered expectations, Plath decided to rebel against the notion that she had to stay "pure" for her marriage and decided that if men could sleep with whomever they wanted, whenever they wanted, so could she. But the summer of 1954 saw Plath move away from more conventional notions of sex into more masochistic views of sex as punishment. She engaged in spanking and rough sex with Sassoon, who wrote to her threatening a more severe punishment: "If you ever anger me greatly I shall have but two alternatives, one of which is to beat you, which is a very different thing from spanking."[22] There is no indication that this was anything other than consensual on Plath's part, but it did begin a pattern that continued for years. In July 1954, while at Harvard Summer School, Plath became involved with a visiting professor. They met up, drank coffee, talked, he drove her to her therapy appointments. However, when they finally had some sort of sexual contact, it was so rough that she suffered a vaginal tear and severe hemorrhaging. When the bleeding wouldn't stop, Plath admitted to her roommate, Nancy Hunter, that she had been manually raped. Within a week of this, Plath was once again dating the professor, which left Nancy in doubt about Plath's claims. Paul Alexander speculated that "she felt drawn to men whose behavior towards her tended to border on abuse."[23] This slightly sinister undertone to some of Plath's sexual experiences, and the silence and uncertainty that surrounded them, seems almost contemporary. A woman who is raped hangs on to her silence because often she will not be believed if she speaks out. Returning to an abuser seems the easier option in a world that refuses to understand or deliberately confuses the notion of consent. Victim-shaming is the norm. The narratives are all too familiar: She can't possibly have been raped if she went back to him. If women put themselves in these dangerous situations, then they can't act surprised if something unpleasant happens. And so on. The onus rarely falls on the aggressor to explain *his* behavior.

Sexton, too, had disturbing sexual recollections, and again in her case opinion was divided as to whether her claims could be believed or not. In therapy she recalled her father entering her bedroom when he was drunk and sexually abusing her. He lay next to her on the bed, touched her genitals, and kissed her on the lips. She also felt that Nana may have witnessed one occasion when this happened and expressed her disgust. The problem for Sexton was that she could not quite establish whether these events really happened. The boundaries between reality and what she thought was reality became blurred. Her worry was that she had made it up: "Do I make up a trauma to go with my symptoms?"[24] Literature dealing with incest, memory, and suppressed trauma indicate this confusion as being common: "The effect of trauma . . . results in a blurring of boundaries between reality and non-reality, about what is real and about what comes to be believed as truth, and about what is perceived as internal and what is external."[25] Sexton's distress at not knowing whether she had made something up or not could well be the direct result of trauma, which can "impair a child's capacity to evaluate reality."[26] Her therapist, Martin Orne, did not believe she had been sexually abused by her father ("It wasn't [his] style when he was drinking") but Orne treated it as if it were true.[27] Sexton's biographer, Diane Middlebrook, also came to the conclusion that Sexton had not been abused, as did her closest friend, Maxine Kumin. But some of Sexton's friends, including Lois Ames, who was a psychiatric social worker and had treated incest survivors, truly believed that this had happened. Linda Gray Sexton points out that Sexton's autobiographical play *Mercy Street* explores an image that her mother "could never pinpoint definitively as memory, but that she could never quite dismiss as fantasy either"—the sexual abuse of a daughter by a father.[28]

This is a theme that recurs in Sexton's poems, too. "The Moss of His Skin" recounts a young girl lying silently in bed, "I held my breath / And daddy was there . . . ," and explores how, by staying quiet, the narrator is able to keep secrets from her sisters.[29] In "Briar Rose (Sleeping Beauty)," the narrator describes how the person who leans over her in bed each night is not her beloved prince but her daddy, drunk and imprisoning her: "my father thick upon me / like some sleeping jellyfish."[30] In the poetic sequence "The Death of the Fathers," Sexton's speaker covers not only disturbing relationships with her father but some of his friends, too, one who picked her up, placed her on his lap, "and his tongue, my God, his tongue, / like a red worm and when he kissed / it crawled right in."[31]

Linda Gray Sexton believed that her mother defined her truths through her poetry, but that this also meant taking literary license. "My mother imparted to me her enduring belief: what actually happened is not nearly so important as how you *feel* about what happened," concluding that even if the sexual abuse did not happen exactly in the way Sexton remembered, it stood as a metaphor for how she feared her father (especially when drunk) yet craved his love.[32]

We can never know for certain whether Sexton was sexually abused by her father or not, but it's perhaps significant that abuse can produce the type of behavior in adulthood that we see in Sexton: behavioral, emotional, and physical problems, as well as compulsive and addictive promiscuity. Repressed and forgotten abuse can result in behavior that is abusive of self and others.[33] Sexton's mother admitted that when her husband was drunk he would verbally abuse his youngest daughter using sexual language in an aggressive manner, telling her one night as she left the house that she looked as though she was going to get fucked. In therapy years later, Sexton would deal with this by creating an alter ego named Elizabeth who, while in a trance, would narrate memories and fantasies about a sexual experience with her father. Referring to herself as "the little bitch" (an insult Sexton's father had hurled at her one night while spanking her for some perceived misdemeanor), she worked through memories of possible sexual abuse and confused feelings about how good it felt to lie and cuddle with Nana. Elizabeth seemed to characterize a transgressive role that she liked to play. Linda Gray Sexton, however, linked the Elizabeth persona with something quite different: "I believe it intertwines with her feelings of being good for nothing with other men and being a prostitute."[34]

Once she married, Sexton did start to display some of the sexual behaviors that would be described in the Kinsey report published five years later. She was perpetually unfaithful to Kayo while simultaneously being highly anxious at the prospect of him being unfaithful to her. She appeared to take a rather casual attitude toward this, writing to W. D. Snodgrass in 1959, "There is a rather nice poet in Boston who is in love with me [George Starbuck]. I guess I'd better give up and sleep with him."[35] Yet her promiscuity did not really seem to bring about that much pleasure, and she repeatedly wrote that she found love exhausting, and lust inadequate. In a candid conversation with Linda when she was a teenager, Sexton admitted that the sex she had with her lovers was never as good as the sex she had within her marriage, leading Linda to wonder that "perhaps there was a great deal of anxiety lying beneath her casual attitude about lovers."[36] What seemed more important was that she was noticed and seen to be special. This could be viewed as the learned behavior of a child who was emotionally neglected (and possibly abused), but instead Dr. Orne insisted on analyzing why she felt she had such a sense of "entitlement." They explored in her sessions why she enjoyed seducing other men so much, but then when it came down to it, did not really enjoy sex with them. The pleasure seemed to be in attracting the partner of another woman. Sexton scholar Dawn Skorczewski, who also links Sexton's childhood neglect to her adult behavior, suggests that "if her power came from seducing men, Sexton said, it was because it was the only thing she had."[37]

But it was not just men whom Sexton seduced. In 1964, she met Anne Wilder, a psychiatrist, and this friendship eventually turned into an affair. The correspondence between the two women is copious and intense. Sexton, despite making the first move, appeared to be in denial that there was anything erotic or sexual between them, and was chided by Wilder for this denial. Yet their exchange of letters is certainly more affectionate than sexual. They called each other "dear" and talked in great depth about their various illnesses, ailments, and emotions. At Wilder's instigation, Sexton talked about why she wanted to die. Yet Sexton was clearly not comfortable with how she felt toward Wilder, asking her, Is it sick? Is it healthy? And she stated emphatically that it was not sexual. Wilder didn't believe her and encouraged Sexton to accept how she was feeling. After they spent some time together on a reading tour, upon returning home Sexton wrote to Wilder that as of a week or two earlier, she regarded herself as bisexual. Sexton's main fear seemed to be that if she indulged in lesbian sex, it might completely extinguish her heterosexuality. Having consummated the relationship, Sexton revealed to her daughter Linda that what two women did to each other when they were having sex was mutual masturbation.[38]

Given that the historical and cultural moment was not especially kind to same-sex relationships, Sexton's reluctance about bisexuality is understandable. Although there was an emerging subculture in America, especially in urban areas, gay and lesbian relationships were generally regarded as degenerate. In fact, to be a lesbian was as bad as being a communist. While McCarthyism was unraveling the lives of those under suspicion, mass interrogations of thousands of gays and lesbians were also happening simultaneously, known as the "Lavender Scare." By the end of the 1950s over five thousand federal workers had been fired or forced to resign for being gay or lesbian. They were seen to be vulnerable to foreign agents who could expose them as "sexual deviants" unless they provided secret information. In Boston, the gay scene was risky and mostly underground but, nevertheless, vibrant and varied. One location where gays and lesbians would congregate after the bars had closed was the Waldorf Cafeteria on Tremont Street, the same café where Sexton, Plath, and Starbuck would go for supper after drinking at the Ritz.[39] But even when bars or spaces were opened, they were predominantly white. One bar in Boston, Playland, allowed gay Black men as patrons, but many Black lesbians were restricted to private house parties and gatherings if they wanted to be out and socializing. While Sexton was willing to go so far with her sexual rebellion, there were boundaries and restrictions that made her uncomfortable being too public about it.

Plath, too, shared this reluctant curiosity about lesbianism. In January 1959 she raised the issue in a session with Dr. Beuscher and wrote afterward in her notebook: ". . . Lesbians, (what does a woman see in another woman that she doesn't see in a man: tenderness)."[40] Yet there is ambivalence. Esther Greenwood is both horrified and fascinated by Joan, the lesbian character in *The Bell Jar*. When Joan declares she "likes" Esther, she receives the response, "That's tough, Joan . . . [b]ecause I don't like you. You make me puke, if you want to know."[41] In fact, Plath affords Esther very little imagination when it comes to same-sex relationships. Sounding like Queen Victoria, Esther declares, "Whenever I thought about men and men, and women and women, I could never really imagine what they would actually be doing."[42] Likewise, in her journals Plath seemed to suffer from a similar lack of imagination regarding intimacy between women: "Why is it impossible to think of two women of middle-age living together without Lesbianism the solution, the motive?"[43] Yet in late 1962, when her marriage ended, Plath wondered whether it would be better to be involved with a woman in the future rather than another man. After her death, any hint of connecting Plath with lesbianism appeared to enrage Ted Hughes. When Plath scholar Jacqueline Rose read Plath's poem "The Rabbit Catcher" through a lesbian lens, in particular arguing that the first stanza referred to oral sex, Hughes wrote to her that this interpretation was grounds for homicide in some countries.

Yet Plath's sexuality did seem to be mainly heterosexual. Her journals are full of sexual fantasies and the ways in which her gender alone curtails her ability to fully act on them: "But women have lust, too. Why should they be relegated to the position of custodian of emotions, watcher of the infants, feeder of soul, body and pride of man? Being born a woman is my awful tragedy."[44] She expressed rape fantasies and wrote about the pleasure she took in her own body, exposing it to the sun, stretching her limbs, feeling desirable. After the end of her marriage she admitted in a letter to Ruth Beuscher that when it came to sex, "I like all sorts of positions at a lot of odd times of day, & really feel terrific and made new from every cell when I am done."[45] Again, after her death, this openness appeared to disturb Hughes. When her abridged journals were published (in the US only), he and the editor, Frances McCullough, admitted they had cut certain passages with the effect of "diminishing

Plath's eroticism, which was quite strong."[46] Even as late as the 1980s, when this edition appeared, women's sexuality was seen as something that needed to be controlled and curtailed.

But controlling their sexuality was not something Plath or Sexton were especially concerned about. In therapy sessions, Sexton would sometimes talk about her overwhelming libido (she called it "feeling sexy") and claimed it took all her willpower to simply not masturbate all day. Given that female masturbation is still something of a taboo, the fact that Sexton wrote about it in her poem "The Ballad of the Lonely Masturbator," in her 1969 collection *Love Poems*, is an indication of how radical this was. The lines "At night, alone, I marry the bed. / Finger to finger, now she's mine" seemed to be even too much for female critics to handle.[47] In her book review, Mona Van Duyn claimed that the poems repelled readers, showed incredible feats of indiscretion, and "have as little to do with believable sexuality as an act of intercourse performed onstage for an audience." The review went further than the poems, accusing Sexton of self-absorption and "her delineation of femaleness, so fanatical, that it makes one wonder, even after many years of being one, what a woman is . . ."[48] In his review Daniel Hughes singles out "The Ballad of the Lonely Masturbator" as being "typical Sextonish extravagance . . . not watercolors but blazing oils whose gaudiness makes one draw back from paint too heavily laid on."[49] Perhaps these sensitive critics should feel lucky that they never had to review *The Journals of Sylvia Plath*. They might have needed smelling salts to recover from such passages as "Oh I would like to get in a car and be driven off into the mountains to a cabin on a wind-howling hill and be raped in a huge lust like a cave woman, fighting, screaming, biting in a ferocious ecstasy of orgasm."[50]

Both Plath and Sexton were not averse to having sex in public, either. In 1956, weeks after meeting at a party in Cambridge, Plath and Hughes were having sex all over the city, perhaps most memorably on a park bench in full university regalia. In 1967, when Sexton traveled to London as one of only two women to take part in the *Poetry International* festival organized by Ted Hughes, she began an affair with the poet George MacBeth. Although she was sharing a room with her friend Lois Ames and recovering from a broken hip, she and MacBeth had sex while Ames was apparently asleep in the next bed. This led to an exchange of correspondence when Sexton returned to America in which MacBeth addressed one of his letters to Sexton's breasts and she replied that having sex with him made her feel like a virgin. Nobody had ever excited her as much as he did. Perhaps, though, such exploits were inevitable, given that all the poets performing at the festival had been booked into the 69 Hotel in Chelsea. The name sent Sexton into "gales of laughter" as she chuckled, "69 Hotel! Don't they know I have a broken hip?"[51]

Not all their sexual exploits were quite so playful, though. In 1966, eight months earlier, when Sexton broke her hip falling down the stairs on her thirty-eighth birthday, she was recovering from rejection by her latest lover. Dr. Frederick Duhl was Sexton's psychiatrist who disturbingly, at some stage during their sessions, started a sexual relationship with her.

Sexton, always desperate for approval and attention, would lie on the couch in his office for the duration of their appointment while they had sex, which he would then charge her for so as not to arouse his wife's suspicions. Sexton's husband, Kayo, wrote the checks for the appointments despite knowing about the affair. Ultimately Duhl terminated his therapy with Sexton, stopped their sexual meetings, and returned to his wife, inspiring Sexton's poem "For My Lover, Returning to His Wife," with the shattering final lines of self-effacement: "As for me, I am a watercolor. / I wash off."[52] Sexton took the rejection badly and with her broken hip lay in bed drinking eggnog and beer, gaining thirty pounds, and neglecting her physical hygiene. Linda Gray Sexton remembers her mother at this time with lank, greasy hair, wearing polyester knit jumpsuits covered in dog hair. The makeup on her dressing table was unused and dry. In "The Break," Sexton opens the poem with "It was also my violent heart that broke, / falling down the front hall stairs."[53] Sexton kept a photograph of Duhl right up until her death. In the image he is facing the camera, head slightly cocked to one side, wearing an open-necked shirt and a buttoned-up mustard-yellow cardigan. It is dated July 1965. On the back, in Sexton's hand, is written *Fred Duhl MiD* [sic], *Man of Many Hearts.*[54]

Although Plath and Sexton were unusually sexually liberated for the time, there were limits to their sexual rebellion. They broke with tradition about sexual control; Plath engaged in sadomasochism and spanking, Sexton in extramarital and lesbian sex. But they were operating in a society that did not value or care about women's sexual pleasure. Sexton's affairs seemed designed to make her feel better about herself, and men were happy to use her in this way. Plath ended up in harm's way, somehow equating sexual pleasure with pain and punishment. In February 1956, when she met Ted Hughes for the first time, she bit him on the cheek until he bled. The first time they had sex one month later, he left her with a battered face and wounded neck. Within weeks, they were married. Violence would play a part in Sexton's marriage as well, often combined with too much alcohol and her deteriorating emotional state. If Plath and Sexton sometimes used sex as a disturbing form of self-harm and violence, they were equally able to draw pleasure from it, most notably through masturbation, when men were not even needed. In "Fever 103°," Plath wrote, "All by myself I am a huge camellia / Glowing and coming and going, flush on flush."[55] Although, of course, there is nothing new about female masturbation, publicly declaring its merits was an absolute taboo, one that Plath and Sexton broke gleefully in their poems.

Negotiating the tricky world of sex in 1940s and '50s America was no easy task. Plath and Sexton gave it a pretty good go trying to prioritize their own pleasure and breaking free from the crippling guilt they were supposed to feel about being sexually adventurous. Figuring out how to become a healthy sexual being, however, was far less demanding than what they both faced when they found themselves with husbands. Then there was a whole new role for them to handle. That of wife.

CHAPTER FOUR

Marriage

He is a violent Adam . . .

—Sylvia Plath[1]

Kayo is a fine person, responsible and kind.

—Anne Sexton[2]

We can perhaps judge the state of white middle-class American marriage from the 1930s onward by knowing that one of the main celebrity guidance counselors, and in fact the first person to set up a marriage counseling center, was by trade a horticulturalist. Paul Popenoe was a well-known and prolific personality offering expert advice on how to strengthen the union of marriage and how to save it when it came under threat. He wrote pieces for the *Ladies' Home Journal* and appeared on media outlets spreading the message that it was, on the whole, a woman's job to maintain a happy marriage and make sure that it did not end in divorce. Not only should women regard marriage as a fulfilling career in itself, they needed to understand that they were in effect responsible for their husbands' careers as well. History professor Kristin Celello outlined in her book *Making Marriage Work: A History of Marriage and Divorce in the Twentieth-Century United States* that matrimonial responsibility started well before any marriage ceremony.[3] It was the responsibility of a woman to earn a marriage proposal and this involved a dedicated program of self-improvement to become worthy of being someone's wife. Lowering expectations, working on appearance, and learning about "intimacy issues" were all suggestions coming from the *Ladies' Home Journal* in 1954 about how best to land yourself a groom. If your marriage started going wrong, if your husband was unfaithful, abusive, or turned to alcohol, what you needed to seriously consider was in what way you likely drove him to it. If your husband was prone to violence, then indulge his whims to avoid arguments so he would relax. If your husband cheated, then work on your appearance and charisma to make sure he gave up his mistress. Furthermore, make it your duty and responsibility to ensure he did not cheat in the future. If this seems outdated, it's worth thinking that these ideas are not so far removed from today's narratives of how to keep your man happy.

"The trouble was, I hated the idea of serving men in any way," says Esther Greenwood in *The Bell Jar.*[4] Rather than being obedient and staying "pure" for a man who almost certainly wouldn't be "pure" himself upon marriage, Esther decided that the best course of action was to forget about staying pure herself and marry someone who also wasn't pure, "then when he started to make my life miserable I could make his miserable as well."[5] When Plath did decide to get married, it was quick, intense, and all rather sudden and secretive. Despite in many ways adhering to the 1950s ideal of the perfect wife who created an intellectually stimulating home, Plath was subject to domestic violence and infidelity. In 1962, after the end of her six-year marriage, she was confronted with the *Ladies' Home Journal* ideals when the local vicar in Devon visited her to find out what was going on in her domestic life. She told him that she had kicked her husband out because he was seeing another woman. When the vicar suggested this might be the result of her not being a good enough wife, Plath's response was to pick up a broom and chase him down the drive of Court Green.[6]

Anne Sexton, too, married quickly and secretly. Unlike Plath, her marriage lasted much longer, almost twenty-five years, but also like Plath's was filled with violence and infidelity (the latter, in this case, on her part): "I was a victim of the American Dream, the bourgeois, middle-class dream. All I wanted was a little piece of life, to be married, to have children."[7] This little piece of life proved to be Sexton's anchor and undoing. Just as she achieved the very things she wanted, they appeared to erode her mental well-being. Yet the point at which she freed herself from their constraints was the point at which she could no longer live.

So, who were these men that Sylvia Plath and Anne Sexton decided to marry? And what was it about them that managed to capture these two women? Both married young; Sexton was nineteen and Plath was twenty-three. Both eloped, and both had been in love with other men shortly before their marriages. Did they gossip about their husbands and dramatic nuptials over their third martini at the Ritz while these very husbands were at home waiting for them to return? What was it about Kayo Sexton and Ted Hughes that made them so *marriageable*?

In 1948, Anne Sexton (then Harvey) was busy learning how to make a decent white sauce at the Garland School in Boston and informing her friends that she was engaged to a nice young man from Wellesley. Despite her engagement, in May she began to exchange letters with Kayo Sexton, whom she was introduced to through a mutual friend. Although at this stage they had not met, Kayo contacted her via letter and received a flirtatious reply from a "mystery woman" (Sexton) inviting him to "come up and see her sometime."[8] They arranged a date at the Longwood Cricket Club in Chestnut Hill in early July and less than three weeks later were seriously in love.

In 1928, Kayo Sexton was born Alfred Muller Sexton II to parents Wilhelmine (known as Billie) Muller and George Sexton. The family had been wealthy, owning the Lower Falls liquor store and living in a mansion on Middlesex Road in Chestnut Hill, complete with a gleaming Buick. Much of their wealth had been lost in the crash, so by 1948 they were less well-off than they had been. As a baby, the nickname "Kayo" was used because, like a character in the comic strip *Moon Mullins*, Kayo was once put to bed in a dresser drawer.[9] The endearing name stuck for the rest of his life. By 1948, Kayo had completed his first year at Colgate University and was hoping to become a doctor, much to the approval of his strict and serious parents. However, after his first date at the cricket club with his future wife, within days he had taken her to meet his parents, who had high hopes of their son marrying a "well-mannered" and "reserved" woman.[10] They were not quite expecting the whirlwind that arrived in their dining room, turning up in her own convertible, smoking, boy crazy, and wearing (in their opinion) too much red lipstick, which stained Mrs. Sexton's best linen napkins.

Despite all family reservations, on August 14, within just weeks of meeting, the couple both secretly dropped from their upper-story bedroom windows and took off for North Carolina, where the legal marriage age was only eighteen. Arriving in a shiny black convertible, they married on August 16, just before sunset, in a small white church in Sunbury. The minister spoke about the seriousness of marriage and arranged three witnesses for the wedding. Kayo wore trousers without a belt that constantly threatened to fall down. Sexton, who forgot to pack suitable footwear, married in a blue dress with clunky black shoes. After the ceremony, with JUST MARRIED signs stuck all over the car, they drove through the pink sunset to Virginia Beach and honeymooned for four days at the Cavalier Hotel.

The shock to both families must have been considerable. When Sexton escaped from her bedroom window to elope, she had at least left a letter "to be put on the table at breakfast"[11] that opened with: "By the time you read this you will have another son-in-law."[12] She proceeded to tell her parents how much she loved them, how she didn't want to have to plan another wedding because she'd already done that with her previous fiancé, and how she'd been thinking about marrying

Kayo for "some time" (a week).[13] Aware that this move would not go down well with the Sexton family, the letter pleaded for understanding and forgiveness. Sexton had no intention of going back to the Garland School, and Kayo had to decide whether or not to go back to college ("He doesn't want to—he wants to marry me").[14] Following the wedding, they sent telegrams to both sets of in-laws. The Sexton family threw theirs away in a fury; the Harveys were more forgiving.

Luckily, within days Kayo's family had calmed down and made peace with the eloping couple, prompting Sexton to write to her parents, "Everything is so perfect now. Knowing that you and the Sextons still love us and are standing by us makes such a difference."[15] The newlyweds were able to spend the next four days enjoying their honeymoon, though according to Sexton, "I'm afraid we are too much in love to pay much attention to the luxury around us."[16] This was confirmed by Richard Sherwood, an old school friend of Sexton's, who ran into them at the Cavalier and was invited to their room for a drink. Unable to contain themselves, he was asked to leave immediately while they had sex and then they had him paged to return once they were finished. He was shocked when Sexton told him they did a lot of "role-playing," a story that Sexton liked to recount with relish.[17]

Sexton believed that in Kayo she had found the sweetest, kindest, most loving man in the world. Certainly, over the ensuing twenty-five years, he would prove to be patient, understanding, and caring in many ways. Toward the end of the marriage, Sexton perhaps underestimated just how much of a supportive force Kayo had been in her life, and by the time she realized this, it was too late for them. But the marriage had also become increasingly troubled by alcohol, terrible violence, and resentment, and Sexton's infidelity was an ongoing source of pain for Kayo.

In the early years they formed a close bond, with Sexton moving to Hamilton, New York, where Kayo continued his premed studies at Colgate, financially supported by his parents. This gave Sexton the first opportunity to try out her new role as housewife, one that began with enthusiasm but didn't last for long. Writing to her parents at the beginning of November, she claimed "I have been MONSTROUSLY busy cooking, washing . . . cleaning, giving parties that don't happen etc. etc. Doing all my little wifely duties."[18] Her domestic life yielded mixed results ("My cooking has taken a slight turn for the better"),[19] though the stories that followed about pineapple muffins and apple pies suggest she was being somewhat kind to herself with this observation.

This was in sharp contrast to Plath, who in the early years of her marriage excelled at and delighted in cooking for her new husband. Born in Mytholmroyd, West Yorkshire, in 1930 to parents Edith and William Hughes, Ted was the youngest of three children; he had an older brother, Gerald, and a sister, Olwyn. The Hughes family was regarded as working-class, though William owned his own business, a confectionery shop, and Edith, an intelligent and well-read woman, had aspirations for all her children. Ted Hughes attended Mexborough Grammar School and won a scholarship for university that saw him graduate from Cambridge in 1954. When Plath met him nearly two years later, he was dividing his time between writing poems in his old university town and doing a variety of odd jobs in London. Their first meeting, in Cambridge, was on February 25, 1956, at a wild and raucous launch for a poetry pamphlet called *St. Botolph's Review*. Somewhat inappropriately, the party, which consisted of heavy drinking, partner swapping, a live jazz band, and smashed windows, was held in the rooms used by the Women's Institute. Plath, who had previously read and admired Hughes's poems, arrived drunk, quoted his poems to him, kissed him, and then bit him on the cheek until he bled. In turn he tore off her hairband and earrings and pocketed them. Then they both drank too much brandy, and a glass got smashed before he returned to his waiting girlfriend in the next room. The next day Plath wrote in her journal, "And I screamed in myself, thinking: oh, to give myself crashing, fighting, to you."[20] This dramatic meeting is often depicted as the turning point for Plath, the moment when she fell in love with Hughes. But her letters and journals do not support this. In fact, she was still deeply in love with Richard Sassoon and yearning to see him. Hughes seemed merely an exciting sideline. In her 1956 poem "Pursuit," Plath's narrator describes the sexual tension of being hunted by a predatory man: "There is a panther stalks me down: / One day I'll have my death of him," ending with the lines "The panther's tread is on the stairs, / Coming up and up the stairs."[21] In her journal she admitted that it was "a full-page poem about the dark forces of lust: It is not bad. It is dedicated to Ted Hughes."[22]

Meanwhile, about Sassoon she wrote, "We came to a point where the first time in my life I felt I actually could see giving my life to this one man; all the nagging conventional society doubts while there, didn't matter a damn."[23] Sassoon, however, had other ideas, and when he realized Plath was coming to Paris that March to see him, he took off for Switzerland to avoid her. Reflecting back years later, he felt that their relationship had been intense and graciously magical, but ultimately egotistical and immature. He was too young to fully understand what he was doing and spent much of his time feeling confused.[24] His friends, though, observed something quite different and claimed it took him ten years to get over losing Plath.

On her way to see Sassoon in Paris, Plath stopped off in London to see Hughes. The night before her journey they sat knee to knee in intense conversation in an upstairs apartment on Rugby Street in Bloomsbury, in a house around the corner from the church where they would marry just three months later. When Hughes walked her back to her hotel, he managed to sneak into her room and they spent most of the night having sex. Upon returning to Rugby Street, Hughes kicked awake one of his friends, Michael Boddy, and told him that he had fallen in love for the first time in his life.[25]

Plath and Hughes recorded this night very differently. In "Rugby Street," in his poetry collection *Birthday Letters*, Hughes wrote, "You were slim and lithe and smooth as a fish. / You were a new world. My new world."[26]

In her journal, Plath wrote that she was exhausted from a "sleepless holocaust night with Ted in London," and that her face was "battered" and "smeared with a purple bruise from Ted and my neck raw and wounded too . . ."[27] This section was removed by Hughes when he published Plath's abridged journals in 1982. In another twist, when Hughes read Plath's journals after her death, he was devastated to learn that after he had fallen in love with her, she was pining for somebody else. In drafts of poems that never made it into *Birthday Letters*, he muses on the power of Richard Sassoon, asking why her love for another man was so simple, and asking, with quite a staggering lack of self-awareness, "What did I do wrong?"[28]

After arriving in Paris to discover that Sassoon had deserted her, Plath collapsed sobbing in the living room of his bewildered concierge while a black poodle patted her with his paw. Plath noted that the radio was blaring "Smile though your heart is breaking." Sounding outraged, she wrote in her journal, "I was really amazed at my situation; never before had a man gone off to leave me to cry after."[29] In the weeks that followed she dated other men, attempted unsuccessfully to travel around various European cities with her old flame Gordon Lameyer, then in April flew from Rome to London, back to Hughes. They were married two months later on June 16, a rainy Bloomsday with Plath's mother in attendance at St. George the Martyr, in Queen Square, Bloomsbury.[30] Hughes wore new trousers and shoes. Plath wore a pink knitted suit dress provided by her mother with a pink ribbon in her hair.[31] She held a pink rose from Hughes and cried as she said her vows. Like Sexton and Kayo, Plath and Hughes had married in relative secrecy; only her mother and brother knew. Hughes did not tell his family for some weeks, and Plath was terrified of the authorities at Cambridge finding out. She seemed to understand that her Fulbright scholarship would be pulled, since marriage was frowned upon, or, as she put it to her brother, "the Victorian virgins wouldn't see how I could concentrate on my studies with being married to such a handsome virile man."[32] Although this turned out not to be the case, after a honeymoon in Spain, for the first six months they lived apart; Plath stayed in her university room at Whitstead and Hughes traveled between London and Cambridge. They exchanged letters almost daily while they were apart, pouring out the agony it was for them to not see each other and how deeply they loved each other. They had pet names, and some of the letters got distinctly racy. They also began a routine that remained for the rest of their married life: exchanging and critiquing each other's poems. By December this living situation had become untenable for both of them so they decided to come clean (nobody cared about the marriage despite Plath's concerns), and they were able to move into a small ground-floor apartment at 55 Eltisley Avenue, in Newnham.[33] They lived mostly from Plath's generous Fulbright grant, with Hughes occasionally doing radio readings in London for the Rank Organisation and taking a teaching job in Cambridge. Plath delighted in reading cookbooks and trying out new recipes for Hughes, which she wrote about ecstatically to her mother. One visitor, however, suggested that all was not as happy as Plath cared to pretend. An old friend from Smith, Sue Burch, recalled visiting Plath and being alarmed at her weeping over her cooking pots, crying for no discernible reason. Hughes ignored this and offered no consolation, as if it weren't happening at all. Burch felt one reason was that Plath had been trying her will out against Hughes and had seen there was "no choice." Burch's take was that some men had such a combination of ego and insecurity that they had to reassure themselves by trampling on others. In her opinion, Hughes was going to be that way with Plath in their marriage.[34]

Although their apartment was rather dingy and damp, they were at least together, financially independent, and starting to make plans for a future life in America. There, Plath felt she would be able to reduce the domestic labor she was forced into while living in England. America had iceboxes, washing machines, and hot water: "I know now that if I want to keep on being a triple-threat woman: wife, writer & teacher (to be swapped later for motherhood, I hope) I can't be a drudge, the way housewives are forced to be here."[35]

Kayo and Sexton, too, in their early years yearned to be financially independent. After only a few months studying at Colgate, Kayo decided to leave and take a job that would allow the couple to support themselves. They moved back to Massachusetts, and Kayo began to work for a wool company in a job that Ralph Harvey secured for him. Sexton worked part-time in Hathaway House Bookshop in Wellesley to supplement their income and joined a modeling agency in Boston with her sister-in-law, Joan. The Sextons stayed with each set of parents for a couple of months at a time, and it was during this period that Billie Sexton began to notice disturbing elements to her daughter-in-law's behavior. First, Sexton openly admitted she had told "dreadful lies" to get a job at the modeling agency, pretending to be much more experienced than she was (which was not at all).[36] But Billie also noticed Sexton was unpredictable and impulsive, with a violent temper. One day while she was cooking, Billie asked her to buy some milk from the store. Sexton's response was to throw herself on the floor in a tantrum, drumming her heels and fists and shouting, loudly. She appeared to swing between deep depression and excitement at rapid speed. But worse in Billie's eyes was the fact that Sexton showed no interest whatsoever in learning how to manage a home. She was much happier lying in bed until late in the morning, reading magazines. Already Sexton was deeply disinterested in what 1950s society had in store for her as a young wife.

Billie may have been even more disturbed had she known that her son's new wife had also recently fallen in love with another man, Johnny, who was training to be a surgeon at Harvard Medical School. Kayo was friends with Johnny's wife, and the two couples began socializing and spending time together. Sexton insisted that the relationship was not sexual, just a romance, but her mother was furious with her, insisting that she stop seeing Johnny and sent her for three months of therapy instead. Sexton's response was to dramatically take an overdose of pills in Johnny's kitchen, where she became dizzy and started to throw up. Johnny walked her back and forth and she appeared to make a recovery from what seemed like an act of resistance rather than a serious attempt on her life. Although therapy helped Sexton decide not to divorce Kayo, who presumably was aware of what was going on, this early love affair set the scene for Sexton's behavior throughout her married life. In later sessions with her psychiatrist Martin Orne, Sexton would argue that her need for attention from men was due to low self-esteem and the feeling that she was "nobody."[37] It wasn't even about sex, it was about being seen. This visibility seemed crucial to Sexton, whose greatest fear was not being desired while simultaneously not really feeling worthy of any man's attention. It was almost as if who did the seeing was not as important as actually just being seen.

Within two years of living with both sets of parents, the Sextons had saved enough money to rent their own tiny apartment in Natick, and in 1950 Kayo was offered an invitation to join his father-in-law's wool company. Starting at the very bottom, Kayo began working for his father-in-law as a road salesman. Just as he accepted this role, the Korean War broke out and Kayo joined the naval reserves, training in navigation. Sent overseas, Sexton once again divided her time between the two sets of parents, and once again began to fall for other men. Eleven years later, reflecting back on her behavior at this time, she claimed that "I don't really *want* to have an affair with anyone, but I have to; it's the quality of action. I first had this feeling, I suppose, when I was dating, after Kayo went into the service."[38] Sexton appeared restless and in need of attention, so in 1952, when Kayo's ship docked in San Francisco, she withdrew all her savings and drove out there, taking five hundred silver dollars to use in the slot machines in Reno in the hopes of winning a home-buying jackpot. Although luck was not on her side, she did immediately fall pregnant when reunited with Kayo, and so returned home to Weston to be taken care of throughout her pregnancy. Her first daughter, Linda Gray Sexton, was born on July 21, 1953, three days before Kayo was released from duty to return to civilian life. Two years later a second daughter, Joyce Ladd Sexton, was born on August 4, 1955.

If Sexton struggled with the 1950s conventions that were forced upon her as a wife, she struggled even more with motherhood. Rejecting certain roles and responsibilities may have been a bold move for Sexton, and in some ways liberating for her, but for others, namely her children, it was distressing and hurtful. Thinking about Sexton's own childhood—her emotional neglect and the learned behavior she took away from that, as well as her troubled relationship with her mother, combined with her unpredictable mood swings—it is possible to see why Sexton felt unable to cope psychologically. But it was not just personal pressure, it was societal pressure too. In a 1968 interview she admitted, "I was trying my damnedest to lead a conventional life, for that was how I was brought up, and it was what my husband wanted of me. But one can't build little white picket fences to keep nightmares out."[39] When she was twenty-eight, shortly after the birth of Joyce (called Joy by her family), Sexton had a psychotic breakdown and tried to kill herself. The children were sent to live with various family members and Sexton was hospitalized. It was during her recovery, after taking a Rorschach test, that her psychiatrist noticed she had untapped creative talent and suggested she start writing. "'Don't kill yourself,' he said. 'Your poems might mean something to someone else someday.' "[40] It was ten years since Sexton had stopped writing poetry after being accused of plagiarism by her own mother. Once she started again, she realized writing gave her life purpose, gave her something to *do*.

But Sexton quickly discovered that writing and being a wife and mother was not easy. As a mother, once she was well enough for the children to return home, she felt as though their demands took priority. In reality, Sexton was lucky to have much more support than many women. Billie Sexton assumed all of the childcare, driving the children to various dancing and violin lessons. A housekeeper, Meme, took care of the laundry and cleaning twice a week, and on the days in between the house would "go to hell."[41] As a wife, Sexton felt that Kayo was not particularly interested in her new career. In a 1968 interview, the interviewer inquired about what Kayo's attitude was to her poetry. She replied, "Well, he's not really that interested. He does occasionally read my books when they're finished, but I don't think he really likes poetry very much."[42] This comment seemed to overlook that Kayo supported Sexton's writing in other ways, by doing the grocery shopping and cooking throughout their marriage, which helped free her from daily chores that would otherwise have eaten into her writing time. Their daughter Linda observed, "As much as Dad resented her poetry, he also helped her out as best he could."[43]

Plath, of course, did not have this problem. In the early years of her marriage, Hughes was the more successful poet, winning prizes and being published widely. After she graduated from Cambridge in 1957, the couple moved to America, where she took up the position teaching English at her old college, Smith, and Hughes also eventually started teaching at the nearby University of Massachusetts, Amherst, for the second half of the year. Both hoped to combine writing with teaching, but for Plath this simply was not possible. Between planning classes and grading papers, she was mostly left too exhausted to then start on her own work. One of Plath's colleagues, George Gibian, observed the couple with interest. He felt that Plath seemed sad and disillusioned with her job, while initially, and unusually for the time, Hughes was financially supported by his wife. Gibian experienced envy, not because Hughes was married to Plath, but because he described him as a consort, a Hapsburg prince free to do what he liked.[44] Although the plan had been for Plath to teach for at least two years, she realized this would make her so miserable that she resigned after one, much to the outrage of her faculty (and mother). Hughes supported her decision to escape the drudgery of teaching, convinced that if they moved to Boston for a year, they would be able to survive using their writing, their savings, and taking part-time jobs.

The year at Smith was not especially happy or easy for their marriage. They were living in a tiny apartment, dealing with exhaustion, trying to write, and plotting their escape from the small, cloistered, gossipy academic world. Throughout the fall of 1957, the pressure seemed to build, and then in May 1958, it exploded. When Hughes failed to meet Plath after her final class at Smith, she caught him strolling the campus grounds with one of his female students from Amherst. Her journals record the shock, despite on one level her intuition telling her at some stage that she would encounter such a scene. The student spotted Plath and immediately ran away, while Hughes nonchalantly offered what Plath referred to as "fake excuses, vague confusions about name & class. All fake. All false. And the guilty look of stunned awareness of the wrong presence."[45] Violence once again entered the relationship, with Plath writing in her journal that she had a sprained thumb and Hughes bloody claw marks for a week. Having thrown a glass at the wall, it failed to break and instead bounced back and hit her on the head, making her see stars. In a curt journal entry Plath wrote, "Air cleared. We are intact."[46]

In 1958, moving to Boston for a year to focus on their writing saw Plath further rebelling against 1950s ideals. Once again she became the breadwinner, taking odd jobs when their savings ran low, and Hughes was happy to be supported by his wife. Aurelia Plath was especially disapproving of this setup, believing at the very least that Hughes should take some responsibility for their income, however irregular that might have been. Plath, on the other hand, saw her husband as a genius who needed to be given the time to write, and she was happy to provide that opportunity. The earning potential for his writing far outweighed hers at this point. This was the year that Plath met Sexton and socialized with other poets in the Beacon Hill area. Dinners were exchanged with Robert Lowell and Elizabeth Hardwick, W. S. Merwin, Stephen and Agatha Fassett, Adrienne Rich, and Marianne Moore. But Plath was crippled by writer's block, what she called the panic bird, and often could not write a word. From a creative point of view, for her, the year had been a waste. The more her panic increased, the less productive she became. It was also an extraordinarily suffocating time, when Plath and Hughes were barely apart. They spent almost all their time together in a small living space, trying to write, but with very little independent time. At the end of her marriage, Plath realized how unhealthy it had been for them, acknowledging that all their experiences were filtered through the other. At some stage in 1959, Plath and Hughes decided to return to England, and they sailed in mid-December, arriving in London in the coldest, darkest month of the year, with Plath five months pregnant. This decision changed Plath's writing fortune: moving into an apartment at 3 Chalcot Square, in Primrose Hill, in February 1960, on the tenth of that month she signed a contract with Heinemann for her first poetry collection, *The Colossus.* On April 1 she gave birth to her daughter, Frieda Rebecca Hughes, and by the following spring had written *The Bell Jar* in six weeks.

For all the unconventional aspects of their marriage, and for all of Plath's ambivalence about which of society's norms she would reject or accept, there were still elements of tradition that stuck. When their sculptor friend Leonard Baskin came to stay in their small London apartment in spring 1961, he recalled that Plath was excited about her work on *The Bell Jar.* Despite relying on Hughes to share the childcare (which unusually for the time he was happy to do), the two men decided to go off for a few days' jaunt to the country. In what Baskin referred to as "insensitivity," they left Plath alone with Frieda, which in effect "short-circuited" her work schedule and killed her "creative thrust." When they returned, Plath was furious and refused to speak to them for twenty-four hours.[47] Like Sexton, Plath quickly discovered that it was far from easy being a mother, wife, and writer. The struggles they faced then are the same ones many women face today, with the onus for childcare most often falling on the mother.

In 1960, Sexton summed up this difficulty in a letter to W. D. Snodgrass: "Kayo (who we all agree is better than I deserve and all) does resent the poetry and sometimes I feel chained to this place . . . not to him . . . but to this suburban place."[48] In an undated anniversary card Sexton sent to Kayo, the front picture shows a woman throwing her arms around her husband and the saying reads "HUBBY! To the GUY who's got what it takes," and the overleaf picture shows a woman sneaking money out of her sleeping husband's pocket with the caption "From the GAL who takes what he's got!" In a handwritten message on the back Sexton hoped that they would always share their understanding, forgiveness, and passion.[49] Even if Kayo failed to fully understand what writing meant to Sexton, she relied on his support with the children and running the house, and initially earning money, which allowed her to write. But Kayo also acted as a lightning rod for Sexton, too, a fact she was aware of when she wrote in 1966, ". . . I am married to a very intense, practical SQUARE. He is good for me for he has complete plans on how to run each day. He is with the world. I am not of it whatsoever."[50] She was also grateful for his love and felt somewhat unworthy: "How in God's name did I ever get such a wonderful husband?"[51]

Despite this, Sexton frequently instigated affairs while simultaneously demanding Kayo stay faithful to her, quite impressively hypocritical by anyone's standards. In 1963, when she was awarded a travel grant from the American Academy of Arts and Letters to spend a year traveling abroad, Sexton's letters home to Kayo pleaded with him to keep loving her and stay faithful. From Belgium she wrote, "Kayo, the night before last I dreamt that you were having an affair with someone and I woke up crying." Yet during this trip Sexton began a relationship with Louis, a German-speaking Yugoslavian man, and when she feared she had become pregnant as a result of the affair, she flew home to Boston, abandoning her yearlong trip after only two months. Chaos and drama were never far away from Sexton on these adventures.

Tensions in the marriage increased as Kayo began to resent the time Sexton spent on writing and grew jealous of her involvement with the literary community around Boston. Feeling excluded and unable to really connect with her new friends seemed to unearth his deepest insecurities, as he felt his wife was leaving him further behind both physically and intellectually. Linda Gray Sexton recalls a terrible argument one Saturday afternoon when her mother was leaving for a meeting with a poet and editor and her father complained that leaving the family on a weekend was selfish. The discussion soon escalated into a serious physical fight, with Sexton throwing her typewriter at the wall and Kayo punching her in the jaw. Wrestling on the floor, Kayo continued to repeatedly hit Sexton until she pleaded with him to "please just kill me."[52] Such physical fights were not uncommon and were often made worse by alcohol. At five o'clock each day Kayo would pour the first drink and it would continue from there. "Booze was a pillar that seemed, at that time, to prop up our family," observed Linda. But with alcohol comes unpredictability. The mood at dinner was sometimes affectionate and humorous; other times it would end in vicious fights, with Kayo choking Sexton and both daughters having to pull their parents apart.

In her therapy sessions Sexton felt as though she was seeking punishment from her husband, and somehow reflecting the ideals put forth by the *Ladies' Home Journal*, worried that Kayo's anger was caused by her own inability to be the perfect sort of wife he expected her to be, "who would market, maintain the house, take care of the children, and keep their guests entertained at dinner parties."[53] The powerful cultural message of what a wife should be clearly preyed on Sexton's mind. She then had to deal with the fallout of not being all the things that were expected of her.

But the violence represented a complex and nuanced picture of two-way aggression that complicated the idea of a straightforward victim/abuser scenario. Sexton always began the altercations, inciting violence, and Kayo responded physically. Their daughter Linda, who witnessed fight after fight, tried to unravel what the violence meant: "They were victims of one another—each equally culpable. I am not excusing my father's behavior, because a man should never turn to physical violence, but she also exerted a kind of violence on him, an emotional and stinging one, that she shouldn't have turned to either. It was so complex."[54]

Sexton appeared to have two responses to dealing with this violence. First, sometimes during fights, and then increasingly in her day-to-day life, she would enter a fugue state in which seemingly she would black out (for up to six hours) and be oblivious to anything going on around her. Sometimes this would enrage Kayo even more, and on one occasion he tried to choke her out of her unresponsiveness. This led Sexton to believe that one day Kayo might kill her. When she raised this fear with Dr. Orne, he suggested they look at what Sexton had done to cause Kayo's behavior. While the dynamics of the relationship were certainly important, so, too, were Sexton's fears. Then, as now, women were often not believed or listened to when domestic violence was presented as a threat to their lives or well-being. In an all-too-familiar refrain, Orne claimed that if Kayo really had been choking Sexton and if she really did fear for her life, then she would leave him.

The second tactic Sexton used that seemed to bring physical fights to an end was to start hitting and hurting herself, punching and slapping her own face and inviting Kayo to finish her off. Her children witnessed the aftermath of these fights, their father placing a cold compress on the injured part of their mother and Sexton kissing the top of his head in forgiveness.[55] Kayo always apologized afterward and eventually, on Sexton's insistence, went into therapy himself to show his commitment to removing the violence from the marriage. The therapy worked and the violence was brought under control, though this produced an odd response from Sexton. She told her therapist that now she had to dream about being tied up and punished because Kayo would no longer beat her up. "When I feel depressed I keep wanting to hurt myself, but he no longer does it. I need to be punished, then forgiven. Never realized he was actually doing this for me."[56] Caught in this toxic dependency, Sexton summed up her marriage: "Sometimes I think he deserves an award for putting up with me. Other times I think he's pretty lucky."[57]

Plath shared Sexton's belief that she was lucky to have married the man she did. Both women, despite their brilliance, appeared to have a sense of being undeserving. Like Sexton, Plath felt nobody else in the world could put up with her the way Hughes did, and for that she was grateful. But like the Sexton marriage, for all the mutual support and affection, the Plath-Hughes relationship had flash points that erupted into violence. Archive notes written by Frances McCullough, who worked with Hughes on the American edition of Plath's journals, recalls a car conversation they had in the 1970s when Hughes admitted he used to "have to" slap Plath out of her rages because she had a "demonic side" like "black electricity," and that one day she voluntarily turned her face into his fist, giving herself a black eye. He went on to claim that Plath then made her injuries look worse than they really were by applying makeup to them because she liked the attention they brought her.[58]

These violent episodes in both Plath's and Sexton's marriages are uncomfortable to read about and consider. Whatever provocation, whatever desire for punishment, it is difficult to read the ways in which men justify hitting women or somehow absolve themselves of responsibility by placing the blame elsewhere. These attitudes are depressingly contemporary, too, with incidents of domestic violence often regarded as a private affair, something that couples should sort out between themselves. Although statistics show violence by an intimate partner is falling slightly, it is still something that affects on average twenty-four people per minute in the United States (twelve million people over the course of a year), with the highest rates among females between the ages of eighteen to thirty-four.[59] The stories that Sexton and Plath have to tell about their experiences of violence and the stories told about them by their partners sound like the same narratives we hear today. *Why doesn't she just leave him? Really, she was asking for it. What did she do to provoke it?*

The tiny Chalcot Square apartment seemed to compound the growing tension in the Plath-Hughes marriage, and although Plath loved living in London with all the cultural stimulation it brought, she agreed to Hughes's request to find a larger house and move to the country. On August 31, 1961, with Plath pregnant again, they packed their belongings and headed to Court Green, a large thatched house in a small market town called North Tawton, in Devon. On January 17, 1962, their son, Nicholas Farrar Hughes, was born in the spare bedroom overlooking the elm trees. Plath immersed herself in decorating their new home, as well as sewing, baking, cooking, planting a garden, and getting to know the neighbors. She would write in the morning while Hughes took care of the children, then they would swap roles for the afternoon. On the surface it all seemed idyllic. They sublet their London apartment to David and Assia Wevill; he was an up-and-coming poet, while she worked in an advertising agency. But the marriage had less than a year to survive. Within six months, Hughes had started an affair with Assia and moved back to London, and Plath was left in the country with two small children and a large country home.

To "fail" at anything was Plath's worst nightmare, and she regarded the end of her marriage as devastating. Upon discovering her husband's affair, letters to her therapist, Ruth Beuscher, show the depths of Plath's despair, given that she regarded her marriage as the "center of her being."[60] Not without humor, Plath nicknamed her rival "Weavy Asshole."[61] Confidence in her desirability was knocked, and Plath's sense of identity confused. Having been wife-mother-poet, this was all now changing, and certain truths were returning to her with clarity. Having yielded to the 1950s belief that a wife should hold the home together and sacrifice her own desires for the good of the family, Plath realized that "I see, too, that domesticity was a fake cloak for me. My trouble is that I can do an awful lot of stuff well."[62] Clean floors, bake a cake, have children, write poems, stitch a nightgown—all these things she claimed she could do effortlessly. In dreadful arguments as the marriage dissolved, Hughes told Plath she was an ugly hag in a world of beautiful women, that he hoped she'd kill herself, and that he'd never wanted children with her. In return, she told him he was a bastard and a selfish liar: "I don't mind knowing a bastard, or having an affair with a bastard, I just don't want to be married to a bastard."[63] In the end she knew he would marry again, acerbically observing that "he has to marry again—who'll cook? . . ."[64] "but . . . I also just haven't the time to be married to a philanderer. That bores me too."[65]

Outsiders saw Plath's reactions as being perfectly justified and normal; Hughes had treated her abysmally and she asked him to leave. David Compton, a writer friend who lived nearby, believed Plath probably expected too much of Hughes, but in return she gave him loyalty beyond the call of duty.[66] Hughes's mother, who watched the marriage unravel with horror from Yorkshire, was sad and furious with her son when she wrote to her daughter, Olwyn, that if Hughes wanted to escape his marriage, why couldn't he do it decently?[67] Years later, when Plath's daughter, Frieda, read about the breakup in her mother's letters, she evenhandedly acknowledged that "undoubtedly, my father would have made it easy for my mother to ask him to leave, through his behaviour, his affair and his deceit."[68] Plath, incandescent with fury, hurt, and weirdly liberated from wifedom, wrote the *Ariel* poems. Poems that would lead Sexton years later to speculate that, far from being depressed, Plath was angry and wrote out this anger in the best hate poetry Sexton had ever seen. In October, Plath produced a poem called "The Jailer," about a sadistic husband who tortures his wife: "I imagine him / Impotent as distant thunder, / In whose shadow I have eaten my ghost ration."[69]

In a letter to poet friend Ruth Fainlight, Plath was fascinated by how domesticity seemed to have choked her like "a gag down my throat," and now that her home life was in chaos she was able to write stuff that had been locked inside her for years. "The muse has come to live, now Ted is gone, and my God! what a sweeter companion."[70] In more dramatic fashion to Olive Higgins Prouty she wrote, "I feel I am writing in the blitz, bombs exploding all round."[71]

In September 1962, the estranged couple made the ill-fated decision to travel together to visit Connemara, Ireland, and stay with poet friend Richard Murphy in his small cottage, the Old Forge, in Cleggan, a tiny fishing village by the sea. The trip was a disaster. Although they visited sites associated with Yeats and sailed on Murphy's boat to Inishbofin island, four days into the vacation Hughes told Plath he was going grouse shooting with a friend for the day and never came back. A distraught and deserted Plath had to make her way home alone to Devon carrying all their luggage. For the next two weeks she had no idea where Hughes was. He had in fact gone on a preplanned jaunt to Spain with Assia Wevill but, in order to conceal this, got a friend to send a telegram to Plath from London pretending he was there instead. Again his mother, Edith, was appalled and wrote to Olwyn that the least Ted could have done was to make sure Plath got home safely. Elizabeth Sigmund, Plath's friend, noted that upon arriving back in Devon, Plath was in an awful state. She started smoking and was terribly upset. The whole incident seemed to confirm that the marriage was well and truly over. To Ruth Beuscher Plath wrote, "The end—the end for me at least—just blew up this week."[72]

When the end of Sexton's marriage came in February 1973 at her own instigation, the only person who thought it was a good idea was Anne Sexton, supported by her best friend, Maxine Kumin. Against the advice of friends and her psychiatrists, and contested by Kayo in the courts, the divorce was finally granted in November. Years of fighting and feeling as though Kayo did not appreciate her as a poet (as well as his wife) led Sexton to believe she needed to find someone who would appreciate all these things much more. Yet it seemed that Sexton had overlooked the support system Kayo offered her, with Dr. Orne believing that the loss of it contributed to her death. Clues about her feelings can be found in a series of poems called *The Divorce Papers*, published posthumously, in which Sexton writes, "More often now I am your punching bag."[73] But the ambivalence and difficulty of ending a twenty-four-year marriage, despite the terrible violence, was never far away. Sexton doubted whether she was doing the right thing, not knowing if they belonged together or apart, writing, "except that my soul lingers over the skin of you / and I wonder if I'm ruining all we had."[74]

Although friends were initially supportive and allowed Sexton to stay with them, they soon became exhausted by her demands and apparent desire for attention. Midnight threats of suicide and her need for constant care meant that sympathy soon fell away, and she returned home, terrified to be alone. In her archive papers there are adverts she has circled for live-in help. She soon realized that as a woman in her midforties, dating wasn't the fun it used to be. Writing to a friend who was experiencing a marriage crisis, Sexton warned that being single was hell. "There are many times when I wish I had not left my husband or at least that I had left him for *somebody*, and although that would have engendered guilt on my part, it might have been easier than this madness."[75] Sexton tried to seduce Kayo back, asking him on dates, but by this stage he refused. It was all too late. "A little love is better than no love at all," she told her daughter Linda. Though their marriage had failed, they loved each other to the end and at her death Kayo cried out, "It's all my fault." He felt her loss keenly.[76]

Though Plath's and Sexton's marriages were different, the ideals underpinning them had similarities. Both women, however much they rebelled, were not fully able to escape what was expected of them; the cultural and historical messages they had absorbed were just too pervasive. It seemed the desperate exhaustion that beset them at the ends of their marriages was not so much that they were no longer with their husbands but rather that the fight and battle to be women in their own right had ground them down. Once their role as wife was taken away, the vacuum that was left terrified them. In one of the last letters she wrote, Plath realized that "I lost myself in Ted, instead of finding myself . . ."[77] Perhaps the sadness here is that Plath and Sexton somehow could not quite gather the strength to truly believe in their self-worth, and in the end neither gave themselves time to. The identity vacuum that was partly filled with writer-poet-mother now seemed to have an insurmountable space, and neither woman quite knew what to do about that. Plath summed it up in her final letter: "I am only too aware that love and a husband are impossibles to me at this time, I am incapable of being myself & loving myself."[78]

And yet Plath and Sexton did lay the groundwork for some of the more familiar breakup narratives we see today. Although there was less understanding of solidarity and self-care, Plath in particular seemed the prototype for the breakup makeover. After kicking out Ted Hughes and going through agonies, she got a fabulous new hairdo, a new wardrobe, new jewelry, and a new sassy attitude. Swanning off to London to attend literary parties and to announce her impending divorce to all their friends, she claimed that Hughes didn't even recognize her when he turned up to meet her at the station. Men driving vans catcalled her (how little changes), and she felt modern and new and desirable. This reclamation of self was at first empowering and exhilarating. Sexton, too, with her newfound freedom, took to staying over at friends' houses, drinking too much, and celebrating what she regarded as her escape.

They may well have thrown off the constraints of marriage and all the difficulties that brought, but crucially a different sort of love still played a central role in their lives—they both were mothers.

CHAPTER FIVE

Mothering

A clean slate, with your own face on.

—Sylvia Plath[1]

I am their mother. Not very good, but I am their mother.

—Anne Sexton[2]

When Sylvia Plath first became a mother in 1960, she found it a profoundly healing and creative experience. When Anne Sexton became a mother to two daughters, she had a psychotic breakdown. The difference between these two women and motherhood seemed to be connected to their ideas of boundaries; Plath had many, Sexton had few.

Even before her daughter was born, in her poem "You're," Plath delighted in the idea of creating a whole new being that would be part of but separate from her. The narrator describes the development of a squirmy embryo: "A creel of eels, all ripples" but, most important, an entity in its own right: "A clean slate, with your own face on."[3] From the moment both her children were born, Plath was able to step back and observe their personalities and quirks come to the fore. She loved to sniff their baby smells and listen to them sleeping. Some of her most tender poems were written to her children as she nursed them by candlelight. But however watchful her eye, she knew at some stage the world would encroach and she would not be able to keep her children safe forever, as reflected by one of the narrators in her radio play *Three Women*: "How long can I be a wall, keeping the wind off?"[4]

Sexton, on the other hand, appeared to have no notion of boundaries, whether emotional, sexual, or physical, with disastrous consequences for her daughters. Although she loved her children deeply and nurtured their development, she struggled to allow them to be separate from her in a healthy way. She engaged in disturbing and damaging physical and sexual behavior, invading their privacy, reading one daughter's diary, and making needy demands that left her children exhausted and bewildered. Her eldest, Linda, wrote, "She tried to be 'a good mother,' but in truth, she was not."[5] Untangling Sexton as mother is a challenging and difficult task, mainly because it involves confronting these conflicting issues of damage but at the same time care, love, and, on many levels, nurturing. Although Linda Gray Sexton has written openly about her mother's sexual behavior toward her, she is clear that she does not see herself as a victim or her mother as a monster. She regards their relationship as rich, troubled, and complicated. Writer Annie Lloyd, however, argues that if Sexton had been a man, we likely would not go near the poetry or celebrate the work. Having previously loved Sexton's writing, Lloyd admitted that when she read about Sexton's behavior, "my affection towards her poetry began rotting under my skin." While Linda argued that for her the only way to transcend her hurt was to tell all, and tell it honestly, Lloyd feels Linda gives away her own sense of self for the genius of her mother's work. For Lloyd, ignoring Sexton's actions was "more vicious than forsaking her," and to culturally prop up an abuser who renders their victim invisible means the virtue of the art ceases to exist.[6] This is a powerful argument, but it is also one that needs to be read alongside the voice of Linda Gray Sexton, for to ignore or override what she has to say about the situation is to once again render her invisible. It also feels important to read this alongside the current climate of cancel culture and its repercussions. The arguments are persuasive on both sides. If high-profile figures engage in transgressive behavior, they should be held accountable. But if holding them to account means canceling them out, then this also cancels out dialogue and the need for a wide range of conversations. The danger is that cancel culture becomes a form of censorship rather than a tool for social justice. There is also an argument that cancel culture traps people in a moment of rage forever, in contrast to conversing about the offense, holding the person to account, and then being able to use the conversation in a transformational way.

This is the approach Linda Gray Sexton took in dealing with what happened to her. Her survival journey from anger to forgiveness is vital to understanding their mother–daughter relationship and Sexton's actions. Linda does not want this part of her life to be simplified and labeled, and she believes that by holding her mother to account, then forgiving her, she can understand her mother better. At the same time, she does not want her mother's art shut down. Far from losing herself, Linda felt that by writing openly about being abused by her mother, she was actually finding herself: "This time I would dare to speak in my own name, to use the gift of words she had made my legacy."[7] Confronting this is not easy or comfortable, nor should it be, but it is essential for a candid understanding of the sort of woman Sexton was. "In the end," wrote Linda, "her love both damaged and nurtured."[8]

Plath and Sexton became mothers at a time when for middle-class white women, having children was seen as the pinnacle of achievement. Once you'd managed to get married and provide a stable, stimulating home for your husband, the next job was to add children to it. Having sex to procreate was, apparently, the best, and not to mention the only, sex to have. The role of the mother was vital for the healthy development of children, and the mother was responsible for creating moral, upstanding members of society. Couples who did not want children were regarded as selfish; women who wanted careers over children were seen as cold and unfeminine. Disillusioned mothers, one of whom was the poet Adrienne Rich, who had three children by age thirty, were made to feel like failures in the all-pervasive idealized view that women were born to be perfect mothers. In fact, motherhood was one area where women seemingly had complete control. In 1963, this view was attacked by Betty Friedan in *The Feminine Mystique*, in which she sarcastically wrote that the only way a woman could become a "housewife heroine" was to keep on having babies. As Plath graduated from Smith in 1955, she would have heard her commencement speaker, Adlai Stevenson, tell all the brilliant young women that they would become housewives and mothers whether they liked it or not, so they had better like it.

Even voices that appeared to dissent from this view didn't really. A December 1956 special double issue of *Life* magazine titled "The American Woman: Her Achievements and Troubles" featured twenty-seven-year-old Jennie Magill, a working mom, on the cover. The picture firmly places her in a maternal role, forehead to forehead, laughing with her young daughter. Eliza Berman, deputy culture editor of *Time*, analyzed the picture and the content and argued that for many Americans (and by this we can assume white, middle-class America) this would have been their introduction to the spectacle of the working mother. In contrast to the stigma surrounding career women in the 1950s, on the surface Berman points out that it appears to be an overwhelmingly positive representation. The article reveals that Magill was able to enjoy a social life with her colleagues in the local department store where she worked, that she provided more disposable income for the family, and that she was able to spend quality time with her children after work. What was missing in the article, however, was the voice of Jennie Magill. The attitudes and ideas expressed in the piece are those of her husband, Jim, who explains that Jennie can really only go to work because he supports her doing so, and because she has a housekeeper to help her. Berman puts the article in its historical context, showing that it was almost seven years before the Equal Pay Act and the publication of *The Feminine Mystique*, and more than a decade before the Equal Rights Amendment. She concludes that "people were talking less about how much women should make than they were about *whether* women should work at all."[9] And if that woman happened to be a wife and mother, then the stigma of the selfish, cold, unfeeling woman soon came into play.

When Plath and Sexton spent time together in 1959, Sexton was already a mother of two; Plath had not yet had children. During this year in Boston, Plath was, according to other women around her, obsessed, fascinated, and horrified at the thought of becoming a mother. A Boston friend, Ruth Whitman, who had two children, said that when she spent time with Plath, motherhood was all they talked about. She felt that Plath desperately wanted to be a mother but was terrified it would get in the way of her poetry.[10] Shirley Norton, the wife of Plath's childhood friend Perry, recounted similar impressions. She had just given birth to twins and Plath would visit almost every day to help out and watch. Shirley felt that Plath was obsessive about motherhood but had absolutely no idea what it entailed and as a consequence appeared both fascinated and repulsed.[11] It was clearly on her mind enough to bring to her sessions with Ruth Beuscher, and her journal notes reveal the extent to which she had absorbed some of the ideals surrounding the role of mother: "For RB: It is not when I have a baby, but that I have one, and more, which is of supreme importance to me . . . [T]o consummate love by bearing the child of the loved one is far profounder than any orgasm or intellectual rapport."[12] Plath then goes on to link the idea of childbearing to death, arguing that she likes the Jamesian view of death as an inaccessibility to experience. If a woman is deprived of becoming a mother, then it is a form of death.

Given Plath's fascination with becoming a mother-poet, and her linking this notion to death, it seems likely that since she spoke to every woman she knew in Boston about combining these two things, she would have spoken about it to Sexton. In fact, as a mother-poet of two, she would be a prime source for Plath to draw on. In her 1962 interview for the British Council, Plath highlights Sexton's dual role, describing her as "the poetess Anne Sexton, who writes also about her experiences as a mother: as a mother who's had a nervous breakdown . . ."[13] Over extra-dry martinis talking about death, poetry, and breakdowns, what might Sexton have told her? Did she speak about her daughters and how she handled being a mother alongside writing poetry? Certainly she told Plath about her breakdown and suicide attempts, but did she reveal when, how, and why these happened? In the spring of 1959, Sexton was mother to five-year-old Linda and three-year-old Joy, and the experience had not been an easy one for anyone involved.

After the birth of her first child, Sexton felt overwhelmed.

She found childbirth horrifying and caring for an infant that seemed to cry incessantly exhausting. Although she was still living with Kayo's parents, she resented their help, support, and advice, which increased her feelings of inadequacy. This was the era when women judged themselves on how naturally they could take to motherhood. It was a measure of their personal success. Sexton failed on all counts; she was not and could not be what culture constructed as a "natural mother." The disturbing hints of behavior that Billie Sexton had already witnessed, tantrums and tears, became more pronounced and took a grim turn as Sexton began to battle serious, clinical depression. Today, this reaction may well be seen in light of postpartum depression, a condition little understood in the 1950s. Coping with this while feeling trapped and like a social failure was a poisonous combination for Sexton and those around her. Despite moving into their own home a month after Linda's birth, Sexton grew increasingly depressed and over the next two years was hospitalized at Westwood Lodge in the suburbs of Boston for depression and attempted suicide. Linda was sent to live temporarily with Billie until things improved at home.

Despite these struggles and difficulties, in 1955, Sexton gave birth to her second daughter, Joy, and the situation worsened. Kayo's job as a traveling salesman took him away from home for sometimes up to a week at a time. During his absences, Sexton found life impossible. Linda recalled her mother pacing the house, crying, and refusing to eat. Her bouts of depression alternated with rage and anger where she would slap or choke her eldest daughter. One day, at the end of her tether, she discovered Linda, who was just a toddler, stuffing excrement into her toy truck. Sexton picked up her daughter and hurled her across the room. The family realized that the children were not safe with their mother and both were initially sent to live with Kayo's mother. But two young children proved too much for Billie Sexton, who was struggling with Ménière's disease, which caused sudden attacks of vertigo and a loud ringing in the ears. Linda was sent to the chilly care of Mary Gray Harvey, where a full-time babysitter named Esther was employed to look after her. But then Mary Gray Harvey could not cope with a young child in the house, so Linda was sent to live with her aunt Blanche (Sexton's sister). Here, Linda was subjected to physical abuse and spanking from her uncle, who was a violent drunk. After six months she returned home, but Joy stayed with her grandmother for two years. During this period, Sexton attempted suicide on a number of occasions, and hospitalizations followed that devastated the family. Fear was a constant state for Sexton, her children, and her husband.

In Sexton's archive are letters and cards written to and from her children.[14] These items seem to poignantly sum up the complicated relationship that was dysfunctional yet at the same time loving. The children sound old and wise beyond their years; resentment and fear is ever-present. In a series of postcards Sexton sent to her daughters from her months traveling in Europe in 1963, she repeatedly tells them that she misses and loves them. She also chides them for not writing to her often enough, until Kayo intervenes on their behalf to say they write once a week, which is more than enough. A card sent to Joy from Brussels has a picture of the *Manneken-Pis* (a small bronze fountain statue of a boy peeing), on the back of which Sexton wrote, "I thought the statue in the middle would make you laugh—what is he doing?!," then urges her daughter to take it to school and show her teachers. Joy dutifully does this and a later letter from Kayo reveals that the teachers didn't share Sexton's sense of humor—Joy was put in detention for taking a rude card to class.

There are also little domestic notes on torn pieces of paper, one from Joy on a bright yellow sheet telling her mother that she has gone to the beach. In a tender detail Joy writes that she's leaving the note because her mother was asleep "but I kissed you three times anyway." There is a handmade get-well card from Joy, a Mother's Day card (with instructions about what a mother should *sometimes* do: make beds, clean dishes, etc.), and a letter of apology for being rude, which contrasts sharply with a crayon-scribbled note in purple with the words I HATE YOU underlined five times. Another letter from Joy to her parents (but seems mainly addressed to her mother) pleads, "Please don't die, I need you," and ends with Joy asking her mother to "stay with me always."

Letters from Linda are much more complicated. One undated note reveals the resentment and hurt that formed part of her childhood. Having been sent upstairs by her mother to think about something she had done wrong, Linda writes, "When you got sick and sent us away, you did something wrong." She follows this up by saying never once has she reproached her mother for this, so the current situation is unfair. One of the things Linda Gray Sexton resents the most about her childhood is that when she got older and read her mother's diaries and listened to the therapy tapes, she discovered that during the six months she was living away from home, her mother was not in the hospital as she had always believed. In fact, Sexton stayed in the hospital for only two weeks. The rest of the time she was having manicures, getting her hair done, writing, and overseeing the house staff. Linda understandably felt as though she and her sister had been "farmed out."[15] In a note Linda sent to her mother while Sexton was traveling around Europe, she says, "I only miss you badly when I see Maxine [Kumin] . . . and strangely enough when people yell at me." Another, longer letter titled "A Mother-Daughter Affair," written by Linda when she was twelve, is heartbreaking in its defiance. She asks her mother to give her space to grow up, to let her make her own decisions, and ends with knowing she will be punished for writing the letter so she offers some suggested sanctions (no phone for a week, no TV, no veg soup). In the postscript Linda declares, "I will always love you even if you are terrible to me." This was the daughter who at eight years old learned how to make her mother's martinis (with an olive) and would deliver them to her study. This was also the daughter who at nine years old had to endure her mother "playing nine" with her, a game that involved Sexton sliding into bed with her daughter and pretending to be nine while Linda had to be the adult. This game ignited fear in Linda, who would plead for her mother to be thirty-four again, and Sexton would refuse. This was also the daughter who had to endure her mother's sexual behavior by being touched in inappropriate ways, and choking with disgust while her mother masturbated next to her in bed.

From Sexton's point of view, she was not really doing anything wrong. The game-playing gave her comfort: "I really liked it . . . I can save myself through my children because there's a bond."[16] The sexual behavior seemed to be a product of no boundaries whatsoever, almost as if Sexton were saying, "I can touch my daughters here to show them how good it feels and liberate their sexuality," with no separation, no notion of how abusive that behavior was. Sometimes in bed Linda felt as though her mother was totally dissociated from the situation as she lay there masturbating silently and glassy-eyed. Given Sexton's own history of suspected sexual abuse by her father and the trauma this caused, repeating the pattern with her own children seems inexplicable but, sadly, not uncommon.

After many years in therapy, Linda acknowledges that her mother's behavior was destructive and abusive. Yet understanding also led to forgiveness and a courageous ability to see her mother operating in a wider picture. As she got older, Linda understood the pressures Sexton was under, the suffering of mental anguish and confusion, the loneliness and fear, all the complexities and frailties that make up a person. Her mother was far from perfect, but she was not a total monster. There were moments of joy and nurturing, and facing up to that complicated mix helped Linda perform some sort of exorcism: "To write about Mother and me would enable me to take control of the demons inside and let them know who was boss."[17] It was not about excusing Sexton's behavior, it was about learning how to survive it, and come out the other side a whole person.

It seems unlikely that Sexton would have told Plath these details about her mothering, or at best she may have filtered out some of the more disturbing elements. Perhaps what she did advise Plath was that if she really wanted to be a poet-mother, then she would need to carve out time to do it. In an interview with Barbara Kevles in 1968, Sexton claimed the only reason she was able to cope with being a mother and a poet at the same time was because of her stubbornness: "When my children were younger, they interfered all the time . . . Now my children are older and creep around the house saying, 'Shh, Mother is writing a poem.'"[18] What Sexton likely did not know about was Plath's determination to be high-achieving at everything. It would be unthinkable for Plath to leave chores undone or neglect her children to write. Rather, everything would be ordered so it worked out to everyone's advantage. This precision and organization was what allowed Plath to become the writer she became, that allowed her and Hughes to live in a clean, tidy house eating home-cooked meals, and that gave her time to spend with her children. It was probably the one thing Hughes missed the most when Plath was gone, so much so that he wrote a list of instructions for Plath's replacement, Assia Wevill, which included demands such as how long Assia was allowed to stay in bed, how much time she should spend with Plath's children, and how often she should try out new recipes.

Plath's joy at being a mother seemed unlimited. Initially, as part of a married team, far from interfering with her poetry, she saw giving birth as enhancing it and releasing some sort of creativity that had previously been dormant. Establishing a childcare routine with Hughes right from the beginning allowed Plath clear writing time in the morning, then the afternoons with the children and doing other household tasks. It was a setup ahead of its time. After the birth of Frieda in London in April 1960, Plath had definite ideas about how mothering and writing would work: Frieda would fit into the schedule. This caused friction on the first visit to her in-laws in Yorkshire, when Edith Hughes wanted to pick Frieda up and nurse her every time she cried. Plath would not allow this, saying she would never get any work done if her daughter got used to it. Edith Hughes's disapproval was clear. But Frieda seemed to slot quite seamlessly into Plath's and Hughes's lives and did not really stop them from doing what they needed to. Three weeks after giving birth, Plath borrowed a baby carry-cot and, along with her poet friend Peter Redgrove, carried Frieda to the lawn in front of the National Gallery to watch the seven-mile-long Ban the Bomb march arriving in London: "I felt proud that the baby's first real adventure should be as a protest against the insanity of world-annihilation."[19] Once again Plath seemed ahead of her time. Today there is the opportunity to attend marches and protests, with a growing global movement to tackle social injustice and environmental issues. Some of the most powerful marches in recent years have been organized and attended globally by younger generations that believe in bringing about much-needed change. Back in 1960, Rachel Carson was still two years away from publishing her study *Silent Spring*, which sparked global concern about the environment, but Plath had read Carson's earlier work and understood the importance of what was happening. Understanding the full effect of nuclear fallout was still in its infancy. That Plath recognized and engaged in protest about these issues highlights that as well as rebelling in her writing, she was happy to rebel in day-to-day life too.

Just over two months after giving birth, Plath was at a Faber party with the likes of T. S. Eliot, Louis MacNeice, and Stephen Spender: "I went to a cocktail party at Fabers given for WH Auden. I drank champagne with the appreciation of a housewife on an evening off from the smell of sour milk and diapers."[20] For a new mother to be attending political marches and champagne parties seems rather glamorous, yet somehow, on the surface, Plath managed it all with ease: "We're just madly in love with her," wrote Plath about Frieda.[21]

Not everything was quite as rosy as it appeared, though. At the end of January 1961, Plath informed her mother that she was due to give birth again in August. On February 5, Plath wrote a newsy, friendly letter to Sexton, telling her all about Frieda ("a marvellous blue-eyed comic"), saying she was convinced she wanted to found a dynasty. Although she did not disclose her new pregnancy, she made clear her plan was to have lots of children. The letter ended with a plea for Sexton to write to her soon: "Please sit down one day between the poem & the stewpot . . ."[22] Within hours of finishing the letter, Plath suffered a miscarriage. Writing, brokenhearted, to her mother the next day, she said the doctor claimed one in four babies are miscarried and often there is no explanation. Plath left it there. It was not until over a year later, after her marriage had ended, that Plath revealed that in the days before her miscarriage, during a terrible fight with Hughes, he had turned violent and beaten her. The fight happened because Plath had taken a part-time job at the *Bookseller* to try and eke out their savings and she was due to work that afternoon. Hughes, who had a meeting with a BBC producer, was to return home in time to take care of Frieda. He arrived back late—by a couple of hours—subsequently making Plath late, and in a fury she tore some of his papers in half ("they could be taped together, not lost . . ."). Plath does not say the beating caused the miscarriage, but she certainly implies Hughes's culpability, adding poignantly, "The baby I lost was due to be born on his birthday."[23] In 2017, when Frieda Hughes first saw these letters and the media got hold of extracts, she felt "other people were now writing my worst fears into them," and reading her mother's words was intensely painful.[24] She felt the context of the fight was important because she wanted people to understand that "my father was not the wife-beater that some would wish to imagine he was."[25] Plath's poem "Parliament Hill Fields" is about a woman who suffers a miscarriage. In the final lines, as the narrator walks home, the poem ends with the unsettling words "The old dregs, the old difficulties take me to wife. / Gulls stiffen to their chill vigil in the drafty half-light; / I enter the lit house."[26]

Within a couple of months, Plath was pregnant again and by September they had moved to Devon. Hughes wanted to be away from the smoggy air of London, and Plath wanted more space for her growing family and, perhaps just as important, a room of her own for writing. Her second child, Nicholas Farrar Hughes, was born on January 17, 1962, in dramatic fashion when initially the baby stuck and her membrane didn't break until "this great bluish glistening boy shot out onto the bed in a tidal wave of water that drenched all 4 of us to the skin, howling lustily. It was an amazing sight. I immediately sat up and felt wonderful . . ."[27] As with Frieda, Plath adored Nicholas and watched their two very different personalities developing: Frieda spirited and lively, Nicholas quiet and smiley, often chuckling. She felt that her son definitely took after her in his love of food. On a visit with Elizabeth Sigmund, sitting at the kitchen table with Nicholas on her knee, Plath pointed out how his eyes followed the food around the table. In photographs, he almost always has a smile on his face, cuddling up to either his mother or his sister. In return they are often looking at him with doting expressions.

Hughes, however, seemed to feel differently and, according to Plath and numerous other sources, was not especially pleased about the birth of his son. The local midwife, Winifred Davies, speculated that as the man of the house he felt threatened by another male presence. With increasing worry, Plath noticed that Hughes rarely touched or spoke to their son. During the times that he minded the children, he remained warm and loving to Frieda, but indifferent to Nicholas. One day, despite repeated warnings, he failed to strap his son into the carriage and Nicholas fell out onto the hard concrete floor. Hughes sat staring at the crying baby while a local woman, Nancy Axworthy, who helped Plath with the house, rushed in to pick him up. Plath, hearing the terrible screaming, ran downstairs to the frightening scene. She wrote to Ruth Beuscher, "He was unhurt. See, said Ted. He could have had concussion or broken his spine. He has never touched him since he was born, says he is ugly and a usurper."[28]

Caring for two young children under the age of three, keeping the house running smoothly, writing poems, and typing up her husband's work pushed Plath to the limit. She took care of the business side of her and Hughes's writing as well as paying all the bills, doing all the shopping, replying to correspondence (often ghostwriting letters for Hughes), making sure poems were regularly submitted to journals and newspapers, as well as proofreading the galleys for her upcoming novel *The Bell Jar* and starting work on a new poetry collection. How disturbing, then, that on top of this, within four months of giving birth, she was faced with a situation that destroyed her. The Wevills came to stay in Devon in May, which sparked the beginning of the affair between

Assia and Ted. In a disappointing lack of female solidarity, Assia returned to London from their weekend, sneering at Plath's appearance (her post-baby weight gain, her apparently sloppy clothes, her exhaustion), and belittling the food Plath had cooked for her and the way Court Green had been decorated. Hughes was captivated and did not hesitate in inciting the affair. Plath was absolutely devastated: "She is so beautiful and I am so haggish & my hair a mess & my nose huge & my brain brainwashed & God knows how I shall keep together."[29] Not for the first time in Plath's life, it feels she would have benefited from Sexton's support at this moment; with her sharp tongue and wry eye she likely would have done Plath's hair and makeup and dragged her out to drink too much and put cheating men in their place.

Instead Plath had other support. The warm friendship of Elizabeth Sigmund, who tried as best she could to steer Plath through the cruel waters of a marriage breakdown; Clarissa Roche, who had always disliked Hughes and had a few choice words about him; Ruth Fainlight, who offered domestic and writing support when she returned from Morocco the following spring; and by letter Ruth Beuscher, who was furious about Hughes's behavior. From Plath's point of view, one of her biggest fears was about to come true: she would end up like her mother, without a husband and a single parent raising the children by herself. Suddenly the prospect of having to do it all hit home and it horrified her. She realized that caring for her children alone was going to be tough: "I love the children, but they do make the plans for a life on my own quite difficult, now they are so small & need such tending."[30] Any practical help from Hughes did not seem to be in the cards, and in a letter to his sister he was already planning to take off around Europe, staying in country after country until he was fluent in all languages. Plath's grief manifested itself in poems such as "For a Fatherless Son," in which the narrator tells her son, "You will be aware of an absence, presently, / Growing beside you like a tree."[31] Another poem, "By Candlelight," features a brass Atlas candlestick holder that comes to symbolize the free man: "No child, no wife."[32] Frieda missed her father terribly and regressed. Plath hardly knew how to deal with her daughter's grief, never mind her own.

A bright moment came in the form of Susan O'Neill Roe, a local nineteen-year-old who was about to move to London to start work as a children's nurse in Great Ormond Street Hospital. She had six weeks to fill before her new job started, so Plath employed her as a nanny. She soon became a pleasant and lifesaving fixture of daily life in Court Green, and her presence seemed to hold Plath together. O'Neill Roe does not recall ever seeing Plath in a state or upset. Rather she has lovely memories of a woman who was energetic and productive, and of the two of them going on lovely picnics with the children.[33] Plath immediately saw her as a younger sister figure, and they would cook in the kitchen and eat lunch together. Plath even dedicated a poem, "Cut," to Susan. She wrote home to her mother, "I love Susan O'Neill Roe, she is a dear with the children. I come down & cook us a big hot lunch and we

& Frieda eat together in the playroom. Then I lie down for an hour's nap. I make a pot of tea in midafternoon & chat over a cup. O it is <u>ideal</u>."[34] O'Neill Roe would also take some of the most tender, poignant photographs of Plath with her children in the sitting room at Court Green in December 1962. The overwhelming color is red: Plath's large red-lipsticked smile as she cuddled her children, the red rug, the red fireplace, the red window seat and curtains, with Frieda and Nicholas each holding toys and cats and their mother. They are difficult images to view with the knowledge of what would happen just nine weeks later.

It does seem unfair, though, to Plath and Sexton to view some of their happier moments with their children through the knowledge that we gain later. Perhaps at the moment the photographs were taken of Plath in December 1962 she was genuinely as happy as she could be. The reading of some of Sexton's poems, such as "Mother and Daughter," "Pain for a Daughter," and "Little Girl, My String Bean, My Lovely Woman," becomes more difficult with the knowledge of how she behaved toward Linda. The focus on her daughter's developing body and identity can feel uncomfortable. But perhaps they were written with tenderness and care and nothing more sinister. In many respects neither Plath nor Sexton was a traditional 1950s mother. They pursued their own careers and did not see children as the pinnacle of their existence but rather part of it.

In the end, Sexton's daughters became exhausted by their mother's demands on them and her repeated attempts to die.

They took it personally because, as Linda pointed out, no one bothered to explain the pain their mother was in. They saw her suicide attempts as bids for pity and sympathy because it was easier to think she was being self-indulgent than that she wanted to leave them forever. As they grew older and pulled away to try and gain some independence, Sexton lashed out, saying hurtful things, accusing them of abandoning her. Yet her final act was to make Linda executor of her estate, the ultimate expression of trust. She believed that her daughter was the one person who best understood her work and would look after it accordingly. A lovely memory Linda has of her mother was a bedtime ritual, when the shades were drawn and the room fell dark, and Linda lay on clean sheets smelling of fresh linen. Sexton would say, "Goodnight house, Goodnight mouse," from a book she used to read called *Goodnight Moon*, and sing a lullaby specially created for her daughter: *"Night-night time has come for Linda Gray . . ."* Sexton's voice was deep and raspy, and Linda would hold on to her mother: "These were the magic times. Safe times. Knowing, for that moment, that I could count on her: she *would* take care of me; she *was* my mother; she was *here*."[35]

Plath never got to spend much time with her children. When she died, Frieda was not yet three and Nicholas had just turned one. The level of Plath's desperation can be judged by the fact that she felt no alternative other than to leave her children. In one of her last poems, "Child," the speaker is full of regret that she cannot give her child all the beautiful things the world holds: innocence, color, new words and experiences. Instead what is offered is "this troublous / Wringing of hands, this dark / Ceiling without a star."[36] The final letter Plath wrote a week before her death was sad, flat, and defeated. But even then, the very last words she wrote in her correspondence were about Frieda and Nicholas: "Now the babies are crying, I must take them out for tea."[37]

CHAPTER SIX

Writing

Arrogant, I think I have written the lines that qualify
me to be The Poetess of America . . .

—Sylvia Plath[1]

I have to be great, that's the entire problem—I want
to leave the impact of my personality carved in marble.

—Anne Sexton[2]

I f Sylvia Plath and Anne Sexton had never known each other,
never read each other's work, literature today would be a
very different place. Theirs was a two-way exchange of ideas,
influences, and writing styles. When they first met, Sexton was
in the more secure position of being a fairly well-known, rising
star of poetry. She was lauded by Robert Lowell, and her original, slangy, open poems burst onto the literary scene, causing
equal parts shock and delight. Plath, too, was well published,
but a more reserved poet at that time, a bit more uptight, dense,
with only occasional flashes of what was to come later. When

Plath first read Sexton, she realized the strength of her work lay in the ease of expression, her honesty, and her ability to get straight to the point. Not only that, she envied Sexton's subject matter: madness, motherhood, sex, parents, therapy, death, suicide. These topics were a breakthrough, not just for poetry in general but for women operating in a male-dominated discipline. To say that Plath and Sexton were in a minority is an understatement, and given that they were both privileged white women really highlights just how bad things were. If they struggled, imagine what it was like for those without that social privilege. Although today there have been improvements, it is still not enough. Transparency about the gendered nature of the literary world shows that misogyny and racism still both play a strong part not only in who gets published but also who gets reviewed and what sort of advances are offered. Those suffering the worst deal are Black, Latino, Asian, and all ethnic minority women writers, while other social characteristics, such as class and age, intersect to create a playing field so unlevel, it is frightening to see how certain groups are just simply pushed off the edge.

The historical moment in which Plath and Sexton were writing, though, is crucial to understanding their work, not only in terms of how radical they were for the time but how they managed this on a personal and professional level. Plath never got to experience second-wave feminism. Sexton did but felt that, despite feeling held back by her gender, she could not fully embrace the movement. What she did realize, though, was the part she played in helping to bring it about. In a 1974 interview with writer

Elaine Showalter, Sexton and Maxine Kumin reflected on how they viewed their lives prior to second-wave feminism:

> SEXTON: You see, when we began, there was no women's movement. We were it.
> KUMIN: And we didn't know it.

And when they were asked how things might have been different had there been a women's movement, they replied:

> KUMIN: We would have felt a lot less secretive.
> SEXTON: Yes, we would have felt legitimate.[3]

Despite rebelling against many of the social norms of the 1950s and '60s, Sexton ultimately sounds as though she would have been more at home with the late twentieth-century/early twenty-first-century third-wave feminism, a movement that went a little easier on men and was more willing to include them. She seemed uncomfortable with the level of anger directed toward men: "I hate the way I'm anthologized in women's lib anthologies. They cull out the 'hate men' poems, and leave nothing else. They show only one little aspect of me. Naturally there are times when I hate men, who wouldn't? But there are times when I love them. The feminists are doing themselves a disservice to show just this."[4]

Although Kumin claimed they were quite secretive, Sexton was not necessarily private about her writing (or indeed anything else). In contrast, Plath definitely was. And she was secretive about all aspects—where she wrote, when she wrote, and what she wrote. When she moved to London in 1959, many people had no idea she was a poet. When she moved to Devon in 1961, her study was kept locked, and hardly anyone was allowed inside. As yet, no photographs have ever emerged of the room, but we can glean the odd bit of information here and there about the space in which Plath produced her *Ariel* poems. It was a large upstairs study with two windows, the front one overlooking the churchyard, the side one overlooking her garden. Ted Hughes planted a peach tree beneath the side window, and Plath had carved out a small flower bed on the front lawn with unusual gray rosebushes. Her desk was a six-foot-long elm plank whose original purpose was for the lid of a coffin. She had a red carpet, and above her desk were newspaper cuttings and quotes. One was a typed copy of a Stevie Smith poem, "Magna Est Veritas" (ending with the line "Great is Truth and will prevail in a bit").[5] Others were newspaper clippings about gruesome murders and serial killers. Her favorite was the story of a young man who kept his mother's corpse in his apartment and tried to electrocute her back to life every evening after work. This lasted only until the neighbors complained about the smell.[6] Thinking about Plath surrounded by this material makes the gallows humor in her late poems much more understandable. Elizabeth Sigmund perceptively noticed that Plath often saw "genuine funniness" in events that others would find horrifying or grotesque.[7]

How Plath negotiated her professional and domestic life is fascinating. Comparing dates on her poetry manuscripts with her Letts wall calendar in 1962 gives a detailed description of some of her days. On Sunday, September 30, 1962, early in the morning she wrote her poem "A Birthday Present," in which the narrator, taunted by an unopened birthday gift, speculates on a previous suicide attempt and says about the present, "If it were death // I would admire the deep gravity of it, its timeless eyes. / I would know you were serious."[8]

Immediately after writing this poem, Plath walked downstairs and prepared roast beef with potatoes, corn, and apple cake, followed by banana bread. At three thirty she hosted afternoon tea for the Fosters, some North Tawton neighbors, who later said, "We did not know she was a poet and she did not tell us." The visit took a disastrous turn when they asked where Hughes was, and Plath informed them that she'd thrown him out. This led to bitter outbursts from Plath about his infidelity and other undesirable habits. Gilbert Foster, seemingly oblivious to Plath's anger, started to give examples of other male writers who lived louche lifestyles. It was not what Plath wanted to hear and her anger increased until two-year-old Frieda, who had been watching her mother closely, said, "Mummy thinks you should leave now."[9]

Other friends of Plath also had no idea what she was writing. Elizabeth Sigmund recalled that Plath never spoke about her poetry or prose, or what went on in her workspace. After Plath's death, when Sigmund moved into Court Green for a short while to housesit, the door to Plath's study had a large padlock on it. London friends the Secker-Walkers, when they read Plath's poems after her death, were taken aback. They knew nothing of this tension between her domestic and professional life, claiming with hindsight, "Hers was a Jekyll and Hyde presentation."[10] Plath's secrecy was taken to a whole new level when her novel *The Bell Jar* was published under the pseudonym Victoria Lucas. She did not want to be associated with it (or anyone who had been lampooned in it to be able to identify themselves).

Sexton, on the other hand, was not really secretive at all. She may have struggled with feelings of not being a legitimate writer, but she held nothing back. Nothing was off-limits to write about either in her own life or her family's. In a 1968 interview with Barbara Kevles, Sexton said, "Part of me was appalled by what I was doing. On the one hand I was digging up shit, with the other hand, I was covering it with sand. Nevertheless, I went on ahead. I didn't know any better."[11] When she was asked how her relatives reacted to her jangling family skeletons, Sexton claimed she didn't write anything hurtful about anyone alive, and she was fine with hurting the dead, since they belonged to her. She did admit, though, that her in-laws did not approve of her poems at all.

The one thing Sexton was private about was her close bond with Maxine Kumin. In the 1950s, if Adrienne Rich felt women should have spoken to each other more and been more supportive, Sexton and Kumin were setting the scene for female solidarity that we take for granted today. They met in a poetry workshop in the late '50s run by John Holmes, and their friendship developed from there. Because they both had young children, it was often difficult for them to get out of the house to meet, so they began a ritual of telephone workshopping every day. Sometimes the calls would last for up to two hours as they critiqued each other's poems, read new work, and spoke about how they were feeling and what their days had been like. Pre–second-wave feminism, Kumin explained that they kept this part of their lives relatively secret because they feared people would lump them together and see them as alike. It was a struggle for separate identities in a literary world that was hostile enough to women. They even went to some trouble not to publish books in the same year. Kumin felt that one of the most positive things about the latter half of the twentieth century was that women were starting to come out of the closet and that this was "maybe the only good thing in a fucked up world." The affection between the two women is obvious toward the end of the conversation with Elaine Showalter when Sexton waxes lyrical about female friendship, and her mother and great-aunt and their screwed-up relationship, ending with: "I think I'm dominating this interview." Kumin replied dryly, "You are, Anne."[12]

Because of her openness, Sexton, more so than Plath, is usually much more comfortably referred to as a confessional poet, but digging about in her interviews suggests that this label may need to be applied with a little more care. In 1970 she boldly told Marjorie Fellow, "I lie in poems" (her tone of voice when she says this is really defiant).[13] Three years later she expanded on this while talking with William Heyen and Al Poulin, claiming that for a long time she resented being classed as a confessional poet until she decided she was the *only* confessional poet. That came with some caveats, though. Often she confessed to things she hadn't done, and indeed she admitted that if she confessed to all the things she had done, then she wouldn't have time to write any poems. Although there's a feeling that Sexton is being playful with her listeners, she makes a serious point that often in her poems she assumes the first person even when it is somebody else's story.

This puts Plath's and Sexton's voices a little closer than they are often regarded, with neither being transparently autobiographical or entirely fictional. It also highlights how the two women played off each other, not only in style and tone but in their actual authorial voices. Poet David Trinidad has published an in-depth look at how Plath and Sexton, to be frank, ripped each other off. Initially Plath was learning from Sexton how to free up her voice, be more slangy, and to play with rhythms and rhymes. The most obvious example cited by Trinidad is Sexton's "My Friend, My Friend," first published in the *Antioch Review* in summer 1959 and almost certainly discussed in the Lowell workshop. Plath knew the poem well. It opens with "Who will forgive me for the things I do? / With no special legend or God to refer to." This not only established the "oo" rhyme, but the opening stanza finished with Sexton pondering whether it would be better to "be a Jew." Compare this to Plath's opening stanza to one of her most notorious *Ariel* poems, "Daddy." "You do not do, you do not do / Any more, black shoe," finishing with the speculation that the speaker thinks she may be a "bit of a Jew."

"That Plath pilfered so heavily from one of Sexton's poems, albeit a minor one," writes Trinidad, "is a bit of a revelation."[14]

It wasn't a one-way pilfering, though. After Plath's death, Sexton started to become heavily influenced by Plath's late work. Sexton was happy to consider that she had given Plath a sort of daring in her work. But she was also happy to admit that Plath had given her the daring to express anger, something she believed she was not able to do in her work or her life (though others might disagree). Sexton cites "Daddy" as an insolent poem, but oddly does not seem to acknowledge the debt Plath owed to her for the structure and rhyme. Rather, she generously credits Plath as a writer who was entitled to use and bury her influences as she wished: "Her poems do their own work. I don't need to sniff them for distant relatives of some sort. I'm against it."[15] Instead, Sexton considers how her own poem "The Addict" borrows something of Plath's open speech rhythms. Trinidad points out other examples where Sexton appears to copy Plath in her use of exclamation marks, dashes, and open metaphors. Sexton's collection *Love Poems* (1969) has Plathian imagery stamped all over it. For Trinidad, though, there were downsides to this influence and ultimately he felt that "Sexton's desire to out-Plath Plath undid her in the end." For him, this was Sexton's use of Nazi imagery, which, while copying Plath, soon got a little out of hand, with poems full of panzer-men, Herr Doktors, and Nazi hooks. He felt that Sexton's attempt to write her own *Ariel* resulted in *The Awful Rowing Toward God*, which Sexton completed in fifteen days. Trinidad, a great fan of Sexton, asks, "But who can write a book of poetry in two weeks?" He notes that the day Sexton corrected the galleys for this collection was also the day she died.

No writer exists in a vacuum, so it is not unusual or surprising that Plath and Sexton bounced off each other in this way. Once Plath got over her jealous suspicion and rivalry, and once Sexton noticed Plath actually did have something to say, their admiration for each other overtook their wariness. Had Plath lived longer, it seems likely their friendship would have continued. Maybe one day they would have been back, not drinking martinis at the Ritz but joining Gloria Steinem in her 1971 protest at the dress code imposed on women in the bar there. Sexton and Steinem exchanged letters about this, with Sexton fully supporting the activism: "I have been boycotting the Ritz for four years but they didn't notice."[16] And maybe Sexton would have thought twice about her agent arranging for her to be published in *Playboy*. Although she didn't approve at the time, she was also excited about becoming part of popular culture, writing, "I'm not sure I approve and God knows what Houghton Mifflin will think when it comes time to publish the book. It worries me a little to be published in *Playboy*. They exploit women, and now I've got a hand in it . . . Still, what the hell. I'd feel a lot worse if they'd turned them [the poems] down."[17]

Plath and Sexton were engaged in their own type of activism, although it is doubtful they saw it that way. Because they regarded their writing as a serious, professional career, and because men in that world often did not really see women as legitimate writers, many of the gender gap issues that still exist today existed then, but with no legislation to acknowledge or support them: lack of diversity, lack of equal pay, lack of recognition, sexist reviews. In 1961, when Plath read "Tulips" live for the BBC from a poetry festival in London's Mermaid Theatre, the poet who introduced her, John Wain, sounded shamefaced when he pointed out she was the only woman writer reading her work. When Sexton appeared at Ted Hughes's London *Poetry International* festival in 1967, she was one of only two woman poets invited to speak. In classic Sexton fashion, when W. H. Auden, who was top of the bill, asked her to cut short her reading of "The Double Image" so he could be home by ten p.m., Sexton offered to change places with him so he could get to bed on time and she would be top of the bill instead. This resulted in Sexton reading "The Double Image" in its entirety and Auden heading home for a late night at ten forty-five.[18]

Yes, there has been some progress since then, but even today when newspapers publish their "Greatest Books of All Time" lists, women from all backgrounds are always underrepresented. In 2019, when the Booker Prize was awarded jointly to two women writers, Bernardine Evaristo (the first Black woman to ever win the prize) and Margaret Atwood, the BBC reported on a live news show that the prize had been won by Margaret Atwood and "another author."

Plath was aware that to succeed as a writer she needed to treat it as a business. Her correspondence shows a highly organized submissions process by which she made sure several of her own (and Hughes's) poems were constantly out for consideration by publications such as the *Atlantic, Harper's,* the *Observer,* the *New Yorker,* and the *Critical Quarterly.* Right up until her death she kept detailed lists showing which poem had been sent where and which had been accepted. She also researched prizes and grants and made sure either her books or Hughes's were submitted on a regular basis. Just over a year before her death she was awarded the prestigious Saxton Grant of $2,000 to support the writing of a novel. Years later, Hughes sounded somewhat disconsolate, complaining that Plath made him "professional," something his Cambridge friends seemed to look down on. They regarded Plath's business acumen as her being a pushy, brash American, as opposed to a woman in charge of her own (and her husband's) career. This acumen is sometimes misunderstood in other ways too. Often dramatic reasoning is given for some of Plath's subject material—that her poems were a murderous art, that her novel came from a place of pain, that at the end of the poetry it is her own dead body on the stage, that she is writing her own death, etc. Apart from pathologizing her writing, this overlooks Plath's savvy eye for the market. Before tackling *The Bell Jar*, she wrote in her journal, "Read COSMOPOLITAN from cover to cover. Two mental-health articles. I <u>must</u> write one about a college girl suicide. . . . And a story, a novel even. . . . There is an increasing market for mental-hospital stuff. I am a fool if I don't relive, recreate it."[19] Plath's friend Clarissa Roche recalls on a visit to Court Green in late 1962 that Plath read aloud her poem "Daddy" in a silly singsong voice, and they both rolled around on the floor with laughter.[20] Of course, some of Plath's later poems came from a place of pain and anguish, but they were also a performance. She was a professional and she knew how to make her poems have the greatest impact. Listening to her reading her own work is all the evidence we need for this. She was one of the first poets to benefit from the BBC promoting the recording and broadcasting of poet's own voices. In an interview for the British Council she spoke about how exciting she found this development: "I feel that this development of recording poems, of speaking poems at readings, of having records of poets, I think this is a wonderful thing. I'm very excited by it. In a sense, there's a return, isn't there, to the old role of the poet, which was to speak to a group of people, to come across."[21]

As well as having a fine business mind, Plath was not overawed by dealing with men in authority. Her lifelong wish was to be published in the *New Yorker*. When she got her first acceptance in 1958, the poetry editor, Howard Moss, wrote to her requesting a few edits to her poem "Mussel Hunter at Rock Harbor." Despite just achieving her life's ambition, she did not agree with his edits and told him so. Her preference was published. She was later offered a first-reading contract with the *New Yorker* that lasted until her death. This meant the magazine got first refusal on any poems that she intended to publish. Anthony Thwaite at the BBC, who worked with Plath on a number of radio programs, recalled her being very businesslike. He quickly realized that she knew exactly what she wanted, and she went about it with no fuss. In his opinion she was quick, capable, and knew her own mind.[22] Before meeting her, Thwaite commissioned Plath and Hughes to do a joint recording for the BBC called "Two of a Kind: Poets in Partnership," in which writers spoke about their lives together.

Internal BBC memos show Hughes writing to accept the commission (almost certainly typed by Plath) and in pencil next to his signature Thwaite has written "What do we have on his wife?"[23] He soon found out.

Sexton, too, was forging her way bravely through the sexist depths of the literary world. Her correspondence reads like she was a one-woman activist fighting for equal pay and recognition years before the Equal Pay Act was introduced, and afterward when it was not really enforced. This was especially obvious in relation to her reading appearances. Well aware that she could make good money on the circuit performing her work, she was also a very nervous traveler and suffered from dreadful stage fright. She had to drink heavily just to get herself to appear and carried a bottle of vodka around in her bag prior to any performance. "It takes a terrible toll on me," she wrote to W. D. Snodgrass in 1961. "I still feel required to get plastered before each reading."[24] On one reading tour in 1966, her daughter Linda (who was thirteen) was put in charge of her mother, making sure she was where she needed to be and that she turned up at the right time. Linda recalled her mother was desperate for the audience to love her, so she drank heavily to bolster her nerves: "She envisioned herself as Judy Garland, one of her favorite singers, and wanted listening to Anne read to be as much of a high as listening to Judy sing."[25] Sexton was open about the terror these readings created: "Readings really unnerve me . . . they actually scare the shit out of me! But it *is* money and I have to have it. . . . Fear, always fear."[26] If she tried to read sober, she would shake and tremble, so she got drunk, which, in her words, made her a bit of a ham. Because these appearances took so much out of her, she decided she needed to charge a high price for them, but, significantly, no higher than male poets who were on the same reading circuit at the time. In 1974, Sexton was charging up to $2,000 plus expenses for an appearance and telling colleges and festivals that the price was good news for them because they were getting a woman reader for the same price as a man. By 1974, Sexton had won innumerable prizes, grants, and awards, including the Pulitzer Prize. Rightly, she saw absolutely no reason why men with lesser achievements should be paid more than her for an identical reading. When she sent out letters outlining her fees and received incredulous replies, she simply responded that if a college couldn't afford her, then what a shame that was for them. On no account would she lower her prices. Likewise, with her first-reading contract with the *New Yorker*, she wrote to Howard Moss a short, sharp letter of five lines, ending with "The point to this letter is a query. Why does Ed Sissman get $300 for signing his contract and I get $100? What more is there to say?"[27] Her archive is full of letter after letter in which she argues her point. It would be good to think that today things have changed, except of course the gender pay gap still exists in almost all areas of work.

Sexton's other battle was teaching creative writing. She gave workshops in colleges all around the country and even ran a series of poetry workshops at McLean Hospital in Belmont, Massachusetts, but the bulk of her teaching was carried out at Boston University. (In a wonderful full circle, she taught her classes in the very room where she first met Plath in Lowell's workshop.) In 1972, when she realized a male colleague was being paid $4,000 per course more than her, she was furious. She wrote to her ex-lover George Starbuck (who was now head of the department), "I know it is a desperate time of money at B.U. but if a man gets it then why doesn't a woman. . . . If I'm important I want to be paid importantly."[28] Less than two months later the issue had still not been resolved and Sexton's irritation and outrage leaps off the page: "Does Boston University want to be written about in my biography as undervaluing me . . . Aside from the fact that I am 'a name,' I am a great teacher."[29] Then claiming that although she did not like to be a troublemaker, if she did not get a response within two weeks she would be taking the matter to the dean and the president. Sadly, one feels she would have gotten no further there. As a female lecturer she seemed to operate under the radar of male academics. When after years of teaching she was finally awarded a half-time full professorship in 1972, a professor from another department wrote to her saying how excited he was that his favorite poet was joining the faculty. She tartly thanked him for his letter and wrote, "It may interest you to know that I have already been there three years as a lecturer."[30]

This lack of recognition seemed to affect Plath and Sexton in different ways. Perhaps because of her lack of formal education, Sexton occasionally suffered from a feeling that she didn't quite belong, wasn't quite worthy, what today would be called imposter syndrome. To W. D. Snodgrass in 1959, and shortly after meeting Plath for the first time, Sexton wrote, "I think I am too mixed up to ever be a good writer."[31] Had workshopping with the immaculately educated Plath and gossiping over martinis afterward left her feeling a little insecure? Even a year later, when her first book came out, she wrote, "Well, it is a difficult period . . . one book out, most reviews in, and the feeling that I'm a fraud, that I didn't write the thing but that I stole it somewhere."[32] Sexton ricocheted between this unworthiness and a desire to be great, a self-belief that even if it couldn't be maintained flashed into being from time to time. In 1959 she wrote, "Jesus, I'm a defensive creature! and in manicy moments I say to myself, I'm better than Lowell!—How is *that* for poetic conceit.!!!"[33] Equally, she was realistic about how successful men in charge would let her be. When she inquired about the application for a grant from the Theodore Roethke Memorial Foundation, she discovered that one of the judges was her nemesis, James Dickey (writer of the devastating review of her first book). Her reply bluntly stated that she found it pointless applying since "I stand no chance of getting it because one of the judges abhors my work. So be it."[34] She longed to aim high and be brilliant, to leave behind the legacy of a great writer. This she saw as inextricably linked to also making money. Like Plath, she knew her work had to be treated like a business to have any chance of being successful. In 1966, she summed this up beautifully in a letter: "I am in love with money, so don't be mistaken; but first I want to write good poems. After that I am anxious as hell to make money and fame and bring the stars all down."[35] The difficulty Sexton faced was feeling as though she didn't quite belong in any world she inhabited. In literary circles she felt her lack of education and faced open sexism, but her domestic life was no better. There, too, she felt like an imposter, not quite herself, not quite belonging. Never a good enough wife or mother, and aware that her poems shocked the locals in Weston and the surrounding towns. Echoing sentiments expressed by Plath's friends, Sexton's neighbors told her that her poems weren't anything like her; that her words were depressing and cruel. But for Sexton, "I know that it is, in truth, like me inside. And, you see, 'inside' is the place where poems come from."[36]

This notion of inside-outside was something that impacted Plath too. Unlike Sexton, she seemed less concerned about imposter syndrome and internalized her writing agonies into something deeply personal, not really connected to the outside world at all. With a solid education behind her, with a reading history that could outdo just about anyone, Plath didn't need to feel threatened by a lack of intellectual clout. Also, for over six years, she had had the support of a poet-husband who was able to understand her writing regime and critique her work. Her difficulties came from a form of writer's block. When she was working a job with no time to write, she desperately wanted to compose poems and stories. When she gave up her job to have time to write, she could not. The year she suffered most was the year she got to know Sexton. Some of the poems Plath took to Lowell's workshop were over two years old, some already published, some not. In a 1960 poem called "Stillborn," Plath compared poems that never came alive to stillborn babies. "These poems do not live: it's a sad diagnosis. / . . . O I cannot understand what happened to them!"[37] She worried that she was not good enough, that she would never be able to make a living from it as well as being a wife and mother. Like Sexton, she saw creativity and money as being linked: "You do it for itself first. If it brings in money, how nice. You do not do it first for money. Money isn't why you sit down at the typewriter."[38] Her journals are full of story ideas that never get off the ground and critiques of poems she was writing, such as "Point Shirley," "Watercolor of Grantchester Meadows," and "Suicide Off Egg Rock," as being too stilted and forced. She felt she needed to get more philosophy into them. Her vision of what she wanted her poems to be is exactly what she finally pulled off with *Ariel*, but that was all still three years away at this point. By the time the poems she dreamed of writing started to appear, Plath's problems were more practical than creative. As her marriage ended and her carefully planned domestic setup slid into chaos, her writing voice finally fully broke free. Her study became the quiet center of the storm going on around her and she truly believed that if she had an ordered study, the rest of her life would settle down pleasantly at some stage: "Here is my hearth, my life, my real self. I have never been so happy anywhere in my life as writing at my desk in the blue dawns, all to myself, secret and quiet."[39]

This writing, however, did not come easy. While fighting for recognition and legitimacy, Plath and Sexton were also trying to run homes, make money, build a legacy, and carve out a place in literature that was resisting their access. Running alongside this were real battles with their own mental health and well-being. Insofar as some of their behavior can be depathologized, it is equally important to recognize that both women had moments of mental anguish and suffering that led to hospitalization, suicide attempts, and deep unhappiness. Today, it is still so difficult for women to "have it all," but back then it was even harder, and this took a toll on most women who tried. There is a reason why Plath and Sexton talked obsessively about breakdowns and suicide attempts over afternoon drinks. These things formed a central part of their existence, and eventually were the things that ended their lives.

CHAPTER SEVEN

Mental Illness

You must not seek escape like this. You must think.
—Sylvia Plath (the last words in her journal
before her suicide attempt in 1953)[1]

The surface cracked when I was about twenty-eight. I
had a psychotic break and tried to kill myself.
—Anne Sexton[2]

I n 1950s America, the treatments for mental illnesses such as
depression, anxiety, suicidal urges, and self-harm were often
as distressing as the suffering caused by the illnesses themselves. Electroconvulsive therapy, insulin injections, physical
restraints, and unreliable drug therapies were all used, sometimes in a rather cavalier way, to try and "cure" patients of any
underlying conditions. Although the psychoanalytic "talking
cure" was increasingly an option, this was often used alongside
other, more invasive techniques, sometimes administered without patient consent.

Living with clinical depression and fear as well as suicidal urges is difficult enough to manage and navigate by itself. Plath and Sexton both engaged in valiant struggles to keep going, to not break, to not succumb to what Sexton called a "leaky ego."[3] Plath's journals see her reasoning with herself over pages and pages why she should not think in a certain way, what she thinks her difficulties are, and what she might be able to do about them. Sexton lamented the energy-sapping nature of "craziness," the time wasted, the opportunities lost. Yet, despite their own attempts to escape the suffocation of depression, both women were at one stage or another subjected to a range of the treatments mentioned above. And retrospectively, both women were failed miserably by the mental health system.

It is a long-argued debate about the nature-nurture aspect of women and mental illness, and the language used can be inflammatory and misleading. Plath and Sexton had no issue using expressions like *crazy* and *mad* to describe how they were feeling, though we shy away from such words today. Even the term "mental illness" is problematic; should it be "mental health"? Sexton acknowledged her own culpability in how she was labeled, given that most of her work dealt with the emotional landscape of her mind: "I am popularly known as the crazy poet . . . And after all, it is my fault. I did write about it thoroughly, explored it so I made my own costume . . ."[4] Connie Taylor Blackwell, a Boston friend of Plath's, described how they would often meet and drink sherry and talk about "the void." It was a big topic, claimed Blackwell, because at the time, in the 1950s, women were being pushed in so many directions that the attraction of nothingness for them was very real. Women, quite simply, got exhausted by it all.[5] This idea that it is indeed society that drives women mad has much credence when you look at the history of diagnoses and treatment. Women were not supposed to be dissatisfied, angry, or outspoken. If they were, they became regarded as a problem. Today, anger in women is still frowned upon. They need to "calm down" and "stop shouting." In short, the message is that women need to stop making a fuss. But to claim that all mental struggles have at their root societal imbalance seems dangerous and reductive. A whole host of other factors can be playing their part alongside this, forming a sort of multidimensional approach to mental health: environment, history, trauma, family, personality, psychology, and even brain chemistry. Taken by themselves, none of these explanations are sufficient, and neither are they without their problems, especially when you throw in other characteristics, such as gender, ethnicity, age, and so on. There is a reason why more women than men are diagnosed with depression. There is a reason why most people diagnosed with depression who are given drugs are women. There is a reason why in mental institutions in America, Black people are among the highest numbers diagnosed with schizophrenia. But there are also theories about brain chemistry and biology, serotonin uptakes, malfunctioning brain synapses, and neurological pathways. Looking at the history of Plath's and Sexton's mental struggles is like carefully piecing together a jigsaw puzzle when we don't even know what the full picture is. How do the pieces fit together? Can we even make sense of the puzzle? A fractured whole can be explored, but there will always be gaps and uncertainties.

There were two noticeable moments in the lives of Plath and Sexton that saw them overwhelmed by emotional difficulties. Plath was twenty when in 1953, after three years studying at Smith and a month spent as a guest editor at *Mademoiselle* in New York, she suddenly felt her emotional resilience collapse, and she made a serious attempt on her life. Sexton was older, twenty-seven, when she suffered a complete breakdown in 1955 following the birth of her second daughter, requiring repeated hospitalization. At this stage, Plath and Sexton had not met. It is possible that they did not even know of each other's existence. Yet the experiences they had would form the basis of their brief friendship, a feeling of having been in the club, a realization that wanting to die had been a big part of their lives. In each other, they saw that understanding, and relished the empathy. In the UK, suicide was still regarded as a crime against the Crown and against God until 1961. It was not until the late 1960s that states in America began to remove the act of suicide as a felony from their legislation, and today it is not listed as a crime in any state. Wanting to die seemed to carry a lack of understanding and a lack of support, so it is hardly surprising that these two women turned to each other.

5.30 pm Mrs Plath of 26 Elmwood Rd. reports her daughter Sylvia Plath age 20 − 5'9" − 140lbs. dark brown eyes, dark blonde hair missing. Propably [*sic*] wearing blue denim skirt, blouse and Jersey. This girl depressed. Route officer and all station a our [*sic*] radio network notified. Teletype item 85. West P.D. notified.

Direct transcription from Wellesley
Police Department records[6]

On August 24, 1953, after attending a screening of Queen Elizabeth II's coronation in Boston's Exeter Theatre, Aurelia Plath returned home to find an unusual note from her daughter: "Have gone for a long hike will be home tomorrow." Alarmed by this out-of-character behavior—Plath never took off like this—and increasingly worried about her daughter's mental state over the summer, Aurelia phoned the police to report her daughter missing.

The police record notes that Sylvia Plath was "depressed." Aurelia Plath, however, knew the extent to which her daughter was struggling against mental and physical exhaustion after intense study at Smith and a month working at *Mademoiselle*. Rather than being swept along by the glamour of the internship, New York City eroded Plath's confidence and optimism. Writing to her brother, Warren, on letterheaded paper from the offices on Madison Avenue, she claimed that the last weeks of college were so hectic with exams and appointments and "the shift to NYC has been so rapid that I can't think logically about who I am or where I am going. I have been very ecstatic, horribly depressed, shocked, elated, enlightened and enervated . . . all of which makes living very hard and newly."[7] In *The Bell Jar*, which fictionalized Plath's New York experience, Esther Greenwood describes the worryingly detached numbness of a sultry summer month in the city: "I felt very still and very empty, the way the eye of a tornado must feel, moving dully along in the middle of the surrounding hulla-baloo."[8] Tossed about between dinners and rooftop parties, frantic writing assignments and dating, Plath's farewell to the city was to feed her entire wardrobe to the night sky from her hotel window in the Barbizon. Esther Greenwood also throws all her clothes into New York's night sky: "Piece by piece, I fed my wardrobe to the night wind, and flutteringly, like a loved one's ashes, the gray scraps were ferried off, to settle here, there, exactly where I would never know, in the dark heart of New York."[9] On leaving the city, Esther's travel bag contained a book of short stories, a sunglasses case, and two dozen avocados.

When Plath returned home to Wellesley for the rest of the summer, she had hoped to start attending a short story class at Harvard run by the writer Frank O'Connor. Her application was rejected.[10] She then decided to learn shorthand as a skill that she could fall back on. She did not understand it. Then she decided to start work on her senior year thesis examining the work of James Joyce. The words seem to slide off the page before her eyes. As a well-published and award-winning young writer, she began to worry that she was no longer able to write poems or prose. She could not eat, and she could not sleep. The hot air of the suburbs smothered her. Her journal shows a mind falling into despair and panic. "You are afraid of being alone with your own mind," she admonishes herself. Instructions are written in capital letters: "NOTHING EVER REMAINS THE SAME." Her handwriting in the journal becomes increasingly erratic. The final entry on July 14 finishes with a desperate plea: "ignore problems—shut walls up between you & the world . . ." She tells herself to think repeatedly, she asks God for help, she tells herself to snap out of it. And her final words are written in shaky black ink: "You must think."[11]

Over the following weeks, the local family doctor referred Plath to a psychiatrist, Dr. Thornton, who was running the Valley Head Hospital in Carlisle, Massachusetts. Plath disliked him intensely. After a few sessions, Thornton disappeared for his summer vacation and turned Plath over to his colleague, Dr. Kenneth Tillotson, who, according to Aurelia Plath, asked his patient to see him as a sort of "fatherly advisor."[12] Tillotson had previously worked at McLean but had left years earlier, causing a national scandal when it was discovered he had engaged in a sexual relationship with one of his patients. After a few sessions with Plath, Tillotson decided she should receive electroconvulsive therapy (ECT) on an outpatient basis.

Although ECT was widely used in American institutions from the 1940s onward, it was not without its problems. Then, as now, opinion was divided between ECT being a somewhat inexplicable but effective treatment against depression versus an ineffectual and barbaric way to treat a mentally distressed patient. The theory is that certain mental health symptoms can be alleviated by sending electric currents through the brain, which induces an epileptic seizure. Beyond this, knowledge is fairly scant. Some psychiatrists believe it is not the electricity but the ensuing seizure that results in an improvement in the patient. Others argue that it alters blood flow and chemical imbalances in the brain, which can be linked to levels of depression. Ideally it is used with the patient's consent, but it can be used without. It is predominantly given to women. In the 1940s, when it was administered without muscle relaxants, the seizures induced were so severe that patients could break limbs. Side effects appeared to be headaches, confusion, aching muscles, damage to the tongue, teeth, and lips, memory loss, and long-term personality changes. Personal testimonies from ECT patients vary widely: some believe it saved them from their depression; others describe the most horrific violation.

This decision by Tillotson to use ECT, and the subsequent botched administration of the treatments, would scar Plath for the rest of her life. Not only did she appear to stay conscious throughout each session, feeling the full force of the electrocution, but afterward she was left alone in a recovery room. "By the roots of my hair some god got hold of me. / I shivered in his blue volts like a desert prophet."[13] Plath felt as though she were being burned alive along every nerve. In *The Bell Jar*, Esther Greenwood describes the experience of having two metal plates fitted to the sides of her head and buckled tightly across her forehead with a strap. A wire was placed in her mouth to bite. "Then something bent down and took hold of me and shook me like the end of the world. Whee-ee-ee-ee-ee, it shrilled, through an air crackling with blue light, and with each flash a great jolt drubbed me till I thought my bones would break and the sap fly out of me like a split plant."[14] She also wondered what on earth she had done to deserve it.

Dreading further electric shock treatments and worrying that she would become a financial burden on her struggling family, on Monday, August 24, Plath left the note saying she was taking a long hike. She then broke the lock on her mother's cabinet, stole a bottle of sleeping pills, and filled a large jug with water. Checking that her grandparents were occupied in the back garden, she went down to the basement. Eight years later, fictionalizing this moment for her novel, Plath wrote: "A dim, undersea light filtered through the slits of the cellar windows. Behind the oil burner, a dark gap showed in the wall at about shoulder height and ran back under the breezeway, out of sight."[15]

Plath moved a pile of wood that was stacked in front of the opening to a dark crawl space and after a few attempts she managed to hoist herself inside with the water and the pills. She then pulled the wood back to conceal the entrance. She had no intention of being found. Months later, in a letter to her friend Eddie Cohen, she described her suicide attempt: "I swallowed quantities and blissfully succumbed to the whirling blackness that I honestly believed was eternal oblivion."[16]

As Plath lay unconscious in the basement, police and neighbors were searching the woods nearby and dragging the local lake, fearing she had hurt herself while out walking. Over three hundred articles appeared in newspapers across the country about the "Missing Smith Girl," with Aurelia Plath explaining that her daughter was anxious and depressed and concerned that she had lost the ability to write.[17] The effect on the family was devastating. They had no idea where Plath was or what had happened to her.

The next day Aurelia discovered the missing pills and called the police station at 6:46 a.m., convinced that her daughter must have broken into her locked cabinet and taken them. The idea that Plath had wandered off on a long walk suddenly took a more sinister turn. Sniffer dogs were brought to try and track her down. Meanwhile, in the cellar of 26 Elmwood Road, Plath had taken too many sleeping pills and began to vomit them up. She described how she "came to consciousness in a dark hell banging my head repeatedly on the ragged rocks of the cellar in futile attempts to sit up and, instinctively, call for help."[18] Nobody heard her until the following day when her brother, Warren, detected moaning coming from the basement. Rushing downstairs, he discovered his sister and immediately phoned for an ambulance. Aurelia Plath called the police station at 12:40 p.m. to tell them she had located her daughter.

Plath was taken to the nearby Newton-Wellesley Hospital with a severe abrasion beneath her right eye, which was allegedly crawling with maggots. Newspaper headlines were now full of "Missing Student Found: Alive but Semiconscious." After an examination in the emergency room, Plath was described as being in fairly good condition with the exception of her cheek wound, which would require shots of penicillin for the infection.

While the family dealt with the aftermath of the suicide attempt, other people were following the story via the papers. One person was Olive Higgins Prouty, the author of books such as *Stella Dallas* and *Now, Voyager*, who also happened to be Plath's benefactor for her scholarship to Smith. Upon reading that Plath had been discovered, Prouty wired Aurelia to say she was on vacation in Maine but would be in touch as soon as she returned home. More important, her telegram contained the words "I WANT TO HELP."

According to Aurelia Plath, when her daughter regained consciousness in Newton-Wellesley Hospital, her first words were "Oh no . . ." Plath recalled the confusion of waking up: "The next days were a nightmare of flashing lights, strange voices, large needles, an overpowering conviction that I was blind in one eye, and a hatred toward the people who would not let me die, but insisted rather in dragging me back into the hell of sordid and meaningless existence."[19] She was placed on twenty-four-hour watch, which became so expensive that her mother and brother replaced nurses to try and reduce the cost. Aurelia Plath had only $600 in savings.

By this time, Dr. Tillotson had also left for his summer vacation, and Aurelia Plath found herself without any psychiatric support. At the suggestion of the local reverend, she contacted Dr. Erich Lindemann, who was head of the psychiatric ward at Massachusetts General Hospital. He examined Plath on September 1 and had no reservations that she needed to be moved to a psychiatric facility. He was willing to admit her to Mass General. On September 3, after eight nights in the local hospital, Plath was transferred to the psychiatric ward, where she underwent extensive—and intensive—examinations. Six days later, Lindemann met with Aurelia Plath and Olive Higgins

Prouty, who had arrived back in Boston from her vacation. Lindemann concluded that Plath was suffering from an adolescent nervous illness and that she should make a full recovery. However, she was not responding well to the environment of the ward. Seeing other patients who were more severely depressed than she was seemed to (not surprisingly) distress Plath, and Lindemann concluded that the best setting for her would be a private institution. He suggested McLean, one of the country's finest mental hospitals.

Olive Higgins Prouty had by now taken charge of all aspects of Plath's treatment, including the medical expenses. An intelligent, formidable, and generous woman, she supported Plath throughout her treatment (and indeed for the rest of her life). Prouty had a personal interest, not only as the benefactor of Plath's scholarship, but in understanding Plath as a young writer struggling against the restrictive social roles of 1950s America. Prouty had encountered similar problems when she was a young woman. Born into a wealthy Massachusetts family in 1882, she married an equally wealthy husband and found her life conflicted between her desire to write and the social obligations expected of a woman in her position. Although on the whole she was happy in her marriage, the poems she wrote expressed her desire for more personal freedom. After a family bereavement, Prouty underwent a nervous breakdown so severe that it lasted for over two years. Her psychiatrist suggested writing as a way out of her depression and Prouty embraced this idea, publishing increasingly successful novels and donating all the proceeds to the various causes she supported. She understood and empathized with the hopelessness that Plath was feeling. Furthermore, she was *furious* about the treatment Plath had received at Valley Head Hospital. Writing a blistering letter to the director, Dr. Thornton, Prouty pointed out that it was the incompetent care at his facility that had led to Plath's suicide attempt. Thornton replied, defending his decision to administer ECT on an outpatient basis, calling Prouty's opinions worthless, and requesting that she never contact his office again. Nevertheless, Thornton reduced his final medical fees by half and Tillotson waived his completely.[20]

This was just the beginning of the highly questionable treatment Plath received in the mental health care system, an experience that would be replicated with Sexton, too, as she navigated her way through unreliable drug treatments and exploitative psychiatrists. Unlike Plath, who was still a student, Sexton had her first major breakdown when she was a wife and mother. And unlike Plath, who seemed to have this one significant suicide attempt and episode, Sexton's mental health issues were an altogether messier and more prolonged affair. It is impossible to diagnose posthumously, but it does seem at least feasible that Sexton's first and most intense period of breakdown was connected to some form of postpartum depression. She was diagnosed as a "hysteric," a label that stuck for years as she moved from one psychiatrist to another. The history and use of this word is significant and directly linked to the gendered nature of what Sexton herself would refer to as madness. The word *hysteria* has its origins in the Greek word for uterus, and historically it was believed that in some women the uterus could detach itself and wander through the body causing havoc, creating disease, and eventually strangling the woman. Because a physical explanation was offered, the cause essentially being the womb, this was seen as an illness that could really only affect women. The term *hysteric* stuck and by the twentieth century was a catchall to describe some kind of emotional excess. Linda Gray Sexton felt that this old-fashioned label hindered her mother's treatment, as psychiatrists focused on the depressive side of Sexton's personality: "Today she might well have been given a diagnosis of some form of bipolar illness, and been treated with the wide variety of mood stabilizers and antidepressants now available."[21] She felt that if her mother had been born twenty years later, she might still be alive.

Instead, between 1955 and 1964, Sexton was taken to the emergency room at Newton-Wellesley Hospital at least five times to have her stomach pumped and was hospitalized on a number of occasions for suicidal impulses and episodes in which she heard voices urging her to kill herself or her daughters. In 1959, Sexton described the development of a frightening new symptom: some sort of blackout or fugue state in which she passed out, sometimes for up to twenty-four hours. With no physical reason for this happening, she supposed in a letter to W. D. Snodgrass that it must be "a hysterical type of thing, I guess."[22] These states could come over her at any time: while driving her car, walking down the street, or immediately following a therapy session. She would have no memory of them happening, or her behavior during them. Often if they

LEFT: The Ritz-Carlton, Boston © Boston Globe, *via Getty Images*

RIGHT: 236 Bay State Road, Boston University, the location of Robert Lowell's poetry workshop
© *Kevin Cummins*

BELOW: Room 222 of 236 Bay State Road, Boston University, where Plath and Sexton met for Lowell's poetry workshop
© *Kevin Cummins*

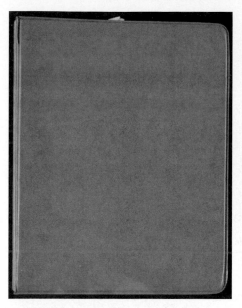

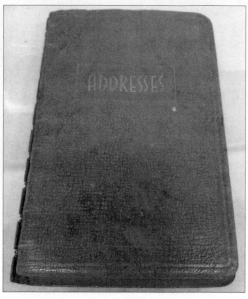

ABOVE: Anne Sexton's red address book, held at the Harry Ransom Center, The University of Texas at Austin © *Photography Collection, Harry Ransom Center, The University of Texas at Austin*

ABOVE: Sylvia Plath's address book, held in the Mortimer Rare Book Collection, Smith College © *Gail Crowther*

BELOW: Sexton on the roof terrace of Oscar Williams's apartment, New York City © *Photography Collection, Harry Ransom Center, The University of Texas at Austin*

LEFT: Plath on the roof terrace of Oscar Williams's apartment, New York City © *Estate of Oscar Williams, courtesy of Lilly Library, Indiana University, Bloomington, Indiana*

RIGHT: Plath and Ted Hughes on the roof terrace of Oscar Williams's apartment, New York City © *Estate of Oscar Williams, courtesy of Lilly Library, Indiana University, Bloomington, Indiana*

LEFT: Sexton at her desk with Plath's *Ariel* visible behind her typewriter © *Photography Collection, Harry Ransom Center, The University of Texas at Austin*

RIGHT: A selection of Sexton's medications and pills © *Photography Collection, Harry Ransom Center, The University of Texas at Austin*

LEFT: Court Green, Plath's home in North Tawton, Devon, taken in April 1963 © *Estate of Elizabeth Sigmund*

RIGHT: Sexton's final home, 14 Black Oak Road, Weston, Massachusetts © *Kevin Cummins*

LEFT: Plath and her children in the garden at Court Green, July 1962 © *Estate of Elizabeth Sigmund*

RIGHT: A contact sheet from a series of images of Sexton. On the back she has written "1/2 hour before leaving husband." © *Photography Collection, Harry Ransom Center, The University of Texas at Austin*

KODAK SAFETY FILM
KODAK TRI X PAN FILM
KODAK SAFETY FILM
KODAK TRI X PAN FILM
KODAK SAFETY FILM
KODAK TRI X PAN FILM
KODAK SAFETY FILM
S C D K D
→7 →6A →6 →5A →5 →4A →4 →3A →3 →2A
→17 →16A →16 →15A →15 →14A →14 →13A →13 →12A
→12 →11A →11 →10A →10 →9A →9 →8A →8 →7A
→22 →21A →20A →20 →19A →19 →18A →18 →17A

RIGHT: 11 St. George's Terrace, Primrose Hill, London, home of the poet W. S. Merwin, where Plath wrote much of *The Bell Jar* in the upstairs study © *Gail Crowther*

BELOW: Fitzroy Road, Primrose Hill, London, Plath's final home, with the blue plaque to W. B. Yeats visible © *Gail Crowther*

RIGHT: McLean Hospital, Belmont, Massachusetts © *Gail Crowther*

ABOVE: The blue plaque on 3 Chalcot Square, Primrose Hill, London, Plath's home from 1960 to 1961 © *Gail Crowther*

BELOW: Sylvia Plath's grave in the churchyard at St. Thomas the Apostle church, Heptonstall, West Yorkshire © *Kevin Cummins*

ABOVE: Anne Sexton's grave in Forest Hills Cemetery,
Jamaica Plain, Boston © *Kevin Cummins*

BELOW: Anne Sexton © *Photography Collection,
Harry Ransom Center, The University of Texas at Austin*

occurred during or after therapy, this interrupted continuity, so her psychiatrist, Dr. Orne, insisted that they start taping their sessions so she could play them back and remember what had taken place during the appointment. As the years went on, some people around Sexton became suspicious about these states, wondering if sometimes they were used as an excuse to escape unwanted or tricky situations. They would often happen after an argument or a difficult therapy session or if Sexton didn't get her way. As late as 1973, when Sexton had been suffering from these blackout states for fourteen years, she was finally sent for a five-day stay at McLean Hospital to undergo examinations. An electroencephalogram checked her temporal lobes for epilepsy, one possible cause of the fugues, but the EEG revealed normal brain functioning. Whether Sexton employed these blackout states consciously or unconsciously, the effect was scary for her children. They worried every time they left the house what state their mother would be in when they returned, or even if she would be there at all. However frustrating their mother could be, Linda recalled one day in December 1973 when she realized just how ill her mother was. Linda overheard Sexton on the phone ordering presents to be delivered for their Christmas stockings. Although Sexton was always prone to agoraphobia and a fear of traveling anywhere alone, Linda found the idea of getting a delivery from a shop less than a mile away preposterous and insisted that they go shopping together. She also just wanted a rare moment of doing normal mother-daughter activities. Determined to have a nice day, she bundled her protesting mother out the door and into the drugstore down the road. While she was choosing a lipstick for her sister, she turned around and found Sexton vomiting, presumably with fear, in the middle of the shop floor: "I put my arm around her and escorted her out into the parking lot, my face red with shame: shame that I had asked her to do something she plainly could not . . ."[23]

Although Sexton's illness was sprawling and unpredictable, there were warning signs that even her young daughters grew to recognize and fear. The small number of household chores Sexton was supposed to do went undone as she sat at the kitchen table all day twirling her hair into knots. Perhaps most significantly, her typewriter fell silent ("She was rarely crazy when she was writing," her daughter Linda noted).[24] It was during these times that Sexton would often look at worksheets she had kept, to remind her how poems came about. Like Plath, when she was feeling depressed, Sexton, too, felt as though she would never be able to write again, and this just compounded the depression. She found her worksheets helped remind her that good poems came out of bad words and bad metaphors, and that even if a poem started wrong, the right process could bring it into being.

If the depression really took hold, then Sexton would take to her bed and start holding conversations with dead people while taking too many pills. Home life would become chaotic, with various family members stepping in to help with childcare and in-laws covering medical expenses. After episodes of hospitalization Sexton would horrify her daughters with stories from the "nuthouse," describing one incident when she was placed on suicide watch with her wrists tied above her head like in a crucifixion. When she asked the nurse for a cigarette, she was refused and told she was being punished and only getting what she deserved.[25]

With violence at home between Sexton and her husband, and periodic physical attacks on her children, Sexton's behavior also played out in the therapy room. In a letter to W. D. Snodgrass in 1959 she recounts (with some humor) a fight she had with her psychiatrist: "One day though I broke out and picked up all the things on his desk and threw them at him (including a lamp and an ink bottle). I'm better some, though. I don't go around trying to kill myself all the time as I once did. (Just him. Ha!)"[26] Between falling into fugue states, physically fighting with her therapist, and being exploited for sex by another psychiatrist and then abandoned, it is hardly surprising that Sexton's behavior was often erratic. Coupled with her low self-esteem, she engaged in dangerous behavior, sometimes seeing herself as being fit for nothing other than prostitution. One evening after a late therapy session, she invited a stranger into her car and performed fellatio on him.

In all this confusion, suffering, and chaos, however, there was a desire in Sexton to make use of these experiences. Linda, too, saw her mother begin to make a career out of her illness. In her public readings she would make light of her visits to various mental hospitals. "I am queen of this summer hotel," she wrote in her poem "You, Doctor Martin," romanticizing her illness, in much the same way George Starbuck remembered her doing on their boozy afternoons at the Ritz.[27] Sexton wrote about her experiences because she felt that one day they might help other people. She firmly believed that "my suffering will reach someone more than my joy."[28] If from time to time she resented being classed as the crazy poet, she equally knew that this was where her power lay. In a 1963 letter to a journalist, she nevertheless complained about *Newsweek* wanting to photograph her in front of a hospital or sitting on the grounds of a hospital for a feature on American poetry. The suggestion, she claimed, was more than she could bear. In a brilliantly tart retort, she refused the photo shoot and instead told them to go and find an existing picture of her, as there were many in "some charming and unusual poses, perhaps some even with the white building in the background that they could <u>pretend</u> was the back entrance to a hospital." She ended assertively: "I am a good poet whether I have my hospital johnny on or not."[29]

Yet Sexton was somewhat prone to glamorize madness, despite the terrible anguish she experienced. Everything about mental hospitals and going crazy fascinated her. Writing about it helped her process what she was experiencing, but equally to build what her daughter described as some sort of "chic cachet."[30] Her long poem "Flee on Your Donkey," which was actually written in a mental hospital, presents her as a veteran patient, familiar with the sights, sounds, and routines of the institution, an old hand at it all: "Six years of such small preoccupations! / Six years of shuttling in and out of this place! / O my hunger! My hunger!"[31] She saw mental institutions as having a certain hierarchy. Having been a patient in places like

Newton-Wellesley and Westwood Lodge, Sexton saw the ultimate glamour in being a patient at McLean Hospital. In fact, she was quite jealous of people, such as Robert Lowell, who had spent time there. She would not get her wish to stay there until just a year before she died.

But if Sexton yearned for a spell in McLean, in contrast, Olive Higgins Prouty was not convinced that this was the best place for Plath to recover from her suicide attempt. On September 14, Prouty drove with Sylvia and Aurelia Plath from Massachusetts General to McLean, where Plath was admitted into the rather grand yellow-stoned administration building and then assigned her private room in Codman House. It was the beginning of autumn, a melancholy time of year, and the trees on the grounds were just beginning to turn orange. Plath would spend many hours looking at them over the coming months. Codman House was an imposing redbrick building, U-shaped, with white pillars on either side of the main entrance. Plath was given two different rooms: the first at the back of the building on the ground floor; the second in the front with a lot more sun. It was regarded as medium security.[32] McLean was regarded as the premier asylum for the best of Boston society.

Shortly after admission, a pivotal moment in Plath's future recovery and life occurred: she was introduced to her psychiatrist, Dr. Ruth Beuscher.[33] Meanwhile, Prouty was in consultation with McLean's director, Franklin Wood, about how the hospital planned to treat Plath's depression. Seemingly they had decided on multiple approaches, some of which would be abandoned over the coming months, others that would be introduced as a final attempt to alleviate Plath's persistent condition.

First, Plath was to undergo intensive psychotherapy; daily sessions with her personal psychiatrist, Dr. Beuscher, and once a week with Dr. Lindemann. Prouty might have been less enthusiastic about Plath's personal psychiatrist at McLean had she known that Ruth Beuscher was not fully qualified and had just started her training residency in the hospital that year. From Plath's point of view, she had a young female doctor (Beuscher was twenty-nine) who seemed to immediately understand and empathize with how she was feeling. Ruth Tiffany Beuscher had a background worthy of working in one of America's top mental hospitals. She was related to the New York Tiffanys and had been educated at Barnard and Columbia. The friendship between Plath and Beuscher would last for the rest of Plath's life. In fact, Beuscher was one of the last people Plath wrote to before she died. From Beuscher's perspective, she felt a strong personal bond with Plath. How professional this was is questionable. Nine years later, when Plath's marriage had failed and she was in despair, Beuscher tried to offer support via their correspondence. In late 1962 she wrote to Plath that if she cured no one else in her life, Plath alone would have been worth it. She even told her she loved her.

Beuscher immediately imposed a strict visiting regime at McLean, allowing only a few people each week to see her patient. Aurelia Plath and Olive Higgins Prouty visited about once every week or ten days, as did an old high school teacher,

Wilbury Crockett. According to Beuscher, Plath was furious. She refused to talk and was angry with her mother. She had been left traumatized by her month in New York. Beuscher recalled, "I was interested not only in her head and her performance but also how she felt."[34]

Alongside psychotherapy, it was decided to give Plath insulin shock treatment. This was a curious decision to make, since it was used predominantly for schizophrenia, a condition that Dr. Lindemann had been keen to stress was not afflicting Plath. Developed in the 1920s by Dr. Manfred Sakel, the idea was to inject patients with increasingly large amounts of insulin each day until a coma was induced. Once comatose (sometimes for as long as an hour), patients would then be pulled out of the coma by intravenous glucose injections. One general theory was that patients were literally shocked out of their mental illness. At the time, there was very little evidence that this technique worked at all, and even less evidence since. It has now been entirely discredited and is no longer used. However, in the 1940s and '50s it was standard practice in American hospitals and Plath was unlucky enough to be one of the recipients. Daily doses of insulin could produce restlessness, perspiration, and invariably significant weight increase—a side effect that did occur to Plath and further impacted on her self-esteem. In a short story, "Tongues of Stone," written two years after her breakdown, Plath describes the experiences of a nameless girl in a nameless mental institution: "She was caught in the nightmare of the body, without a mind, without anything, only the soulless flesh that got fatter with the insulin and yellower with the fading tan."[35] In *The Bell Jar*, Esther Greenwood receives insulin injections until she experiences a reaction, pulling out of a deep sleep and beating her bedpost with her fists. When she is asked if it made her feel better, the hopelessness of it is evident: "I did for a while. Now I'm the same again."[36] Olive Higgins Prouty was not convinced by this treatment. She had been trying to learn more about the reasoning and purpose behind the injections and had even visited her library to carry out further research. In any event McLean did not persist with the insulin therapy beyond early November.

The final treatment McLean chose for Plath on her admission to the hospital was unstructured free time every day during which, if she felt like it, she could undertake occupational therapy. This met with strict disapproval from Olive Higgins Prouty, who felt Plath's days had become aimless, and furthermore, this lack of purpose was exacerbating her depression. In a stern letter to Dr. Beuscher, Prouty reported that during her last visit Plath had complained about long hours spent in her room, her failure to mix with other patients, and the desire to have some structured activities to make her days more bearable. Beuscher did nothing to change Plath's routine beyond suggesting perhaps she could type up some of Prouty's manuscripts on a typewriter provided by Aurelia Plath.

This conflict about Plath's treatment continued throughout October and November. A letter dated October 22 from Olive Higgins Prouty to Aurelia Plath described how much happier Plath seemed as she had been weaving on the looms in the occupational therapy rooms. Plath's family and friends, though, saw no improvement in her condition and by mid-November she appeared to still be significantly depressed. Writing to Dr. Lindemann, Olive Higgins Prouty continued to be concerned about the lack of structure. Because Plath was so depressed, she did not have the motivation to organize her time, but Prouty felt certain if she were given a light schedule, Plath would certainly cooperate. McLean, on the other hand, did see some improvement and stopped the insulin shock treatment on November 7. They continued to resist inflicting a schedule on Plath's days, fearing the pressure might set her back. Seeing part of her problem as having been an "accomplisher," they wanted to remove any obligation for Plath to fulfill—or perhaps worse still, fail—any expectations placed on her. Plath herself lends some credence to this view. When the unnamed girl in "Tongues of Stone" attempts to learn knitting and fails, it brings about uncontrollable crying and a further sense of despair. Paradoxically, though, the lack of schedule equally leads to listlessness: "It was sometime in October; she had long ago lost track of all the days and it really didn't matter because one was like another and there were no nights to separate them because she never slept anymore."[37]

For most of November, after stopping the insulin shock therapy, McLean regarded Plath's primary and most effective treatment as being psychotherapeutic. However, in a letter dated November 25, Franklin Wood informed Olive Higgins Prouty that they had started Plath on a drug called chlorpromazine (also marketed under the name Thorazine). Although today chlorpromazine is regarded as one of the safest antipsychotic drugs on the market, incredibly when it was given to Plath in 1953 it appeared to have undergone no clinical trials whatsoever in the United States.[38] Originally synthesized in 1950 in France, chlorpromazine was developed as an antihistamine to treat nausea and allergies. It was first administered in a Parisian hospital in 1951 with the noticeable effect that it induced calmness in patients prior to surgery. As a consequence, Henri Laborit, one of the surgeons behind the creation of the compound, suggested it might be of use in psychiatry. Chlorpromazine was first used to treat mania and schizophrenia later in the year at St. Anne's Hospital in Paris. The two psychiatrists to prescribe it, Jean Delay and Pierre Deniker, published a report in 1952 citing its effectiveness in controlling agitation and excitement. Over the following years the use of the drug began to spread throughout Europe and the United States. There can be no doubt that McLean, which prided itself on being at the forefront of psychiatric treatments, was following the progress of the drug's use in Paris and was presumably one of the first institutions across the Atlantic to prescribe it. While this pioneering attitude is laudable, looking back, it is also a reminder of just how experimental many of the psychiatric treatments were at the time. What is now known is that chlorpromazine has various dose-dependent risks attached to it that were presumably just being discovered from clinical use during the early 1950s. Dizziness, seizures, weight gain, stiffening of muscles, and drowsiness were all side effects that came to light. Franklin Wood seemingly felt the effects of chlorpromazine were unknown, since he informed Olive Higgins Prouty that if the drug did not work, then McLean would use the final resort of ECT.

Sexton, too, was subject to a range of drug treatments, many of which seemed somewhat experimental, with unknown side effects that often left her wondering whether her feelings of craziness were in her own head or had to do with the cocktail of drugs she was on. Like Plath, she was given Thorazine, which did appear to stabilize her moods and stop the sudden fugue states, but there were downsides. Sexton felt that somehow the drug blocked her creativity, and people around her noticed a change in her personality: "Rita [her neighbor] told me today that I've changed on Thorazine. She says I'm more childlike. She also says she bets I haven't had one original idea since then . . . Rita right [*sic*]. No ideas. None. Of my own. NOT ONE."[39] The other downside was that the drug made her skin photosensitive, making two of Sexton's favorite activities—swimming and sunbathing in her garden—impossible. The impact of this drug ruined a vacation for her in 1969 with unpleasant-sounding physical effects: "The Thorazine is poisoning the whole vacation. I sting. I hurt. There is no shade."[40] But on the whole she appreciated the calmness that the little orange pills seemed to offer, and even credited it with saving her life on more than one occasion. The haphazard nature of her drug therapy did not escape her, though, as she acknowledged it had taken over ten years to find a drug that seemed to help with her symptoms.

The sheer amount of drugs Sexton consumed was astounding. In a 1964 therapy session, Sexton spoke to Dr. Orne about the drugs she was on, saying Nembutal (a barbiturate) made her hallucinate, and that, among others, her twice-a-day Librium (a sedative) was leaving her lethargic and demotivated. She described not being able to sleep, as she felt ants were crawling all over her skin. She had not been getting dressed but rather writing in her bathrobe or bathing suit. Although she described Librium as being a good calmer-down, there seemed a fine line between being calm and being too drugged to do anything at all. By 1966, she wrote that in order to get to sleep at night she had to take eight pills, and in order for the Thorazine to work she had to take huge amounts of it at least five times a day. The bottles lined up on her bedside table terrified her children. They knew at any moment she could take them to end her life, and this left them fearful and jittery.[41]

Along with Thorazine, Sexton was also given another relatively new drug called Tofranil. This was a tricyclic antidepressant discovered in 1951 and introduced for medical use in 1957, eventually reaching the US in 1959. Three years later Sexton was on it but not enjoying the effect it had on her at all. In a letter to fellow poet Tony Hecht, her distress is evident and a reminder that while some psychiatrists were dishing out drugs without fully knowing the effects, the impact on mental health was often detrimental. Sexton described how Tofranil "makes me feel queer . . . kind of outside life . . . maybe it is just me or maybe it is the drug." This bewilderment is hardly surprising given the list of possible side effects: dry mouth, drowsiness, low blood pressure, rapid heart rate, blurred vision, nightmares, and confusion. No wonder Sexton wrote, "I seem to be a ship that is sailing out of my own life."[42]

If these vast quantities of drugs left Sexton feeling blurred and confused, she then added to the problem by drinking alcohol, the one thing that should have been avoided. In particular, alcohol combined with Tofranil increased the intensity of the side effects. It's easy to see why Sexton relied on alcohol to self-medicate, when the very treatment she was being given sometimes left her feeling as bad as the underlying condition itself. Both she and her therapist knew that she used and abused alcohol in this way, yet there never seemed to be any attempt or instruction for her to give it up. In 1968 she wrote, "Right now it's noon and I'm drinking—I use booze like medication, Duhl [her doctor] says. Oh well." But the combination was toxic in all sorts of ways and only seemed to create problems, not alleviate them. In the same letter, she wrote that her panic about not sleeping led her to take so many drugs that even when she was asleep she thought she wasn't. And as she drifted in and out of sleep she found herself banging on the bedroom walls, or smoking and dropping cigarettes, burning things all around her. It sounded exhausting for everyone involved. Sexton received little sympathy about these side effects from her range of psychiatrists. When she complained to Dr. Duhl that despite not being prone to headaches she had been suffering from one for days that felt like a knife in one eye, he replied, "Well you can have one in your life can't you?"[43] She was also given an anti-seizure drug, Dilantin, which often causes extreme nausea. When Sexton complained about feeling sick all the time, she resorted to more alcohol, which worsened the nausea and ran the risk of affecting her blood levels too. If, in comparison to insulin treatment and ECT, drugs seemed to be somehow the softer option, living with bad and uncontrolled reactions to them seemed unrelenting and barbaric.

Unfortunately for Plath, she was subjected to the lot at McLean. Although regarding it as a last resort because of her previously traumatic experience with it, Beuscher agreed that ECT should be used to try and alleviate Plath's depression. On December 10, Plath received her first session. Patients were led down white-tiled concrete underground tunnels to the treatment and recovery rooms. According to Beuscher, they had worked together for months preparing Plath for this moment, with Beuscher convinced that if Plath ever wanted to get out of McLean this would be the best way for her to achieve it.

Understandably, after her first experience with ECT just a few months earlier, Plath was terrified. It is perhaps a testament to her trust in Beuscher that she agreed to a course of treatment at all. Although Beuscher recalls Plath had very few sessions—"I don't think she had more than two or three"[44]—on a postcard sent to her mother on December 17, Plath wrote, "I am doing occasional work over at the library—and am having my 6th treatment tomorrow I hope I won't have to have many more . . ."[45] Plath's fear and reluctance is evident, but at best the sessions seemed to have been without the violent trauma Plath had experienced earlier in the year at Valley Head Hospital.

By late December, there had been a radical improvement in Plath. From Beuscher's point of view, it seemed ECT had some sort of psychological impact, as though once Plath believed she had been punished she was able to get well. But as a psychiatrist, Beuscher remained surprised by the speed of Plath's recovery: "I can't tell you what happened . . . She just didn't want to have any more shock treatments, so she reorganized herself inside so she wouldn't have any more. I never saw it happen with anybody else, but I wouldn't be surprised if it did happen."[46] In other words, it appeared that Plath so despised the treatments that she willed herself to be well (or indeed pretended) in order to escape the hospital. Another Smith student, Jane Anderson, who was a patient at McLean during the same time as Plath, believed this. She subsequently felt Plath had avoided facing up to the therapy that she desperately needed to truly get well, and that she took the easy route out by leaving too soon.[47] Plath's medical record tells a slightly different story. The ECT stopped because apparently Plath openly refused to have any more sessions, and thankfully they did not administer it without her consent.[48]

However, following the ECT in December, Plath suddenly began to write letters from the hospital to friends and family after months of silence. For the first time, we hear how she felt about McLean and what her daily routine was like, how she viewed her environment, and perhaps more important, how she was feeling. By the time Plath began communicating with the outside world she had moved from Codman House to the relatively more relaxed South Belknap House for women. This was—and still is—a large redbrick building with white-trimmed windows containing a walled-in courtyard and a narrow front lawn with a border of bushes. Whereas Codman

House was set back among the trees, South Belknap is right next to the administration building in the center of the hospital grounds. As if reflecting this move to a less isolated place, Plath began to socialize a little more and started spending time with other patients in the communal areas. In a letter to Eddie Cohen written on December 28, Plath felt as though the worst was over and that she could "get pleasure from sunsets, walks over the golf course and drives in the country."[49] She described a ward of ten women who shared a dining room, two bathrooms, and a living room that contained bridge tables, a piano, and a TV. The windows overlooked the golf course and down to the lights of the town below. On his visits Wilbury Crockett reported that he often found Plath playing bridge or talking to other girls around the piano. Plath was well aware how lucky she was to be there: "As the basic fee for room and board alone is $20 a day, the backgrounds of most here is [*sic*] quite different from mine."[50] If not for Olive Higgins Prouty, Plath might well have found herself locked away in the type of institution that used to give her nightmares. Other girls Plath met in the ward were from Vassar, Radcliffe, and Cornell. Outside her ward she met several concert pianists and a physics whiz kid from MIT. Nevertheless, she confessed to Cohen, "I long to be out in the wide open spaces of the very messy, dangerous, real world which I still love."[51]

Once Plath started feeling better, she was granted ground privileges and able to walk unaccompanied in the gardens and frequent the coffee shop, library, and occupational therapy rooms. In a letter to her erstwhile boyfriend Gordon Lameyer, she highlighted the sociability of McLean, playing up its reputation as a country club for the richly insane: "I spend a good deal of my time in the coffee shop, a pine-paneled den of smoky sociability, and have struck up a fast friendship with the librarian here."[52] She described becoming adept at ceramics, working on the hospital newspaper (the *McLean Gazette*), listening to organ concerts and piano recitals in the music department, and making use of the enormous record library on rainy afternoons. By mid-January, in a letter to her college friend Enid Mark, Plath seemed to be entering full poetic mode, describing the view from her hospital window overlooking the chapel and the golf course: "The lights have just come on and hang suspended in luminous haloes of honey-colored brilliance on the path leading down to the town."[53] She described her daily routine as rather unscholastic, instead filling her time with tobogganing, badminton, bridge, gossiping in the coffee shop, and watching good movies: "It's such fun."[54] If there is a forced air of jollity about this, Plath was still nevertheless honest about her eagerness to leave McLean and return to Smith. She felt an air of serenity, she confided in Mark, at the thought of returning to her friends and her academic routine.

Beginning with day visits home, and then extending to full weekends, McLean gradually began to ease Plath back into the outside world. Consulting with Smith College, they agreed she should return to her studies in late January, but with a lighter workload.[55] In terms of follow-up care, McLean and Smith agreed that Plath should see the college psychiatrist, Dr. Booth, once a week. Olive Higgins Prouty was incredulous. Her plan had been to send Plath to another hospital of her choice, Silver Hill, as a post-McLean recuperation. Having paid nearly $4,000 to McLean for Plath's treatment, she remained as dissatisfied upon Plath's release as she was at her admission.

One result of the mental struggles that both Plath and Sexton experienced was a shutting down of their creativity and a fear that it would not return. Given that writing was so integral to their sense of self, the idea that it might be lost forever understandably shook them deeply. Sexton began writing seriously as a form of therapy in her twenties, to release energy and give her life a purpose. Plath had always wanted to be a writer from a young age. There was a saving quality about it for them. Plath regarded writing as essential to her life as breathing and eating bread. Sexton was even more open about it: "Poetry and poetry alone has saved my life."[56] These were sentiments that both expressed on a number of occasions.

Sexton was aware that poor mental health was, for her, fruitless. "Madness is a waste of time. It creates nothing. Even though I'm often crazy, and I am and I know it, still I fight it because I know how sterile, how futile, how bleak . . . nothing grows from it and you, meanwhile, only grow into it like a snail."[57] She dismissed the myth that creativity and genius are inextricably linked, arguing that the genius of well-known poets like Lowell and Roethke was more important than their "insanity." She felt that poets had to have a heightened awareness but in her opinion this seldom sprang from mental illness. Besides, she argued, there are plenty of insane people who are not writers or artists, leading her to conclude that "I don't think genius and insanity grow in the same bed."[58]

What these mental struggles did offer Plath and Sexton, though, was creative material to use in their writing. After four and a half months in McLean, on January 29, Plath was released. During that time she had emerged from a suffocating depression, engaged in psychotherapy every day, been injected with insulin, swallowed chlorpromazine, and had electric currents sent through her brain. In all her months there, at some point, her poetic imagination sparked to life, because what she witnessed and experienced, she retained—not written down in her journals or even in letters, but in her memory. This would only emerge some years later in poems, short stories, and a novel. With emotional distance, Plath was able to engage a more detached viewpoint of her stay at McLean. In many cases, she was even able to use humor. And the same with Sexton. At first she could only write about her breakdowns after they had happened, but eventually she almost grew to live with them, and provided she had enough energy, she even began producing the odd poem while still a patient during her many hospital stays. Pumped full of drugs with occasional destructive therapy experiences, like Plath, Sexton was treated shoddily by the mental health care system. Whatever underlying issues were going on often seemed to be inflamed by treatment rather than calmed. There seemed no easy answer to the struggles that she faced daily, and realizing this led her to claim, "I think it will be a miracle if I don't some day end up killing myself."[59]

On January 30, through snow and ice, Plath's brother, Warren, drove her back to Smith College. As they entered the campus in a blizzard and drove down the hill near Paradise Pond, the car flew into a dramatic skid and sped down the slope sideways, tilting, completely out of control. Eventually, they spun to a standstill, facing up the hill they had just slid down. As if summing up the whole episode, and indeed her almost five months at McLean, Plath wrote in a letter: "All's well that ends well, as the cat said as he devoured the last of the canary."[60]

CHAPTER EIGHT

Suicide

I am scared to death I shall just pull up the psychic
shroud & give up.

—Sylvia Plath[1]

But I've had a good life—I wrote unhappy—but I
lived to the hilt.

—Anne Sexton[2]

One of the greatest injustices of the legacies of Sylvia Plath
and Anne Sexton is the infamy of their suicides. Sensa-
tionalized, romanticized, pathologized, these two women have
become defined, and known, by the manner of their deaths.
This is not to say their suicides are not important, or how they
chose to die has no significance. Far from it. The problem has
been that their lives get read backward. All their productive,
happy years, each word they wrote, every hope they had for
the future, every illness or recovery, is seen as foreshadowing
their deaths, in a way they did not experience themselves. Plath

hoped to live to a ripe old age, to have blue-rinsed hair and a lapful of grandchildren. Sexton did not plan to get old but was in full, firm, and happy control of how she planned to get one over on death. Yes, they died young; Plath at age thirty in 1963, and Sexton eleven years later in 1974, at age forty-five. But it seems deeply unfair to them and their work to understand their lives and achievements through the final act they chose to carry out.

Equally, the trope of the doomed, romanticized writer is dangerous and unhelpful. Exploring the weeks leading up to Plath's and Sexton's deaths, in the way we might explore any other week in their lives, shows nothing glamorous about their decision to die. For both it was a sad and desperate time, a loss of their previous life spark and vitality into a dull flatness and exhaustion that neither could escape. Their loneliness was appalling. Then the aftermath of their deaths destroyed family members, leaving lifelong grief and conflict. Suicide detonates an emotional explosion sweeping up everybody involved into it, scattering the debris of devastation across years, even generations.

Of course, once they died, Plath and Sexton immediately became statistics, slotting into the cultural pattern and story of who was dying where, when, and how. The week Plath died in February 1963 there would have been at least ninety-nine other suicides, and an extra twenty-five to fifty who did not make the official lists. In 1974, when Sexton died, she fell into the category most prone to kill themselves, forty-five to sixty-four-year-olds. This impersonal information shows that, sadly, there was nothing unique or doomed-genius-woman-writer about their deaths. They were, along with many other people, too desperate and wrought to continue living.

The desire to die was not sudden or new for either Plath or Sexton. In 1959, during those afternoon drinking sessions, with their fingers clutching martini glasses, Sexton recalled how they sucked up every small detail of each other's suicide attempts, "as if death made each of us a little more real at the moment," treating the whole thing like some addictive gossip. "But I do say, come picture us exactly at our fragmented meetings, consumed at our passions and at our infections, as we ate five free bowls of potato chips and consumed lots of martinis."[3] It was this that formed the center bolt of the relationship, the death connection, and the admiration for each other's writing.

One other person that Plath spoke to in detail about death was the poetry critic Al Alvarez. Perhaps this was because he, too, had survived a suicide attempt. In 1960, during a difficult period in his life, with a failing marriage, he took an overdose of forty-five sleeping pills. Like Plath, he took too many and vomited some back up but was found in time and taken to have his stomach pumped. While recovering in his hospital bed, he was visited by the police, since it was still illegal to attempt suicide in the UK at that point. When he tried to explain why he had done it, they hushed him and said, "It was an accident, wasn't it, sir?"[4] Too exhausted for anything else, he agreed that was indeed the case. He noted that Plath had a certain self-respect about her 1953 overdose, regarding it as a serious act to end her life and "an act she felt she had a right to as a grown woman and a free agent . . ."[5] In her poem "A Birthday Present," Plath's narrator claims, "After all I am alive only by accident." It was this attitude that led Plath to speak about suicide with a wry detachment and, as Alvarez noted, with no mention of suffering or drama. It was this level of control that he believed informed her final poems. She developed the ability to take her internal horrors and with factual skill transform them in the coolest way possible into half-rhymes, startling imagery, and subtle associations. It was almost as if Plath's close brush with death had left her somewhat fearless. This was confirmed by her last doctor, John Horder, who felt that she coped with the stresses of life by realizing she could end it anytime she felt like it: "Either I'll get better or I'll kill myself." She was playing it both ways.[6]

In the ten years between her 1953 suicide attempt and her death, Plath's mood was, like anyone else's, up and down. Often her down spells were linked to writing difficulties, or a creative block, but for the most she seemed fairly stable and able to cope with day-to-day life, taking responsibility for running her home, all cooking and domestic chores, writing, sending out poems for publication, and, after the end of her marriage, full-time childcare. Neighbors in London and Devon remembered her as sociable and easy to talk to, and only noticed a change once her marriage fell apart around July. Then she seemed more tense and drawn-looking, and over the summer of 1962 lost more than twenty pounds. The end of any relationship is a traumatic time, but Plath was a world away from her family across the Atlantic, dealing with an errant husband who kept disappearing and emptying their bank accounts, while she was trying to keep the house running, the bills paid, and the children happy. On top of this, during the fall of 1962, she contracted double pneumonia, followed a few months later by a nasty bout of influenza. She worried about money. She worried about whether Hughes would contribute toward the children. She worried she would not be able to write enough to keep things afloat. She was living four hours away from London, where her regular work opportunities were. The anger and despair she felt about her abandonment and Hughes's betrayal filled her days, nights, and poems. Presumably it filled her final journal, too, though in the years after her death Hughes "lost" it, so perhaps we shall never know.

What the end of her marriage seemed to bring about was at first a coruscating fury, then a deep despair, then a partial acceptance and jubilant recovery when she decided to leave Devon and move back to London in December. This jubilance, however, was followed by a catastrophic emotional crash. But it was not just the end of her marriage. There was a terrible combination of events that truly seemed to be working against her: respiratory illness; the children getting colds and the flu; pretty much the worst weather on record toward the end of 1962, bringing the country to a standstill; a heavy rejection of her latest poems; a lukewarm reception to the publication of *The Bell Jar*; and dealing with the gossip about her estranged husband, who appeared to be sleeping his way around London (or in his own quite staggering words, he had ten thousand desires that he had repressed for six years in a "gentlemanly considerate way," but found they had suddenly appeared and were absolutely insatiable).[7] Plath's death is often linked to her marriage breakdown, and Hughes, too, wrote to Aurelia that Plath should have just told him she couldn't live without him. But there were much more complicated factors playing out than a cheating husband. Plath was more than capable of living without Hughes and supporting herself, but exhaustion is exhaustion and we all only have so much energy before something gives. What Hughes's betrayal appeared to do was poke at old wounds: fear of abandonment; the death of her father; her shaky sense of self; a lack of self-esteem; and the need to build a new, independent identity. Writing to Ruth Beuscher, Plath understood all of these problems and was distressed by them: "I am, for the first time since my marriage, relating to people without Ted, but my own lack of center, of mature identity, is a great torment. I am aware of a cowardice in myself, a wanting to give up."[8]

The idea that Plath was on an inevitable course toward suicide is simply not true. Her insight, her bravery, and her ability to be practical and analyze situations and her own behavior meant that she, more than most, stood a good chance of coming out of a terrible situation in better shape than others. It seemed, then, a cruel twist of fate that so very many things were thrown at her simultaneously, things that would overwhelm anyone. Toward the end of her life, weakened by illness, living in London, which was under deep snow in what came to be known as "the Big Freeze," she experienced one of the coldest winters on record in the UK. Power outages, frozen pipes, and no running water were a daily occurrence. Standpipes were set up in the street for people to go and fill buckets with fresh water. Together with looking after sick babies, and isolated from family, it is hardly any wonder that in the same letter to Beuscher she wrote, "Just now it is torture to me to dress, plan meals, put one foot in front of the other."[9]

The energy it takes to move home at such a time is not to be underestimated either. Throughout her married life, the longest Plath stayed in one place was eighteen months. She seemed to be constantly packing up, shifting her possessions, crossing both ways across the Atlantic, moving from city to country and then back again, twice while pregnant. The home-making, the unpacking, the painting, decorating, buying furniture and rugs, making an empty space a cozy place. And the last time she did it, she did it alone, with two children under the age of three. Single-handedly she packed up Court Green for the winter and moved back to London into an unfurnished three-bedroom maisonette at 23 Fitzroy Road, in Primrose Hill. The house had a blue plaque on the front wall announcing that W. B. Yeats used to live there. Plath felt that surely this was auspicious. But first she had to paint floors, buy furniture, decorate an otherwise empty space, and yet again make a home for her and the children. Her Letts wall calendar for December is exhausting, crammed with daily lists of what she needed to do to make the flat habitable. Her checkbook shows how much she was spending on chairs, rugs, cabinets, and tables. In between she was trying to fulfill writing commitments to keep the money coming in.

All these factors played a part in eroding Plath's resilience. It is true she was prone to depressive spells, but she was also sensitive to her environment. So much going wrong and so much to try one's patience and nerves while dealing with a marriage breakdown would overwhelm anyone. The highs and lows of her last six months are exhausting to read about as she reasoned with her situation, railed against it, and tried to come to terms with the direction her life was suddenly going. Having been raised by a single mother who sacrificed her life for her children, Plath was terrified she would end up in the same position, creating the same toxic dependency and need.

Her Devon friend Elizabeth Sigmund saw Plath's physical and mental well-being undergo a change toward the end of 1962. From being a lively, engaged, contented woman, Plath became more anxious and distracted, and somehow more inward-looking. Her hair lost its life and she became painfully thin, with bones sticking out of her hands and wrists, and dark circles beneath her eyes. More disturbing for Sigmund was Plath's psychological distancing, which she described as some sort of absence, as though Plath were not really in the room with her. Although she was there getting the cups ready for tea and concentrating on what she was doing, Sigmund strongly felt that Plath was communing with something so dark and distracting that it was impossible to reach her. On her social visits, Sigmund felt completely irrelevant and hardly seen. The word she used to describe Plath's presence was "forbidding."[10]

It was during these fall months that an aborted suicide attempt possibly took place. Alvarez writes in his memoir that Plath told him she had driven off the road in Devon, "deliberately, seriously wanting to die."[11] For some reason, Alvarez was convinced that this was not a serious attempt and that Plath was not really contemplating suicide. The incident seems to have taken place just outside North Tawton on an airfield strip at Winkleigh, a location that puzzled Elizabeth Sigmund when she found out years later because the road there is wide-open and flat, with no walls or trees on either side. In fact, Sigmund explained, people went there to learn to drive *because* there was nothing to hit. There appeared to be no damage to the car, and with the exception of Alvarez, Plath did not tell this story to any of her other friends. While it may be easy to consider that this was Plath exaggerating for effect while drinking whiskey with Alvarez, cross-legged on his studio floor, it does after all seem that there was a witness to this event, though the details are still rather mysterious. Her neighbor Gilbert Foster was walking by Court Green in late 1962 just as Plath pulled into the driveway in her black Morris Traveller. She got out of the car looking shaken, disheveled, and very upset. He asked if she was all right and she said she had just tried to harm herself by driving the car off the road. He went home and told his wife, Marian, who wanted to know if Plath was hurt. Gilbert said no, and it was left at that.[12] There was something about the nature of the event that left both the Fosters and Alvarez thinking this was a minor incident. But whatever happened, it revealed that around September 1962, Plath's mental state had deteriorated so significantly that she was engaging in some form of risk-taking self-harm.

This type of behavior was evident in Anne Sexton's last months as well. Initially jubilant after ending her marriage in 1973, by the following year the reality of the situation was hitting home and Sexton became desperately lonely. Both her daughters were now away for most of the year studying; Linda at college and Joy at a private school in Maine. Kayo had moved out of the house, and for the first time Sexton found herself living alone. This seemed to be the catalyst for increasingly erratic and demanding behavior as Sexton, in the words of her daughter Linda, "began to spin out of control, faster and faster—a tornado in the making."[13] Just prior to her divorce, Sexton made the decision to stop taking all medication. Given how it made her feel, this is hardly surprising, but equally what we now know is how dangerous it can be to suddenly stop taking pills in an uncontrolled way, particularly ones that offer some form of tranquilizing effect. The impact can be so severe it can even cause psychotic episodes. Whether Sexton began to experience withdrawal symptoms, which does seem likely, she tried to counteract the fallout from this by self-medicating with increasingly large amounts of alcohol. Although she had always been a heavy drinker, now it tipped into alcoholism, and from 1973 onward she was drinking from the moment she woke up until she went to bed. This had an even worse impact on her behavior, and Linda described how her mother became more needy and outrageous. The drama increased, and wherever she went she carried vodka with her—even into faculty meetings at Boston University. She began to demand certain seats on airplanes. She would order the most expensive food in a restaurant and then send it back, making a public scene. Before a reading, it became essential that she was provided with a fried egg sandwich and four or five double vodkas, and after the reading she insisted on a certain brand of pen to sign her books. Her doctor abruptly ended their therapy sessions in late 1973, claiming Sexton was too overwhelming and demanding, and her friends and family began to withdraw. This exacerbated Sexton's loneliness and she started arguments, even with her closest friends, which further drove people away.

In 1974 she made three suicide attempts. The alcohol made her angry, argumentative, and unreasonable. She needed her friends to talk to her for hours on end, but they had their own lives and families, and if they were not able to provide the support she demanded, they were cast aside. Her daughters, exhausted by the years of care they had given their mother, no longer wanted to return home on weekends. Home no longer felt like home to them. Sexton was drunk all the time, sleeping around and dating men she met through newspaper advertisements, and engaging in reckless behavior with money, such as burning a hundred-dollar bill in a restaurant with her cigarette lighter and ordering vast quantities of champagne. The child support that Kayo sent for Linda and Joy never seemed to make it to them. In the last year of her life, Sexton spent $50,000 on therapy alone.

Today, it would be hoped that this sort of self-destructive and erratic behavior could be treated with more vigilant mental health care. In the 1970s, that would have meant rehab to get Sexton's drinking under control. If the drugs she was given seemed experimental, her manner of withdrawing from them was highly dangerous, especially for someone so prone to mood swings. Combined with excessive alcohol, Sexton's emotional state must have been unbearable for her. And the intense pain she felt was taken out on those around her, which made it impossible for them to want to be with her. It was a dangerous, toxic, heartbreaking cycle. And yet again she found herself being treated somewhat irresponsibly by a therapist who abruptly ended their sessions when it all got to be too much. Even if her behavior was, to put it mildly, unhelpful, Sexton's loneliness was mentally crippling. Her impulsive urges and alcoholic haze led her to make bad decisions and feel that the end was near. Seven months before she died, she wrote in a letter, "Yes, for me death is always very close."[14] Life felt very fragile and impossibly painful.

This closeness of death was something her family had lived with for many years, distraught at her pain and exhausted by their own. Linda described it poignantly: "Her mental illness was a terminal illness; our family stood by [as] helplessly as that of a cancer patient, trying to keep her comfortable, trying to beat back death for just one more year. Trying not to say goodbye. Trying to say goodbye."[15] They knew, somehow, that one day Sexton would kill herself, and in the meantime everything centered around looking after her: "Death lived at our house . . ."[16]

In a 1970 interview with Marjorie Fellow, Sexton revealed in insightful depth her relationship to death and dying.[17] It is an audio interview and throughout there is a clock chiming, dogs barking, and a clinking of ice against the side of a glass. Sexton's voice is deep and smoky. At one point her daughter Joy interrupts the interview. There are loud feedback noises because Fellow has pressed the wrong buttons on the recording machine ("Play and record shouldn't be on at the same time," chides Sexton). It is introduced as an interview about death and Sexton opens it with a showstopping admission: "I'm constantly aware I'm going to die. Every time I look at the green leaves I think 'I'm going to die.' I'm obsessed with death." What then unfolds is Sexton putting this obsession into some sort of context. She talks about the death of Nana, her beloved great-aunt, as being one of the biggest blows of her life, not least because her death was so degrading. At eighty-six years old she had suffered from arteriosclerosis and been hospitalized for eight months. Sexton felt that everybody died on her, but Nana's death was "the most shattering thing I went through." This sort of death seemed to horrify Sexton, who decided she wanted to be in full control of how and when she died. The thought of being killed in a car accident terrified her: "I don't want to die scared." Neither could she bear the thought of waiting around for death to be dealt by something else; she didn't want cancer, she didn't want an unexpected death. In fact, her take was, if you kill yourself, death doesn't get you at all. In a defiant tone of voice she says, "I'm gonna run the whole show." She wanted to die "young and whole," and the way to do this was suicide. When Fellow asked her whether this was a good idea because she had children and a family, Sexton seemed to reason this away saying somewhat disingenuously that she didn't think about the effect on her family since she would have to die one day anyway.

In contrast, Plath was terrified about what would happen to her children if she died. Shortly before her death, she turned up at the door of her downstairs neighbor, Trevor Thomas, in tears and sobbing loudly, "I am going to die and who will take care of my children?"[18] Taking her inside and pouring her a glass of sherry, Thomas asked if she had received some terrible health news, but Plath explained it was nothing like that at all, she simply felt as though she could not go on. In the hour she stayed there her mood swung from despair to anger to bitterness and back to hopelessness. What she wanted was unrealistic, to somehow rewind to a time when everything was happier and none of the bad things had happened. Initially her doctor, John Horder, saw no evidence of clinical depression when she moved back to London in December 1962. On the contrary, he found her full of plans and determined to succeed. But it was clear to others that by the end of December she was beginning to struggle. Al Alvarez, who called to see her on Christmas Eve, found her much changed. The flat was silent, bare, white, and bitterly cold. She seemed lonely and desperate, asking him to stay, but he was going to dinner with some friends. After drinking some wine and hearing her latest poems, he left. "I knew I had let her down in some final and unforgivable way. And I knew she knew.

I never again saw her alive."[19] One friend, Catherine Frankfort, invited Plath and the children to her house for supper on Boxing Day, and Frankfort's mother-in-law noticed that Plath seemed incredibly sad and tortured. But Catherine did not notice this side of Plath at all. She could see that from time to time she was miserable, but she put this down to her marriage breakup and insisted that "Sylvia could behave in this most gay and natural way up until the very end."[20] Other friends, such as Lorna Secker-Walker, described experiencing a similar situation to Elizabeth Sigmund; the sensation that Plath was both there and not there. She appeared vague and distracted. The Wednesday before her death, Lorna had arranged to babysit so Plath could go shopping for curtain fabric. But when Plath appeared at Lorna's apartment with the children she sank into a chair, saying, "Oh I feel so weary. I think I am not going to go and choose fabric. I'd rather just sit and have tea with you."[21] It was as though all her life force was somehow spent.

This change in Plath is even evident in her poetry manuscripts. The *Ariel* poems are mostly written on vibrant pink Smith College memorandum paper. Plath's writing swirls and spikes as though the pages are alive and jumping. They almost breathe. The final poems she wrote in London are on stark, white, blank paper. Her writing looks flat and lifeless, the language chilly and detached in poems such as "The Munich Mannequins" and "Words," and summed up in the final bleak lines of "Contusion": "The heart shuts, / The sea slides back, / The mirrors are sheeted."[22]

Battling with regular power outages, no running water, and no telephone in her apartment due to backlogs and delays, she caught the flu in early January and was ill and cut off. Days later, the children came down with heavy colds when Plath was still so weak she could hardly get out of bed. Dr. Horder sent a nurse to help. She had deadlines to meet and broadcasts to make. Money was a constant worry. In the last recording she made for the BBC, on January 10, her voice sounds thick and nasally as she struggled with respiratory illness. Hughes took off to Spain with Assia Wevill for some winter sun and left her to cope with the children alone. Exhausted and scared, her mood began to sink further.

Piecing together what happened in the last week of Plath's life is difficult. She wrote a few letters, and there are interviews with friends who were around her at the time, but really there was nobody there that she was close to. Her final journal was, according to Hughes, "lost" along with the journal before. The incomplete manuscript of the novel that she had been working on since the fall of 1962 called *Double Exposure* was also "lost." This she regarded as a strong and witty piece of work, about the breakdown of a seemingly idyllic marriage due to a lying, cheating husband. So, with her voice curiously silenced, her last days are filled in by secondary sources relying on notoriously unreliable memories and stories that change over time. There are also existing fragments from Hughes's diaries covering that time, as well as his version of events in drafts and poems for his collection *Birthday Letters*, dealing with his life with Plath.

It appears that, exactly a week before Plath's death, Dr. Horder, realizing that her mood had taken a serious turn, put her on medication and arranged for her to see a female therapist. Yet more bad luck ensued. The appointment to see the psychiatrist was sent to the wrong address and turned up only after Plath's death. The medication she was given was marketed under a different name in the UK and she had been taken off it during her first breakdown in the US due to a bad reaction. Horder also contacted various mental hospitals about possible admission, but he regarded them all as too grim and believed that the children would keep her going. He did not want to take action to hospitalize her without her consent, as this would not only involve putting the children into care but would also increase her anxiety and despair.

During this week her car broke down, and a live-in au pair she had employed just a couple of weeks earlier left the children alone while Plath was out and so was fired. Once again, Plath was at home alone trying to work and look after her children. On Tuesday, February 5, Hughes, back from Spain, called round to the apartment and suggested they go on vacation together. The following day he called round again, this time in a very different mood. Assia had told him Plath had been speaking badly of him to her friends and he turned up threatening to sue her and told her he was engaging a lawyer to sue her friends as well. She fell apart.

The following day, in a terrible state, she called her friends Jillian and Gerry Becker and asked if she could go and stay with them for a couple of days, as she was no longer able to cope at home. Taking the children, she stayed at their house in Islington until Sunday night. Those few days were exhausting for Jillian as she looked after her own children and Plath's too. By this stage, Plath was heavily reliant on drugs to sleep and drugs to wake her up, and in between she seemed in a febrile state.

So much seemed to be working against her, yet still she battled against it. On Friday the eighth, she had a meeting with the poet Patric Dickinson, who wanted her to present an evening of American poetry at the Royal Court Theatre over the summer. That night she went to dinner with some friends from America, Patty Goodall and her family. She also called her friend Lorna Secker-Walker to tell her she was feeling better and that she had resolved all of her problems. Then she mentioned she would be staying with the Beckers and was calling to say goodbye to her. It was only three days later that Lorna understood the nature of this call.[23] Sometime during the day, she mailed a letter to Hughes saying that she was leaving the country. It arrived the same afternoon and something about the tone must have spooked him. He turned up at her apartment and by luck found her there. She burned the letter in front of him and sent him packing. He went off to spend the weekend with another woman he was seeing, Susan Alliston, deliberately dodging being available for Plath in case she tried calling him (a decision that would torture him for the rest of his life, judging by his poetry manuscripts, which return to this obsessively). Another fact, though it is unclear whether Plath knew about this before her death, is that Assia Wevill was pregnant with

Hughes's child. Even if Plath had entertained any notions of rekindling her marriage, this would have ended those hopes.[24] Elizabeth Sigmund believed that if Plath did find out about this, she would have been inconsolable.

Reports differ for the following day. Some claim Plath stayed in all day and spent the evening being looked after by a student of the Beckers, listening to music and drinking wine. Other reports claim she disappeared all day, but nobody knew where to. On Sunday, though, following a large lunch, she slept heavily and well in the afternoon and declared she was ready to go home. Dr. Horder was sending a nurse the following morning to help her and the children, and she had a meeting with her publisher. The Beckers did not want her to go but she insisted, so Gerry drove her and the children back to Fitzroy Road. She cried all the way and he tried his best to make her go back home with him, but she would not. He stayed with her a little while until she felt better and then told her he would call the next day.

The last person to see Plath alive appears to be her downstairs neighbor, Trevor Thomas. She knocked on his door in their shared hallway just before midnight and asked for some stamps. He noticed that her speech was slurred and she appeared to be heavily drugged. During the exchange she insisted on paying for the stamps, otherwise her conscience would not be clear with God. Worried, he asked if he should call Dr. Horder, but she insisted she was fine. Ten minutes after their conversation he noticed the hallway light was still on and opened his front door. Plath was still standing there, just staring into space, and again he asked if she needed the doctor. She assured him she was having a wonderful dream, a wonderful vision, and then she disappeared upstairs.

In Plath's thirty years she threw everything into her life and work. Resilient, strong, intelligent, caring, political, and no-nonsense, she captured the richness of her experiences and transformed them into poetic brilliance. Her love of life was immense, and even up to her last days, she did not want to die. But sometime in the early hours of Monday, February 11, her resilience ran out and she could not go on. Her last acts involved her work and her children. She left on her desk, neatly encased in a black spring binder, her final version of *Ariel*, beginning with the word *love* and ending with the word *spring*. She wrote a note, "Please call Dr Horder," and included his telephone number. Then she buttered bread for the sleeping children, made bottles of milk for when they woke, and opened their bedroom window. After saying goodbye, she taped their bedroom door shut and sealed any remaining gaps with towels and cloths. Then she went downstairs to the kitchen and sealed herself in with tape around the doorframe and the window. She opened the oven door, turned on the gas, lay on the floor, and placed her head on a small folded cloth inside the oven. According to the coroner's office, she would have been incapacitated within twenty seconds, and beyond resuscitation within thirty. That is how quickly a life can be wiped out.

The following day Hughes sent a telegram to Plath's family in America simply stating, "Sylvia died yesterday." Her death shocked everyone, including her doctor, who felt she had slipped through the net. Hughes moved into the apartment to take care of the children, and Plath's brother and wife made plans to fly over from America. The nature of Plath's death was kept quiet, and after her body had been autopsied and embalmed it was taken by rail from King's Cross Station in London to Hebden Bridge in Yorkshire. Her cause of death was suicide by carbon monoxide poisoning (domestic gas). An obituary by Al Alvarez ran in the *Observer* that weekend, titled "A Poet's Epitaph," but that was the only one. Any death notices that appeared in American newspapers cited her death as due to viral pneumonia. Even three years later, in June 1966, the *Boston Globe* reported that she had died from ill health and melancholia. From the day of her death, silencing was enforced, and this would take a much more sinister turn as her work began to be tampered with and lost.

Although Plath had started divorce proceedings, she was still legally married at the time of her death. Seemingly she left no will (a fact that many of her friends found astounding, since it was out of character), and so Hughes got full control over all her assets and copyrights to her work. She left at least two letters in her apartment the night before she died, one addressed to her mother. Ted Hughes would not allow Aurelia to see the letter, and when she pushed he told her if she did not back off she would never see her grandchildren again. She left it at that, and never discovered the contents of the letter. Days earlier, Aurelia had sent $4,000 to her daughter as a gift. She noted that she never received this money back either.

Al Alvarez speculated whether Plath really intended to die. He felt she was playing Russian roulette, not much caring whether she won or lost. Dr. Horder felt the care with which her children had been protected and the way the kitchen was prepared meant this was a serious attempt to die. There is evidence, though, that Plath may well have wanted someone to be able to get into the apartment. She left her coat with a set of keys in the pocket at the Beckers'. She checked with Trevor Thomas what time he would be up for work the next morning. But another source suggests she may have hidden a set of keys under her doormat. A novel by Jill Neville, *Last Ferry to Manly*, includes a fictionalized account of Plath's last days written by someone who was there. Although names and occupations have been changed, the rest of the facts add up. Neville, an ex-girlfriend of Alvarez's, worked with Assia Wevill at the same advertising agency and also, if her account is to be believed, had sex with Hughes at the beginning of 1963. There is a scene in which the protagonist, Lillian (Neville), arranged with Katherine (Plath) to visit her to discuss the possibility of doing some administrative work and generally helping out. The meeting was to take place early on a Monday morning and Lillian was instructed that if she could not get into Katherine's apartment she would find some keys under the doormat. Feeling guilty about having slept with her husband, Lillian decides at the last minute not to go to the meeting and hears later that day that Katherine has killed herself. Lillian keeps this secret for many years. Given how all the other "facts" in the novel check out, it would be odd if this was the only one that did not.

But even if all these details are correct, and Plath left various sets of keys about, it may well have been to ease entry to the apartment to rescue the children rather than herself.

The shock of Plath's death in London literary circles led to all sorts of gossip and sensationalist intrigue. But among all of this was genuine upset and horror. Anthony Thwaite, who had worked with Plath at the BBC, recalled sitting in a pub with a group of male poets reeling with the colossal shock of it all. Douglas Cleverdon, another BBC producer who had commissioned a radio play from Plath called *Three Women*, walked in enormously shaken and upset. When one of the men made a "male shit" comment based on sexist assumptions along the lines of "Women poets, what do you expect?," the poet Louis MacNeice rounded on him and demanded he shut up.[25] Even in death, Plath faced appalling sexism from a male-dominated literary circle.

Many of her Devon friends only discovered she had died when they read the *Observer* that weekend. Elizabeth Sigmund recalls the unbelievably brutal shock of opening the paper and seeing a picture of Plath holding Frieda with news of her death: "I remember walking the dark country lanes, and saying over and over to myself, 'Where is she?' There were tracks of a fox in the snow, wandering this way and that, sniffing for answers to its own secret questions. I bent over the prints making holes in the snow. She would have understood."[26] The following month, Sigmund moved into Court Green to look after the house and was distraught to see Plath's shoes lined up in the bathroom. There was something oddly intimate about it that she felt her loss even sharper. Worse was to come a few weeks later when she received by mail the gas bill for 23 Fitzroy Road covering the time of Plath's death. Assia Wevill, who by then had moved into Plath's London apartment with Hughes, had scribbled on it, "She was your friend—you pay it."

Across the Atlantic news of Plath's death reached Sexton, who immediately felt a sort of envy. She told her therapist that she felt Plath had stolen something that was hers—*that* death was hers. And over the coming year she reflected on it more and more, in one therapy session admitting, "I'm so fascinated with Sylvia's death. There's so much. It really needs to be analyzed. The idea of dying perfect, certainly not mutilated."[27] At this stage, and for a couple of years afterward, Sexton would know the manner of Plath's death only through gossip circles. Even in 1965, two years after the event, she wrote in a letter, "The gossip-truth is that she killed herself, as she tried this once before one cannot be too surprised—by turning on the gas."[28] Sexton hoped that Aurelia Plath still did not know the truth. She did. Plath's brother arrived in London a few days after her death and was told of her suicide not by Hughes but by Plath's lawyer. But Sexton's reaction to Plath's death was unusual. While she recognized the sadness of it all, she felt both jealous and somehow shut out from the experience. She included these feelings in her poem "Sylvia's Death": "Thief!—/ how did you crawl down into, // crawl down alone / into the death I wanted so badly and for so long . . ."[29]

The fact that Plath quietly stole this death also unearthed feelings of admiration and defiance in Sexton: "About her death she was silent. Damn it. And then, maybe—maybe not—it was her business. Everyone runs around condemning her for it and I say[:] She had a right!"[30] But it was not just Plath's death that created envy in Sexton: her daughter Linda noticed that professionally her mother became extremely jealous of Plath, mainly because after the publication of *Ariel* it "quickly reversed their positions on the visibility ladder in the contemporary poetry community."[31] But Sexton did not let that color her ability to praise as well. She knew Plath's last poems were something outstanding and she did not stint on her admiration: "Her last poems are amazing. True-blue things! I wish I might write her to tell her how I admire and love them. But one can't (although I do in my poems) write to the dead."[32]

Although Sexton got involved in helping out with a memorial service for Plath in Wellesley, back in England, Plath's actual funeral was a muted affair. Taking place in Yorkshire, hardly any of her London or Devon friends had enough time to travel there—only the Beckers. In terms of family, only her brother and his wife, Margaret. The few other people who attended were members of the Hughes family. Plath was buried in an Oxford coffin wearing a white shroud with a fake Elizabethan ruff around her neck. There was snow on the ground. After a short service in the funeral home at Hebden Bridge, which Warren described as looking like an upturned boat, another service took place in St. Thomas the Apostle church at Heptonstall, before the burial. Afterward, Hughes announced to the gathering, "Everyone hated her." "I didn't," replied Jillian Becker.

Neither did Sexton, who over the coming years wrote the elegy "Sylvia's Death" (quoted earlier) and summed up their attitudes to life and death in her poem "Wanting to Die." An affectionate memoir called *The Barfly Ought to Sing* was published in 1966, detailing their poetry capers in Lowell's workshop and three-martini afternoons at the Ritz. In a letter to Al Alvarez written June 1963, Sexton included a copy of "Sylvia's Death" and praised him on "A Poet's Epitaph." She lamented that a similar obituary had not appeared in the American press for such a great poet. Almost predicting what Plath's posthumous future would hold, Sexton claimed that Plath was a better poet than Hughes and it annoyed her when Plath was dismissed as just Ted Hughes's wife. She felt her loss keenly and told Alvarez that although they did not know each other very well they had felt an intimate bond both as women and poets.[33] Alvarez replied almost two months later, saying Sexton's poem had upset him, not because it was bad but because it brought Plath's death crashing about his ears again, and because the words felt so right. He also told Sexton that after his obituary for Plath had been published along with three of her last poems, he was deluged with abuse—people complaining about the bad taste of it all.[34] Seemingly, *Observer* readers were not too taken with the unsettling power of Plath's final words.

It was really only in the last year of her life that Sexton seemed to grow tired of Plath, but then she grew tired of many other things too. In June 1973 she was contacted by the BBC and asked to choose her favorite Plath poem, which she could then read for broadcast. In a weary-sounding letter Sexton refused, saying she really wasn't in the mood to do the whole Plath deal and anyway she was busy getting a divorce and giving readings of her own work.[35]

In fact, in the last year of her life, Sexton was busy barely holding herself together. If Plath's death came as somewhat of a shock, for Sexton's family the shock was that Sexton had not died sooner. As her alcoholism took more of a grip following her divorce, Sexton's physical health began to fail and she started substituting alcohol for food. This resulted in severe weight loss, which left her haggard and with a tremor and a twitch. Linda noticed that her mother's "metabolism seemed to be moving at a furious pace: she was so thin she seemed like a blowtorch at white heat."[36] When Sexton could persuade her daughters to come visit, they were greeted with aggressive behavior and tantrums. They would witness outbursts where their mother would throw glasses against the fireplace or collapse on the floor, beating her fists and drumming her feet, yelling how much she hated her children. She began to have indiscriminate sex with men and women and became increasingly desperate. Finally, she managed to persuade her youngest daughter, Joy, to stay with her over the summer of 1974, which resulted in disaster. Drama after drama ensued, and when Sexton yet again attempted suicide, Joy had to accompany her to the emergency room and watch while she had her stomach pumped. During this procedure Sexton suffered an epileptic fit, witnessed by Joy, a trauma that has stayed with her. After Sexton self-discharged early, an argument exploded between them and Joy was booted out of the house with Sexton yelling, "Fuck you! You think I'm going to put up with this shit? I hate you! Get the hell out of here! And don't come back!"[37] Sexton had in effect brought about her own abandonment. What it was not possible for Joy and Linda to see at the time (they were still such young adults) was the torture their mother was experiencing. With age and hindsight, Linda was able to understand that this wild behavior was almost certainly her mother just trying to feel something beyond the black curtain of depression. She believed that, in the end, her mother was killed by depression.[38] Like Plath's death, anyone wanting to romanticize the suicide of Sexton need only read about the misery and agony for all involved. There was nothing remotely glamorous about this; it was unbearable for everybody.

There were moments of reprieve, though. In July, Sexton seemed to regain some of her verve and flair and managed to score free tickets, hotel, and travel from the *Boston Globe* to go see one of her favorite singers, Ella Fitzgerald, perform on Cape Cod. This was in return for her writing a review (which was published on July 28). Likewise, as the summer ended and her poetry classes started up again at Boston University, her adoring students recalled she was as witty and sassy as ever. She was so much fun that they all looked forward to going out drinking with her after class. It was only two days before her death that they noticed a real change in the workshop. Sexton apologized for making a mess of the class. She explained that she was exhausted and not quite in the mood, which she described as being "cryie" and "drifty as hell."[39]

Having tried to tackle her loneliness, Sexton advertised for live-in help mainly for company and to stave off the fear of being alone. One couple came and went. By October a second couple was living with Sexton in her house at 14 Black Oak Road, but this seemed to do little to ease her despair. When the end came, it came quickly and quietly. After all the years of drama and scenes, Sexton died privately and without fuss. The afternoon of October 4 was spent having lunch with her close friend Maxine Kumin and working on the proofs for her last collection, *The Awful Rowing Toward God*. At some point later in the afternoon, Sexton wrapped herself in her mother's old fur coat and, with vodka martini in hand, went into the garage to her red Mercury Cougar. She turned on the engine and the radio, then lay on the back seat and waited for the fumes to overwhelm her. Outside, it was a beautiful afternoon and the oak and maples trees were just changing color.

The young live-in couple found Sexton's body sometime later and carried her into her study. Then they called Billie Sexton, who came and sat on the couch next to her former daughter-in-law's body, waiting for the coroner. In the end, nobody in her family was really surprised, but there was a poignancy that she had quite simply slipped away by herself. Linda observed that "Mother did not want to remain reliant on sedating drugs or alcohol. Her life did not have quality sufficient to create the desire to continue. She wanted to die, and her desire came not from anger but from despair."[40] She believes that her mother, realizing that all the therapy in the world could not save her, died of untreatable, unceasing depression.

Sexton's daughters looked for, and found, a full-length red polyester dress with slits up the side and a low neckline that their mother had worn for her readings. They felt that this was quintessentially "Anne Sexton." Then they took this to the funeral home, where Sexton was placed in a cremation casket in the dress. Although Sexton had left all her business affairs in order, she was less directive about her funeral wishes. In the end, her ashes stayed in the family home for two years, until a unanimous decision was made and they were buried in the Sexton family plot in Forest Hills Cemetery, in Jamaica Plain, just outside Boston.

Plath's and Sexton's graves have become pilgrimage sites. Any visit at any time of year reveals objects left by visitors who have paid their respects: pens, pebbles, shells, rosary beads, candles, and cards. Often letters and poems are left, declaring love and thanks. The poems they wrote save people. Their lives may have ended suddenly, but there was nothing doomed about these two women. With extraordinary strength, they were able to use their struggles and difficulties to create something that filled their lives with satisfaction and pleasure. Then they gifted this to their readers.

Plath's wish for her work came true. She believed that the greatest use of poetry lies in its pleasure: "Certain poems and lines of poetry seem as solid and miraculous to me as church altars . . . ," and if they reach few people, well no matter, because they already go surprisingly far all around the world, "farther than the words of a classroom teacher or the prescriptions of a doctor; if they are very lucky, farther than a lifetime."[41]

These two women need neither our pity nor the insult of being written off as crazy poets. They deserve our respect and awe. Just four months before she died, Sexton summed up what it all meant in a letter: "But here I sit in my kitchen with the winter sun coming in through the window. The sugar bowl, fat sugar, squatting in front of me and beside me, pasted up on the refrigerator is someone's letter. It says (in only one line) 'Thank you, Anne Sexton, for the poetry of your life.'"[42]

Epilogue

Often the fallout from a suicide is a mess.

The years after Plath's death are characterized by grief, conflict, anger, and suppression. After the publication of *Ariel* in 1965, she seemed to explode into popular and literary culture with a voice that fit perfectly into the social changes that were taking place. It was almost as if she had anticipated second-wave feminism and suddenly there were her poems, waiting to be found. There was the voice of Esther Greenwood in *The Bell Jar* pulling apart gendered power relations and mocking ridiculous double standards. We cannot know whether Plath would have embraced the feminist movement, though perhaps there are hints that she would have been interested given in her final interview, where she clearly stated that she was "rather a political person."[1] We also cannot know what work she would have gone on to produce and what turn this might have taken away from the white heat of those last poems. We do know that, somewhere, there is an incomplete manuscript of a novel titled *Double Exposure*. In September 1962 she wrote to her poet friend Ruth Fainlight that she had a second novel that she was dying to write but was struggling to find the time between being ill, doing the income tax, laundry, and looking after the children. Throughout the fall and winter of 1962–63, her letters refer repeatedly to the novel she has started working on but just doesn't have the time to write. We get glimpses of the plot here and there as she describes writing it at 5 a.m. before the babies wake up. On two occasions she mentions how it makes her laugh; that it is set in Devon and is "semi-autobiographical about a wife whose husband turns out to be a deserter and a philanderer although she had thought he was wonderful & perfect."[2] She admits she will be writing it under a pseudonym as she did *The Bell Jar*, but tells her brother, Warren, in September 1962 that "I think I'll be a pretty good novelist, very funny—my stuff makes me laugh & laugh & if I can laugh now it must be hellishly funny stuff."[3] Letters written by Olwyn Hughes held in the British Library reveal that she saw the manuscript and described two scenes from it; one chapter was a blow-by-blow account of the Wevills' visit to Devon when the affair began between Hughes and Assia, the second a chapter dealing with a tense train trip from Devon to London made by the married couple. Assia Wevill also saw the manuscript and was appalled at how she was represented, and what she was called (one half of the Goof-Hoppers). The whereabouts of this unfinished novel are unknown, with Ted Hughes claiming that the manuscript "disappeared somewhere around 1970."[4] Along with the missing journals, Al Alvarez believed that there are missing poems, ones she read to him that he never saw again (he cites one example as being a poem about the trees in her Fitzroy Road garden). He did not believe that any of this work would have been destroyed.[5] Somebody, somewhere, knows where these items are.

But the battle over legacy does not stop with Plath's work. It has also raged over her as a woman and cultural figure. Biographers from the late 1960s onward were met with obstruction and silence. It has really only been in recent years that a revisioning of her is able to take place, where a more balanced focus can be placed on her wit and humor, and a more nuanced look at her life and achievements that does not focus solely on her suicide or mental health. Questions are now asked about this representation of her as a tragic, doomed figure on an inevitable slide toward suicide. Reading her work and life through the lens of her death shuts down so many other possible readings and interpretations. It also wipes out her complexity, strength, and love of life. Her friends always saw this and spent years writing letters to newspapers, trying to establish some sort of memorial, trying to get a different narrative out there that would do her justice. Private correspondence between two of her friends, Elizabeth Sigmund and Clarissa Roche, reveals not only the amount of energy they poured into getting Plath a fair hearing but how upsetting it was for them to see her portrayed as a vindictive, jealous, crazy, suicidal woman.

When Ted Hughes died in 1998, Plath's estate passed to her children, Frieda and Nicholas. Then, when Nicholas died in 2009, Frieda was left with the responsibility of running the estate herself.[6] It is difficult to image how a daughter lives with the legacy of her parents' lives and reputations, particularly when it must seem as though complete outsiders know more about the lives of your parents than you do. In 2016, when Plath's letters to Ruth Beuscher, previously thought to have been destroyed, were discovered to be in the possession of a Plath scholar, Frieda was understandably shaken by this: "There was something deeply saddening about this; I felt excluded from my own mother's personal feelings, feelings that other people—strangers—had already pored over."[7] But perhaps more poignantly, her mother's death led to a frozen moment in time. Plath's final poems and letters never fully resolve her anger. Frieda is left with that perpetual conflict, which presumably, had her mother not died, would have worked itself out at some point, or at least lost some of its immediate power. Even Plath herself realized the hurt would pass, claiming rather poignantly in the last letter she ever wrote that she could see her and Hughes becoming great friends one day. And even right in the middle of the bitter breakup she wrote to Ruth Beuscher, "What kills me is that I would like so much to be friends with him, now I see all else is impossible. I mean my God my life with him has been a daily creation, new ideas, new thoughts, our mutual stimulation."[8] Under Frieda's guardianship, the estate has become much more open, and in recent years has allowed the publication of certain letters that almost certainly would never have seen the light of day decades earlier. This has allowed a more rounded view of Plath and a less partisan view as well. However frustrated readers and scholars may feel about some of Ted Hughes's decisions, and angry about his behavior, with the publication of the love letters Plath sent to Hughes we can now get a much clearer understanding of their relationship and what he meant to her. This cannot be dismissed. And although the frustration remains, there is now a chance to reduce the conflict that has raged for decades. In a fair summary of her parents, Frieda Hughes believed them both to be flawed and impassioned, and this makes her love them more. She wrote, "They both suffered, they both made mistakes, they were going through the same kind of hell that literally thousands of couples go through every day, and, in fact, the letters are profoundly illuminating in this respect."[9] This revisioning of a less combative approach seemed to be quite literally represented in 2018 in an auction room in Bonhams in London. In order to ensure safekeeping for future generations (Frieda is the last of the Plath-Hughes line), many personal effects and manuscripts were put on sale. Walking into the display room where all the items could be reviewed revealed Hughes's writing desk with his green typewriter and well-worn Windsor writing chair. Directly opposite was Plath's desk, a sturdy wooden affair with four drawers down either side and her light green Hermes 3000 on top. There were books dedicated to each other, the much-sought-after red rug that took pride of place in their living room, and an ink-stained tray that Plath would serve afternoon tea on. For a while their marriage, like any other, was happy and productive, then it was not. From this, Plath wrote the ultimate, searing breakup poems about life, love, and loss that have helped so many readers get through their own difficult times. Not many people can do or say that.

Sexton, too, has suffered from misrepresentation, both in her lifetime and afterward. Her name, like Plath's, has become some sort of shortcut to describe a particularly lazy, sexist trope of a doomed woman writer. In contrast to Plath, though, Sexton did not have a posthumous life of being silenced. Shortly before she died, she made her twenty-one-year-old daughter Linda executor of her estate, and Linda immediately understood that to do her mother justice would involve having to remove her own feelings and honor the words of Sexton-as-writer. Realizing that in life her mother had no sense of privacy, Linda saw no reason to invent one after her death. If Ted Hughes was criticized for the suppression of Plath's voice, in the years after her mother's death, Linda would be questioned about not supressing enough, namely releasing the recordings of her mother's therapy sessions. When Diane Middlebrook researched and wrote her 1991 biography, she drew on this resource, and this decision made the front pages of the American press. The accusation was that this was a violation of Sexton's rights, and that even after death she should be afforded doctor-patient confidentiality. In a foreword to the biography, Sexton's psychiatrist, Dr. Martin Orne, explained his reasons for sanctioning the release of the tapes, having been given Linda's blessing to do so. It was his firm belief that, through her work, Sexton wanted to help people: "Soon after her poetry began to be published, she found that many troubled individuals sought her guidance and counsel. Indeed, she took great pride in being able to help others with similar pain. She spent an inordinate amount of time answering letters from strangers, and undoubtedly helped many of them."[10] Orne appeared to be right in saying this. In a 1970 interview, Sexton argues that her pain will reach more people than her happiness. She recounts getting lots of letters from suicide survivors and taking the time to send one young girl a dandelion.[11] This does not mean the therapy tapes are a free-for-all. They are under restricted listening and permission is required to quote from them. Listening to the copies held at the Harry Ransom Center at the University of Texas is a curious experience. Sexton's voice sounds different: more relaxed and chatty, less stagey. The sound of a striking match and a lit cigarette can clearly be heard, and the creaking of chairs and shifting about. In presumably one of the first sessions to be taped, Sexton is irritated by the noise of the recording. Some of the tapes have been doubly taped over, so from time to time there is almost a sonic double exposure and ghostly traces of music burst through into the session. At one point before Sexton starts speaking, there are a few minutes of a jaunty version of "A Very Nice Man" from the musical *Carnival* playing.

But these are not the only recordings that offer an intriguing insight into Sexton. There is also a tape of the first public concert given by her group Her Kind (undated) at the deCordova Museum in Lincoln, Massachusetts, where Sexton performs a jubilant and uplifting version of "Music Swims Back to Me," building up to a massive crescendo in the lines "Imagine it. A radio playing / And everyone here was CRAAAAAAAZY!"[12]

Another recording of a tipsy-sounding Sexton singing an impressively off-key version of "Deck the Halls" at her neighbors' house on Christmas Day reveals why she probably chose to speak her poems in the band performances rather than sing them. And in another very playful recording Sexton can be heard moving about her study, seemingly waiting for a phone call to give an interview. There's bumping around and a creaking chair and Sexton says, "I feel like I need to burp." It sounds as though she sits down and has dumped her feet where she always dumped them, on the shelf adjacent to her desk, and starts singing, "I am calling yoouuuu-yooouuu-yoooouuu, won't you listen tooooo tooooo toooo?" Then the phone rings and she immediately switches into professional mode, talking about the development of her second poetry collection, *All My Pretty Ones.*

The audio resurrection is powerful, and we get this with Plath too. The final recording she made for the British Council in October 1962, in which she reads some of her *Ariel* poems, feels oddly intimate. Her breathing is audible, as is her shifting and turning of papers. Her voice sounds tense and emotional, though reading her letters from this time, perhaps that is hardly surprising. There is a more relaxed recording from April of that year made by the BBC for a program called *A World of Sound*, the episode titled "What Made You Stay?" This series interviewed people who had come to live in England from elsewhere and why they chose to make it their home. This was recorded in Plath's living room in Devon and she sounds completely at ease, wittily pointing out numerous Britishisms she finds entertaining. In one story she recounts her first night spent in England as a student in a slightly run-down guest-house in London. When she went to bed in the freezing-cold house, the landlady offered her either a hot-water bottle or a cat. Plath wryly chuckled in response, "I chose the cat."

Personal effects and photographs in archives also bring these two women back to life with startling immediacy. Smith College holds the six-foot elm plank desk that Plath wrote her *Ariel* poems on, the odd ink stain preserved, each bump and knot in the wood visible. One of Plath's silvery prom dresses, resplendent in its taffeta glory, lies encased in a tissue-papered box, showing us the physical outline of her body. Her Girl Scout uniform, complete with an impossible number of badges, is perfectly preserved. Furniture that she painted for Court Green is still vibrant, with her design of red hearts and blue-birds. Photographs of her as a baby through to a young woman with her own children visually unfold the story of her life, in black-and-white and color. In contrast to the often serious pictures used on book covers, here are Plath's smiling beach images, moments laughing with friends and boyfriends, lovingly cuddling with her children. There is a feeling that she could suddenly materialize at any moment and pick up where she left off. This was felt strongly by Frieda Hughes upon handling and reading her mother's letters: "I was struck by the sensation of standing in the room with my mother; I could almost smell her."[13]

Linda Gray Sexton wrote powerfully about organizing her mother's things to divide between family members and to build an archive. Two weeks after Sexton's death, Linda entered her mother's writing room and found traces everywhere. Shelves stuffed with books, filing cabinets overflowing with manuscripts and letters, and the curve of her chair still holding the imprint of how Sexton would sit with her feet up on the desk. Elsewhere in the house, ashtrays overflowed, dirty clothes were strewn on the bedroom floor, the kitchen sink was filled with coffee cups, "and her chair at the rectangular table was pushed back, as if she had just left the spot where we had shared so many difficult and yet wonderful talks when I was living at home."[14] Some of these items are now stored in the Harry Ransom Center: Sexton's spectacles, her daily calendars, scrapbooks, years of correspondence, and intimate family notes. Photographs show a glamorous Sexton, often with a cigarette or drink in hand, laughing, sitting at her typewriter, or swimming in her pool. Some of her remaining clothes were sent to a charity shop. It is fascinating to think that somewhere out there, someone completely unsuspecting might have been wearing a blouse or skirt that once belonged to one of America's greatest twentieth-century poets.

Although it is now many years since their deaths, in so many ways it feels as though Plath and Sexton are still with us, agitating with their voices, exposing all those wrongs that still exist, and all those universal themes that will never go away: love, death, sex, pain, joy. They were so ahead of their time and the ripple effect of their rebellion travels through the decades, playing its own part in the long, slow struggle that is social change. Yes, there is still so much work to be done, and today it feels, as ever, that as soon as progress is made the backlash **creates steps** backward. But if history shows us one thing, it is that social change never comes about easily. It is messy and it comes in waves. It takes time and an extraordinary amount of energy. Today when people take to the streets to make their voices heard, when people battle for a platform, when women fight for a world that finally values them, they are using the space that has been created for them by earlier rebels while simultaneously creating space for those to come in the future. Social rebellion is cumulative and collective. It takes everyone playing their part to bring it about. For Plath and Sexton, their poems, stories, plays, novels, and letters are their legacy that they have gifted us. They played their part in blasting open taboo subjects that have allowed the rest of us to walk much easier down a path that was pretty much forbidden to them.

You truly get a sense of what it took for them to do that through the endless manuscripts they left behind, worked, and reworked—in the thousands of letters, teaching notes, business contracts, household bills, bookkeeping—but also, as Plath said, in the lares and penates of a woman's life: lipstick smears on envelopes, cigarette burns on letters, coffee cup rings on poetry drafts, their personal libraries, recipe books, and in their perpetual struggle against the male-dominated discipline they were so determined to succeed in.

They may be long gone from the streets of Boston and the martini-drinking, red-carpeted hush of the Ritz-Carlton bar, but in so many other ways they are still with us. And they are here to stay.

Acknowledgments

Throughout the research for this book, I have been lucky to work with the most incredible archive and library staff. Sam Maddra and Sarah Hepworth at University of Glasgow Library; Karen V. Kukil and Barbara Blumenthal at Smith College Archives (back in 2011); Caroline E. Johnson, Mariah Wahl, Kathryn Millan, Kelly Kerbow-Hudson, Ancelyn Krival, Linda Briscoe Myers, Amy Wagner, Michael Gilmore, and Andi Gustavson at the Harry Ransom Center, The University of Texas; Emily Banks, research proxy at Rose Library, Emory University; Jessica Smith and all reading room staff at the John Rylands Library, Manchester; all staff in the Manuscripts Reading Room at the British Library; and staff in the Lilly Library, Indiana University.

I am grateful for the friendliness and welcome shown to me by Catherine Flora Con at the Creative Writing Department of Boston University, who allowed me to look around the room where Plath and Sexton met for the Lowell writing workshop.

In my day-to-day life, the invaluable family and friends who sustain me and help so much with dog care on research visits:

Carole and Ces Crowther, Joanne and Peter Whiteside, Rob Sanders, John Avery, Cathy McKenna, Carolyn King, Suzanne Demko (gin, vegan gift baskets), Christine Buckley, and Vanessa Curtis (snacks and shopping).

People in the Plath and Sexton communities who have directly shared knowledge, links, and material: David Trinidad, Emily van Duyne, Andrew Wilson, Carl Rollyson, Di Beddow, Julie Goodspeed-Chadwick, William Sigmund, and all the wonderful scholars whose brilliant work has gone before and will come after. Thank you also to the massively supportive Plath/Sexton communities on social media. Thank you to everyone who sent me links and encouragement. I would also like to thank Cal Morgan for his generosity in reading an earlier book proposal and whose perceptive feedback led to the development of this book.

A big thank-you to Peter K. Steinberg for years of friendship, Plathing, and generous sharing of resources and knowledge.

A special thank-you to Kevin Cummins for help, support, champagne, and the best photography.

I am hugely grateful to Linda Gray Sexton for her support throughout the writing of this book; always gracious, always generous, always kind, and whose wise advice in certain areas has made this a much better book.

At Gallery Books and Simon & Schuster: Maggie Loughran for editorial support, Dominick Montalto for superb copyediting, and the production and marketing teams.

This book about two spectacular women would not have happened without two other spectacular women. My agent,

Acknowledgments

Carrie Kania, at C&W Agency, who originally came up with the idea. Long may our afternoons in the French House continue. And my editor, Alison Callahan, at Simon & Schuster, whose witty, insightful, perceptive, and always kind guidance has made this the book that it is. Both women are a dream to work with.

Finally, my George, who structures my writing days with delight. We walk on the beach; he rolls in dead things. We come home. I write, he snores. (He's a black Labrador, by the way.)

Notes

INTRODUCTION KICKING AT THE DOOR OF FAME

1   Sylvia Plath, *The Bell Jar* (London: Faber & Faber, 1986), 74.

2   Plath, *The Bell Jar*, 79.

3   Plath, *The Bell Jar*, 71.

4   Anne Sexton, *A Self-Portrait in Letters*, ed. Linda Gray Sexton and Lois Ames (New York: Mariner Books, 2004), 82.

5   Anne Sexton, *No Evil Star: Selected Essays, Interviews, and Prose*, ed. Steven Coburn (Ann Arbor: University of Michigan Press, 1985), 3.

6   Kathleen Spivack, *With Robert Lowell and His Circle: Sylvia Plath, Anne Sexton, Elizabeth Bishop, Stanley Kunitz, and Others* (Boston: Northeastern University Press, 2012), 34.

7   Sexton, *A Self-Portrait in Letters*, 49.

8   Sylvia Plath, *Journals of Sylvia Plath*, ed. Karen V. Kukil (London: Faber & Faber, 2000), 475.

9   Anne Sexton, *The Barfly Ought to Sing* in *The Art of Sylvia Plath: A Symposium*, ed. Charles Newman (London: Faber & Faber, 1970), 174. George Starbuck (1931–96) was a

fellow poet and a junior editor at the publishing house Houghton Mifflin.

10   Correspondence between Anne Sexton and Robert Lowell, Box 22, Folder 3, Harry Ransom Center, University of Texas.

11   Plath, *Journals*, 476.

12   Peter Davison, *The Fading Smile: Poets in Boston, from Robert Frost to Robert Lowell to Sylvia Plath* (New York: Knopf, 1994), 139.

13   Plath, *Journals*, 478. Although Plath planned to write about the affair, there appears to be no surviving story.

14   Sexton, *The Barfly Ought to Sing* in *The Art of Sylvia Plath*, 174.

15   Sexton, Ibid.

16   Sexton, Ibid., 175.

17   Sexton, Ibid., 174.

18   Sexton, Ibid., 176.

CHAPTER ONE   REBELS

1   Sylvia Plath, *Letters Home: Correspondence 1950–1953*, ed. Aurelia Plath (London: Faber & Faber, 1988), 40.

2   Anne Sexton, *A Self-Portrait in Letters*, ed. Linda Gray Sexton and Lois Ames (New York: Mariner Books, 2004), 33.

3   The Better Buying Service was an organization that sold products at a 15 percent discount if cash payment was made within seven days of delivery. Plath lists the address as 56 Grosvenor Street, London, W.1.

4 The *Bookseller* is a British magazine reporting news on the publishing industry. It produces biannual issues, and Plath had been employed to copyedit and lay out the children's section for the spring edition in 1961.

5 Anne Sexton, *The Complete Poems* (New York: Mariner Books, 1999), 85.

6 Linda Gray Sexton, *Searching for Mercy Street: My Journey Back to My Mother, Anne Sexton* (Boston: Little, Brown, 1994), 190.

7 Sexton, *A Self-Portrait in Letters*, 270.

8 It is important to note just who this propaganda actually included and excluded. While white, wealthy, heterosexual women might be afforded this option, it was not a realistic ideal for African American women, working-class women of all ethnicities, or lesbians.

9 Sylvia Plath, *The Letters of Sylvia Plath, Vol. II: 1956–1963*, ed. Peter K. Steinberg and Karen V. Kukil (London: Faber & Faber, 2018), 760.

10 Plath, *The Letters of Sylvia Plath, Vol. II*, 738.

11 Exchange of emails between author and Marian Foster, June 2015.

12 Janet Badia, *Sylvia Plath and the Mythology of Women Readers* (Amherst and Boston: University of Massachusetts Press, 2011), 26.

13 Susan Wood cited in Badia, *Sylvia Plath and the Mythology of Women Readers*, 7.

14 Sylvia Plath interviewed by Peter Orr for the British Council, October 30, 1962.

15 Sexton, *The Complete Poems*, 88.

16 Plath's and Sexton's language and observations about racial issues are worthy of deeper study than is within the scope of this book. Reading articles and pieces, for example, of how Black or Latino people read Plath is essential. Many readers say they are able to overlook her occasional use of questionable language (see the poem "Ariel") and identify with the universal themes of suffering and oppression. See for example, Vanessa Willoughby, "Black Girls Don't Read Sylvia Plath," *Medium*, November 12, 2014, accessed February 16, 2020, https://medium.com/the-hairpin/black-girls-dont-read-sylvia-plath-1a8034c986b6. Other readers find they are not able to overlook certain racist tropes used, for instance, in *The Bell Jar* and, at best, think it should be reclassified as a problematic favorite. See for example, Crystal Contreras, "It's Time We Had A Talk About 'The Bell Jar,' the White Feminist, Racist Literary Icon," *Willamette Week*, October 4, 2017, accessed July 19, 2020, https://www.wweek.com/arts/books/2017/10/04/its-time-we-had-a-talk-about-the-bell-jar-the-white-feminist-racist-literary-icon/.

17 Jane C. Hu, "The Overwhelming Gender Bias in *New York Times* Book Reviews," *Pacific Standard*, August 28, 2017, accessed June 18, 2020, https://psmag.com/social-justice/gender-bias-in-book-reviews.

18 John Thompson, "Two Poets," *Kenyon Review* 21, no. 3 (Summer 1959): 482–90.

19 J. D. McClatchy, *Anne Sexton: The Artist and Her Critics* (Bloomington: Indiana University Press, 1978), 117.

20 Hu, "Overwhelming Gender Bias." This research also explores the lack of diversity in publishing and reviewing, generally pointing out, for example, that women of color in particular form an overlooked and underrepresented group.

21 John Boyne, "Women Are Better Writers Than Men," *Guardian*, December 12, 2017, accessed June 18, 2020, https:// www.theguardian.com/books/2017/dec/12/double-x -factor-why-women-are-better-writers-than-men.

22 Ibid.

23 Plath, *The Letters of Sylvia Plath, Vol. II*, 812.

24 Al Alvarez was himself prone to clinical depression and had survived a suicide attempt. He recounts this in his book *The Savage God*, which is a study of cultural and theoretical attitudes toward suicide.

25 Charles Newman, *The Art of Sylvia Plath: A Symposium* (London: Faber & Faber, 1970), 202–203.

26 John Holmes to Anne Sexton, February 8, 1959, Box 20, Folder 6, Harry Ransom Center, University of Texas.

27 Sexton, *The Complete Poems*, 34–35.

28 Katie Goh, " 'I Made Lemonade': The Female Confessional in the Twenty-First Century," *Inciting Sparks*, October 11, 2016, accessed June 18, 2020, https://incitingsparks.org /2016/10/31/i-made-lemonade-the-female-confessional- in-the-twenty-first-century/.

29 Poems such as "Mystic," "Balloons," "Words," and "Edge."

30 Sylvia Plath, *Collected Poems* (London: Faber & Faber, 1988), 15.

31 Ibid., 224.

32 Ibid., 217.

33 "Profile: Olwyn Hughes Grande Dame, Under Siege," *Scallywags* (May 1992), 24.

34 Anne Sexton to Susan Fromberg Schaeffer, December 1968, Box 24, Folder 4, Harry Ransom Center, University of Texas.

35 Linda Gray Sexton, *Half in Love: Surviving the Legacy of Suicide* (Berkeley, CA: Counterpoint, 2011), 63.

36 Plath, *The Letters of Sylvia Plath, Vol. II,* 817.

37 Ibid., 874–75.

38 Peter Davison, *The Fading Smile: Poets in Boston, from Robert Frost to Robert Lowell to Sylvia Plath* (New York: Knopf, 1994), 203–204.

39 Sylvia Plath, *The Journals of Sylvia Plath,* ed. Karen V. Kukil (London: Faber & Faber, 2000), 480.

40 Plath, Ibid.

41 Plath, Ibid.

42 Plath, Ibid., 483.

43 Plath, Ibid., 494.

44 Kathleen Spivack, *With Robert Lowell and His Circle* (Boston: Northeastern University Press, 2012), 35.

45 In fact, "Sow" had already been published in *Poetry,* July 1957, though Plath seems to have kept quiet about this in the workshop.

46 Plath, *The Letters of Sylvia Plath, Vol. II,* 812.

47   Al Alvarez records his first meeting with Plath in *The Savage God*, 23. Despite having published one of her poems in the *Observer*, he failed to recognize the wife of Ted Hughes as the writer Sylvia Plath.

48   For a full account of this movement, read Maggie Doherty's excellent *The Equivalents* (2020).

49   Maggie Doherty, *The Equivalents: A Story of Art, Female Friendship, and Liberation in the 1960s* (New York: Knopf, 2020), xii.

50   Davison, *The Fading Smile*, 204.

51   Plath, *Journals*, 98.

52   Hu, "Overwhelming Gender Bias."

53   Plath, *Collected Poems*, 221–22.

54   Sexton, *The Complete Poems*, 77.

55   Plath, *Collected Poems*, 206.

56   Plath, *Journals*, 151.

57   Anne Sexton interview with Marjorie Fellow, May 22–23, 1970, Sound Recording C0159, Harry Ransom Center, University of Texas.

58   Plath, *Journals*, 151.

CHAPTER TWO   EARLY DAYS

1   Sylvia Plath, *The Journals of Sylvia Plath*, ed. Karen V. Kukil (London: Faber & Faber, 2000), 44.

2   Anne Sexton, *No Evil Star: Selected Essays, Interviews, and Prose* (Ann Arbor: University of Michigan Press, 1985), 176.

3 Diane Middlebrook, *Anne Sexton: A Biography* (London: Virago, 1991), 4.

4 Anne Sexton, *The Complete Poems* (New York: Mariner Books, 1999), 4.

5 Sexton, *No Evil Star*, 177.

6 Anne Sexton interview with Marjorie Fellow, May 22–23, 1970, Sound Recording C0159, Harry Ransom Center, University of Texas.

7 Sexton, *No Evil Star*, 177.

8 Linda Gray Sexton points out, "Note the cuddling aspect of the lesbian relationship in 'Rapunzel' (*Transformations*), where Mother Gothel pushes past sexual boundaries into a more erotic relationship." Notes to author, May 20, 2020.

9 Linda Gray Sexton, *Searching for Mercy Street: My Journey Back to My Mother, Anne Sexton* (Boston: Little, Brown, 1994), 15.

10 Middlebrook, *Anne Sexton: A Biography*, 10.

11 Ibid., 13.

12 Sylvia Plath, *Letters Home* (London: Faber & Faber, 1988), 10.

13 Ibid., 13.

14 Otto Plath material, Harriet Rosenstein Papers, Box 3, Folder 7, Rose Library, Emory University.

15 Sylvia Plath, *Johnny Panic and the Bible of Dreams* (London: Faber & Faber, 1977), 124.

16 Sylvia Plath McLean Hospital Record, Harriet Rosenstein Papers, Box 3, Folder 10, Rose Library, Emory University.

17 Anne Sexton, *A Self-Portrait in Letters* (New York: Mariner Books, 2004), 12.

18 Middlebrook, *Anne Sexton: A Biography*, 20.

19 Gray Sexton, *Searching for Mercy Street*, 80.

20 Sexton, *A Self-Portrait in Letters*, 339.

21 Her father died in June 1959 from a stroke.

22 Sexton, *The Complete Poems*, 37–38.

23 Sexton, *A Self-Portrait in Letters*, 229.

24 Sexton wrote many poems dealing with her mother's death. See for example, "The Division of Parts," "Dreaming the Breasts," and "Leaves That Talk."

25 Sylvia Plath, *Collected Poems* (London: Faber & Faber, 1988), 117.

26 Observation by Marcia Brown, one of Plath's college friends, at the Sylvia Plath 75th Year Symposium, Oxford University, October 25–29, 2007.

27 Interview with Marcia Brown Stern, Harriet Rosenstein Papers, Box 4, Folder 16, Rose Library, Emory University.

28 Plath, *Journals*, 429.

29 Plath, *Letters Home*, 38.

30 Sylvia Plath McLean Hospital Record, Harriet Rosenstein Papers, Box 3, Folder 10, Rose Library, Emory University.

31 Plath, *Journals*, 429.

32 Ibid.

33 Bridget Anna Lowe, "Burning Free: Sylvia Plath's Summer 1962 Bonfires and the Strange Case of the Surviving Christmas Card," *Plath Profiles* 5 (Summer 2012): 57–82, 65.

34 Plath, *Journals*, 432.

35 Plath, *Letters Home*, 32.

36 Plath, *Journals*, 435.

37 Ibid., 437.

38 Sexton, *A Self-Portrait in Letters*, 262.

39 Linda Gray Sexton points out a family parallel between her mother and her younger sister, Joy. Both were social butterflies at school, regarding it as an opportunity to socialize, and both were put in therapy. Indeed, it would be easy to confuse their report cards held at the Harry Ransom Center, University of Texas, since they cite almost similar observations about mother and daughter.

40 Sexton's report cards can be found in Box 31, Folder 6, at the Harry Ransom Center, University of Texas.

41 Sexton, *No Evil Star*, 141.

42 Notes from Linda Gray Sexton to author, May 20, 2020.

43 Sexton, *The Complete Poems*, xxvii–xxviii.

44 For example, letters and teaching notes held in the Harry Ransom Center at the University of Texas show Sexton well ahead of her time in developing educational programs engaging in practices such as scrapping student grades and getting students to grade themselves. This was in 1967.

45 Sexton, *A Self-Portrait in Letters*, 316.

46 Anne Sexton to Anne Wilder, September 21, 1967, Box 43, Folders 5–8, Harry Ransom Center, University of Texas.

47 Julie Kane, "Julie Kane on Anne Sexton," *The Dark Horse*, accessed February 26, 2020, https://www.thedarkhorse magazine.com/Featured/Julie-Kane-on-Anne-Sexton.

48 Plath, *Letters Home*, 37.

49 Ibid., 40.

50 Ibid.

51 Paul Alexander, *Rough Magic: A Biography of Sylvia Plath* (New York: Penguin, 1991), 59.

52 Plath, *Journals*, 37.

53 Ibid., 618.

54 Plath, *Letters Home*, 40.

CHAPTER THREE SEX

1 Sylvia Plath, *The Letters of Sylvia Plath, Vol. II: 1956–1963*, ed. Peter K. Steinberg and Karen V. Kukil (London: Faber & Faber, 2018), 798.

2 Anne Sexton, "My Husband Hates the Way I Read Poems," *Los Angeles Times*, video clip, accessed November 20, 2019, https://latimesblogs.latimes.com/jacketcopy/2010/08 /anne-sexton-poet.html.

3 Joanne Meyerowitz, "The Liberal 1950s? Reinterpreting Postwar American Sexual Culture," in Karen Hagemann and Sonya Michel (eds.), *Gender and the Long Postwar: Reconsiderations of the United States and the Two Germanys, 1945–1989* (Washington, D.C.: Johns Hopkins University Press and Woodrow Wilson Center Press, 2014), 297–319, 295.

4 Sylvia Plath, *The Journals of Sylvia Plath*, ed. Karen V. Kukil (London: Faber & Faber, 2000), 20.

5 Ibid.

6   Dawn Skorczewski, *An Accident of Hope: The Therapy Tapes of Anne Sexton* (New York: Routledge, 2012), 163.

7   Correspondence held in Box 23, Folder 5, Harry Ransom Center, University of Texas.

8   Anne Sexton, *A Self-Portrait in Letters* (New York: Mariner Books, 1999), 8.

9   Sexton's scrapbook is found in Box 48 at the Harry Ransom Center, University of Texas.

10 Plath, *Journals*, 11.

11 Ibid., 12.

12 Linda Gray Sexton writes that her mother miscarried as her parents were eloping, but this did not deter them from going ahead with the marriage. Notes to author, May 20, 2020.

13 Plath, *Journals*, 99.

14 Paul Alexander, *Rough Magic: A Biography of Sylvia Plath* (New York: Penguin, 1991), 56.

15 This story is recounted in Diane Middlebrook, *Anne Sexton: A Biography*, 19.

16 Plath had other significant relationships, too; for example, with Gordon Lameyer, who took a series of color photographs of Plath, and with Myron Lotz. Although Plath clearly cared about these men, they did not seem to have the same lasting effect on her as Norton and Sassoon.

17 Plath, *Journals*, 452.

18 Sylvia Plath, *The Bell Jar* (London: Faber & Faber), 85.

19 This conversation was also fictionalized and included in *The Bell Jar*, 58.

20 Plath, *Journals*, 155.

21 Sylvia Plath, *The Letters of Sylvia Plath, Vol. I: 1940–1956*, ed. Peter K. Steinberg and Karen V. Kukil (London: Faber & Faber), 733.

22 Alexander, *Rough Magic*, 153.

23 Ibid., 147.

24 Diane Middlebrook, *Anne Sexton: A Biography* (London: Virago, 1991), 56.

25 Clara Mucci, "Trauma, Healing and the Reconstruction of Truth," *American Journal of Psychoanalysis* 74, no. 1 (March 2014): 31–47, 35.

26 Mucci, "Trauma, Healing and the Reconstruction of Truth," 36.

27 Middlebrook, *Anne Sexton: A Biography*, 58.

28 Linda Gray Sexton, *Searching for Mercy Street: My Journey Back to My Mother, Anne Sexton* (Boston: Little, Brown, 1994), 38.

29 Anne Sexton, *The Complete Poems* (New York: Mariner Books, 1999), 27.

30 Sexton, *The Complete Poems*, 294. It is worth noting that Dawn Skorczewski points out this slimy imagery is how semen might seem to a child.

31 Sexton, *The Complete Poems*, 328.

32 Gray Sexton, *Searching for Mercy Street*, 38–39.

33 See Robert Timms and Patrick Connors, "Adult Promiscuity Following Childhood Sexual Abuse," *Psychotherapy Patient* 8, no. 1–2 (1992): 19–27.

34   Linda Gray Sexton, notes to author, May 20, 2020. For transcriptions of Sexton's therapy sessions dealing with "Elizabeth," see Middlebrook, 56.

35   Sexton, *A Self-Portrait in Letters*, 75.

36   Linda Gray Sexton, notes to author, May 20, 2020.

37   Skorczewski, *An Accident of Hope*, 146.

38   Linda Gray Sexton, notes to author, May 20, 2020.

39   Information on Boston's queer history from Mark Thomas Krone, "Boston Queer History," https://markthomaskrone .wordpress.com/tag/the-punch-bowl/.

40   Plath, *Journals*, 460. Note that this exchange appears almost word for word in *The Bell Jar*.

41   Sylvia Plath, *The Bell Jar* (London: Faber & Faber, 1986), 232.

42   Ibid.

43   Plath, *Journals*, 528.

44   Ibid., 460.

45   Plath, *The Letters of Sylvia Plath, Vol. II*, 798.

46   Ted Hughes and Frances McCullough, *The Journals of Sylvia Plath* (New York: Ballantine Books, 1982), xii.

47   Plath, too, alluded to masturbation in her poem "Fever 103°."

48   Mona Van Duyn in J. D. McClatchy, *Anne Sexton: The Artist and Her Critics* (Bloomington: Indiana University Press, 1978), 141.

49   Daniel Hughes in McClatchy, *Anne Sexton: The Artist and Her Critics*, 141.

50   Plath, *The Journals of Sylvia Plath*, ed. Karen V. Kukil (London: Faber & Faber, 2000), 174.

51 Sexton, *A Self-Portrait in Letters*, 318.

52 Sexton, *Complete Poems*, 190.

53 Ibid., 190.

54 This photograph is held in Sexton's papers at the Harry Ransom Center, University of Texas.

55 Sylvia Plath, *Collected Poems* (London: Faber & Faber, 1988), 232.

CHAPTER FOUR MARRIAGE

1 Sylvia Plath, *The Letters of Sylvia Plath, Vol. I: 1940–1956*, ed. Peter K. Steinberg and Karen V. Kukil (London: Faber & Faber, 2017), 1165.

2 Anne Sexton, *A Self-Portrait in Letters* (New York: Mariner Books, 2004), 13.

3 See Kristin Celello's book *Making Marriage Work: A History of Marriage and Divorce in the Twentieth-Century United States* (Chapel Hill: University of North Carolina Press, 2009).

4 Sylvia Plath, *The Bell Jar* (London: Faber & Faber, 1986), 79.

5 Plath, *The Bell Jar*, 85.

6 Story told to author by Elizabeth Sigmund.

7 Anne Sexton, *No Evil Star: Selected Essays, Interviews, and Prose* (Ann Arbor: University of Michigan Press, 1985), 84.

8 Diane Middlebrook, *Anne Sexton: A Biography* (London: Virago, 1991), 21.

9 Details here taken from Middlebrook, *Anne Sexton*, 21.

10   Sexton, *A Self-Portrait in Letters*, 13.

11   Ibid.

12   Ibid.

13   Ibid., 14.

14   Ibid., 15.

15   Ibid., 16.

16   Ibid., 18.

17   Linda Gray Sexton, notes to author, May 20, 2020.

18   Sexton, *A Self-Portrait in Letters*, 19.

19   Ibid., 20.

20   Sylvia Plath, The *Journals of Sylvia Plath*, ed. Karen V. Kukil (London: Faber & Faber, 2000), 212.

21   Sylvia Plath, *Collected Poems* (London: Faber & Faber, 1988), 22–23.

22   Plath, *Journals*, 214.

23   Plath, *The Letters of Sylvia Plath, Vol. I*, 1131.

24   Correspondence with Richard Sassoon, Harriet Rosenstein Papers, Box 4, Folder 6, Rose Library, Emory University.

25   From Elaine Feinstein papers, Box 73, EFP 4/4/2, the John Rylands Library, Manchester, UK.

26   Ted Hughes, *Birthday Letters* (London: Faber & Faber, 1998), 24.

27   Plath, *Journals*, 552.

28   *Birthday Letters Manuscripts*, MS88918/1/7, the British Library.

29   Plath, *Journals*, 553.

30   Bloomsday is a celebration and commemoration of the life of the Irish writer James Joyce. June 16 is the day on

which his novel *Ulysses* takes place, but it also commemorates the first date with his wife-to-be, Nora Barnacle.

31 The Hughes scholar Keith Sagar owned a wedding photograph of Plath and Hughes and claimed that Plath's dress resembled a bathrobe.

32 Plath, *The Letters of Sylvia Plath, Vol. I*, 1207.

33 In a strange coincidence, the person living in the apartment above them was a cousin of Richard Sassoon, a fact Plath kept quiet.

34 Interview with Susan Weller Burch, Harriet Rosenstein Papers, Box 1, Folder 13, Rose Library, Emory University.

35 Sylvia Plath, *The Letters of Sylvia Plath, Vol. II: 1956–1963*, ed. Peter K. Steinberg and Karen V. Kukil (London: Faber & Faber, 2018), 110.

36 Middlebrook, *Anne Sexton*, 24.

37 Dawn Skorczewski, *An Accident of Hope: The Therapy Tapes of Anne Sexton* (New York: Routledge, 2012), 113.

38 Middlebrook, *Anne Sexton*, 27.

39 Anne Sexton, *No Evil Star: Selected Essays, Interviews, and Prose* (Ann Arbor: University of Michigan Press, 1985), 84.

40 Sexton, *No Evil Star*, 85.

41 Linda Gray Sexton, notes to author, May 20, 2020.

42 Sexton, *No Evil Star*, 113.

43 Linda Gray Sexton, notes to author, May 20, 2020.

44 Interview with George Gibian, Harriet Rosenstein Papers, Box 1, Folder 30, Rose Library, Emory University.

45 Plath, *Journals*, 391.

46 Ibid., 392.

47 Interview with Leonard Baskin, Harriet Rosenstein Papers, Box 1, Folder 7, Rose Library, Emory University.

48 Sexton, *A Self-Portrait in Letters*, 114.

49 This card is held in the Sexton archives, Box 25, Folder 4, at the Harry Ransom Center, University of Texas.

50 Sexton, *A Self-Portrait in Letters*, 293.

51 Ibid., 168.

52 Linda Gray Sexton, *Searching for Mercy Street: My Journey Back to My Mother, Anne Sexton* (Boston: Little, Brown, 1994), 87.

53 Skorczewski, *An Accident of Hope*, 84.

54 Linda Gray Sexton, notes to author, May 20, 2020.

55 Linda Gray Sexton, *Half in Love: Surviving the Legacy of Suicide* (Berkeley: Counterpoint, 2011) 59.

56 Middlebrook, *Anne Sexton*, 156.

57 Sexton, *A Self-Portrait in Letters*, 352.

58 Frances McCullough papers, notes from July 7, 1974, Box 8, Folder 54, University of Maryland.

59 These figures are taken from the National Domestic Violence Hotline, https://www.thehotline.org/resources/statistics/ (accessed July 28, 2020).

60 Plath, *The Letters of Sylvia Plath, Vol. II*, 793.

61 Ibid., 797.

62 Ibid., 878.

63 Ibid., 878–79.

64 Ibid., 878.

65 Ibid., 879

66 Interview with David Compton, Harriet Rosenstein Papers, Box 1, Folder 18, Rose Library, Emory University.

67 Letter from Edith Hughes to Olwyn Hughes, October 2, 1962, Add MS 88948/2, the British Library.

68 Plath, *The Letters of Sylvia Plath, Vol. II*, xx. The foreword to Volume II is written by Frieda Hughes and describes her reaction to reading the letters her mother wrote to Ruth Beuscher. This is a raw, honest, and stunning piece of writing and essential for understanding the legacy that children of well-known parents have to live with and negotiate.

69 Plath, *Collected Poems*, 227.

70 Plath, *The Letters of Sylvia Plath, Vol. II*, 882.

71 Ibid., 896.

72 Ibid., 827.

73 "The Wedlock," in Anne Sexton, *The Complete Poems* (New York: Mariner Books, 1999), 510.

74 "Waking Alone," in Sexton, *The Complete Poems*, 514–15.

75 Sexton, *A Self-Portrait in Letters*, 419.

76 Linda Gray Sexton to author, May 20, 2020.

77 Plath, *The Letters of Sylvia Plath, Vol. II*, 967.

78 Ibid., 969.

CHAPTER FIVE MOTHERING

1 Sylvia Plath, *Collected Poems* (London: Faber & Faber, 1988), 141.

2 Dawn Skorczewski, *An Accident of Hope: The Therapy Tapes of Anne Sexton* (New York: Routledge, 2012), 6.

3 Plath, *Collected Poems*, 141.

4 Ibid., 185.

5 Linda Gray Sexton, *Searching for Mercy Street: My Journey Back to My Mother, Anne Sexton* (Boston: Little, Brown, 1994), 281.

6 Annie Lloyd, "When the Sexually Abusive Artist Is a Woman," *The Establishment*, February 28, 2018, accessed January 31, 2020, https://medium.com/the-establishment/when-the-sexually-abusive-artist-is-a-woman-b12f6fd49ece.

7 Gray Sexton, *Searching for Mercy Street*, 300.

8 Ibid., 298.

9 Eliza Berman, "Life Before Equal Pay Day: Portrait of a Working Mother in the 1950s," *Time*, April 13, 2015, accessed February 18, 2020, https://time.com/3759822/working-mothe/.

10 Interview with Shirley Norton, Harriet Rosenstein Papers, Box 4, Folder 22, Rose Library, Emory University.

11 Interview with Shirley Norton, Harriet Rosenstein Papers, Box 2, Folder 27, Rose Library, Emory University.

12 Sylvia Plath, *The Journals of Sylvia Plath*, ed. Karen V. Kukil (London: Faber & Faber, 2000), 495.

13 Plath interviewed by Peter Orr, October 30, 1962, British Council.

14 All items held in Box 25, Folder 5, at the Harry Ransom Center, University of Texas.

15 Linda Gray Sexton to author, May 20, 2020.

16 Gray Sexton, *Searching for Mercy Street*, 60.

17 Ibid., 296.

18 Anne Sexton, *No Evil Star: Selected Essays, Interviews, and Prose* (Ann Arbor: University of Michigan Press, 1985), 100–101.

19 Sylvia Plath, *The Letters of Sylvia Plath, Vol. II: 1956–1963*, ed. Peter K. Steinberg and Karen V. Kukil (London: Faber & Faber, 2017), 462.

20 Plath, *The Letters of Sylvia Plath, Vol. II*, 484.

21 Ibid., 469.

22 Ibid., 575–76.

23 Ibid., 830.

24 Ibid., xvi.

25 Ibid., xxi.

26 Plath, *Collected Poems*, 153.

27 Plath, *The Letters of Sylvia Plath, Vol. II*, 714.

28 Ibid., 830. To be fair to Hughes, this letter was written while the marriage was breaking down, and whatever Plath and neighbors were witnessing between Ted Hughes and his son in 1962 did not seem to be a feature for the rest of his life. Hughes and Nicholas had a close father-son relationship after Plath's death.

29 Plath, *The Letters of Sylvia Plath, Vol. II*, 844.

30 Ibid., 830.

31 Plath, *Collected Poems*, 205.

32 Ibid., 237. There was something about this poem that profoundly upset Hughes when he read it after Plath's

death. Although he never fully explained why, he crypti-
cally refers to the candlestick holder as having some deep
personal significance in their marriage.

33 Interview with Susan O'Neill Roe, Harriet Rosenstein
Papers, Box 1, Folder 11, Rose Library, Emory University.

34 Plath, *The Letters of Sylvia Plath, Vol. II*, 883.

35 Gray Sexton, *Searching for Mercy Street*, 26.

36 Plath, *Collected Poems*, 265.

37 Plath, *The Letters of Sylvia Plath, Vol. II*, 969.

CHAPTER SIX WRITING

1 Sylvia Plath, *The Journals of Sylvia Plath*, ed. Karen V.
Kukil (London: Faber & Faber, 2000), 360.

2 Linda Gray Sexton, *Searching for Mercy Street: My Journey Back to My Mother, Anne Sexton* (Boston: Little, Brown,
1994), 130.

3 Anne Sexton, *No Evil Star: Selected Essays, Interviews, and
Prose* (Ann Arbor: University of Michigan Press, 1985),
172–73.

4 Ibid., 179.

5 Florence Margaret Smith (1902–1971) was an English
poet and novelist known as Stevie Smith. In late 1962,
Plath and Smith exchanged letters, and Plath hoped they
might meet for tea when she moved back to London from
Devon. This meeting never happened.

6 Interview with David Compton, Harriet Rosenstein Papers,
Box 1, Folder 18, Rose Library, Emory University.

7   Interview with Elizabeth Sigmund, Harriet Rosenstein Papers, Box 4, Folder 10, Rose Library, Emory University.

8   Sylvia Plath, *Collected Poems* (London: Faber & Faber), 208.

9   Marian Foster, "Devon Days (1959–1963): North Tawton, Dartmoor and Sylvia Plath," accessed February 24, 2020, https://www.robley.org.uk/devon-days.html.

10 Interview with David and Lorna Secker-Walker, Harriet Rosenstein Papers, Box 4, Folder 7, Rose Library, Emory University.

11 Sexton, *No Evil Star*, 87.

12 Ibid., 176–77.

13 Sexton interview with Marjorie Fellow, May 22–23, 1970, Sound Recording C0159, Harry Ransom Center, University of Texas.

14 David Trinidad, "'Two Sweet Ladies': Sexton and Plath's Friendship and Mutual Influence," *American Poetry Review*, November 1, 2006, accessed February 21, 2020, https://www.thefreelibrary.com/%22Two+sweet+ladies%22%3A+Sexton+and+Plath%27s+friendship+and+mutual...-a0155145734.

15 Anne Sexton, *The Barfly Ought to Sing* in *The Art of Sylvia Plath: A Symposium*, ed. Charles Newman (London: Faber & Faber, 1970), 178–79.

16 Letters held in Box 28, Folder 1, at the Harry Ransom Center, University of Texas.

17 Anne Sexton, *A Self-Portrait in Letters* (New York: Mariner Books, 2004), 356.

18 J. D. McClatchy, *Anne Sexton: The Artist and Her Critics* (Bloomington: Indiana University Press, 1978), 113.

19 Plath, *Journals*, 495.

20 Interview with Clarissa Roche, Harriet Rosenstein Papers, Box 3, Folder 14, Rose Library, Emory University.

21 Interview with Peter Orr, October 30, 1962, the British Council.

22 Interview with Anthony Thwaite, Harriet Rosenstein Papers, Box 4, Folder 17, Rose Library, Emory University.

23 BBC Written Archives Centre, Reading, UK.

24 Sexton, *A Self-Portrait in Letters*, 130.

25 Gray Sexton, *Searching for Mercy Street*, 119.

26 Sexton, *A Self-Portrait in Letters*, 163.

27 Ibid., 333.

28 Ibid., 385.

29 Ibid., 393.

30 Anne Sexton to Orlo Strunk Jr., February 15, 1972, Box 28, Folder 1, Harry Ransom Center, University of Texas.

31 Sexton, *A Self-Portrait in Letters*, 74.

32 Ibid., 116.

33 Ibid., 79.

34 Anne Sexton to Mrs. John L. Shek, August 3, 1967, Box 28, Folder 5, Harry Ransom Center, University of Texas.

35 Sexton, *A Self-Portrait in Letters*, 287–88.

36 Ibid., 147.

37 Plath, *Collected Poems*, 142.

38 Plath, *Journals*, 436

39   Sylvia Plath, *The Letters of Sylvia Plath, Vol. II: 1956–1963,* ed. Peter K. Steinberg and Karen V. Kukil (London: Faber & Faber, 2018), 891.

CHAPTER SEVEN   MENTAL ILLNESS

1   Sylvia Plath, *The Journals of Sylvia Plath,* ed. Karen V. Kukil (London: Faber & Faber, 2000), 187.

2   Anne Sexton, *No Evil Star: Selected Essays, Interviews, and Prose* (Ann Arbor: University of Michigan Press, 1985), 84.

3   Sexton, *No Evil Star,* 98.

4   Anne Sexton, *A Self-Portrait in Letters* (New York: Mariner Books, 2004), 396.

5   Interview with Connie Taylor Blackwell, Harriet Rosenstein Papers, Box 1, Folder 9, Rose Library, Emory University.

6   Records from Wellesley Police Department, Wellesley, MA, in "Sylvia Plath Collections: Wellesley Police Department Records," by Peter K. Steinberg, *Sylvia Plath Info Blog,* posted October 10, 2016, accessed November 29, 2017, http://sylviaplathinfo.blogspot.co.uk/2016/10 /sylvia-plath-collections-wellesley.html.

7   Sylvia Plath, *The Letters of Sylvia Plath, Vol. I: 1940–1956,* ed. Peter K. Steinberg and Karen V. Kukil (London: Faber & Faber, 2017), 642.

8   Sylvia Plath, *The Bell Jar* (London: Faber & Faber, 1986), 3.

9   Plath, *The Bell Jar,* 117.

10   Plath took this rejection badly and saw herself as not good enough to make the class. Years later, a distraught Frank

O'Connor revealed that he had rejected her from the class because she seemed way too advanced and well published and would have outshone all the other students.

11 All journal quotes taken from my archival notes in order to describe the appearance of Plath's writing but can be found in *The Journals of Sylvia Plath* (London: Faber & Faber, 2000), 186–87.

12 Information obtained from a letter written by Aurelia Plath to Olive Higgins Prouty, September 29, 1953, held in the Lilly Library, Indiana University.

13 Sylvia Plath, *Collected Poems* (London: Faber & Faber, 1988), 141.

14 Plath, *The Bell Jar*, 151.

15 Ibid. 178–79.

16 Plath, *The Letters of Sylvia Plath, Vol. I*, 656.

17 See a full summary of all known articles in national and local papers at https://www.sylviaplath.info/fsa.html, accessed April 27, 2020.

18 Plath, *The Letters of Sylvia Plath, Vol. I*, 656.

19 Ibid.

20 Paul Alexander, *Rough Magic: A Biography of Sylvia Plath* (New York: Penguin, 1991), 129–30.

21 Linda Gray Sexton, *Half in Love: Surviving the Legacy of Suicide* (Berkeley: Counterpoint, 2011), 103.

22 Sexton, *A Self-Portrait in Letters*, 51.

23 Linda Gray Sexton, *Searching for Mercy Street: My Journey Back to My Mother, Anne Sexton* (Boston: Little, Brown, 1994), 151.

24 Gray Sexton, *Searching for Mercy Street*, 92.

25 Gray Sexton, *Half in Love*, 70.

26 Sexton, *A Self-Portrait in Letters*, 95.

27 Sexton, *The Complete Poems*, (New York: Mariner Books), 3.

28 Interview with Marjorie Fellow, May 22–23, 1970, Sound Recordings C0159, Harry Ransom Center, University of Texas.

29 Letter from Sexton addressed to "Dear Sport's Writer" (real name unknown), April 10, 1963, Box 17, Folder 1, Harry Ransom Center, University of Texas.

30 Gray Sexton, *Half in Love*, 47.

31 Sexton, *Complete Poems*, 99.

32 This information, with photographs, can be found in "Sylvia Plath and McLean Hospital," by Peter K. Steinberg, *Sylvia Plath Info Blog*, posted October 20, 2016, accessed December 13, 2017, http://sylviaplathinfo.blogspot.co.uk /2016/10/sylvia-plath-and-mclean-hospital.html.

33 Later known as Ruth Tiffany Barnhouse (1923–1999).

34 Alexander, *Rough Magic*, 130.

35 Sylvia Plath, *Johnny Panic and the Bible of Dreams* (London: Faber & Faber, 1977), 268.

36 Plath, *The Bell Jar*, 212–13.

37 Plath, *Johnny Panic and the Bible of Dreams*, 268.

38 This was confirmed by Suzanne Demko, clinical team leader, FDA, who wrote, "The first marketing approvals for Thorazine in the US were on September 18, 1957 (for capsules) and November 20, 1957 (for tablets, injections) under New Drug Applications (NDA) 011120 and 009149,

respectively. This means that any use in the US before the earliest date had to be investigational, or for experimental purposes. Even if it was approved for marketing elsewhere in the world, its use would have been illegal in the US other than under an IND application (investigational new drug), which was necessary for investigational purposes." Email exchange with author, April 26, 2020.

39 Sexton, *A Self-Portrait in Letters*, 259.

40 Anne Sexton to Lois Ames, February 1969, Box 17, Folder 3, Harry Ransom Center, University of Texas.

41 After Sexton's death, when her daughters, Linda and Joy, cleaned out her closet and bathroom, they found enormous jugs of drugs, the type that pharmacists use for bulk storage. Her psychiatrists had been prescribing in large quantities and she had stored enough to easily kill herself. Linda noted, "I do not understand how any good, reputable physician would do such a thing with a patient who was suicidal. It still makes me angry. As you can see, our earlier 'fears' were well founded." Notes to author, July 30, 2020.

42 Sexton, *A Self-Portrait in Letters*, 239.

43 Anne Sexton to Anne Wilder, January 1966, Box 43, Folders 5–8, Harry Ransom Center, University of Texas.

44 Alexander, *Rough Magic*, 134.

45 Plath, *The Letters of Sylvia Plath, Vol. I*, 651.

46 Ruth Tiffany Barnhouse cited in Alex Beam, *Gracefully Insane: Life and Death Inside America's Premier Mental Hospital* (New York: PublicAffairs, 2001), 155.

47 See the Jane Anderson papers held at Smith College.

48 Pages from Plath's medical record were stolen by Ruth Beuscher when she stopped working at McLean and appeared for sale with the Harriet Rosenstein Papers, now held at the Rose Library, Emory University.

49 Plath, *The Letters of Sylvia Plath, Vol. I*, 657.

50 Ibid.

51 Ibid., 658.

52 Ibid., 652.

53 Ibid., 665.

54 Ibid.

55 These hospital notes are now held at the Rose Library, Emory University.

56 Sexton, *A Self-Portrait in Letters*, 81.

57 Ibid., 267.

58 Sexton, *No Evil Star*, 71.

59 Sexton, *A Self-Portrait in Letters*, 255.

60 Plath, *The Letters of Sylvia Plath, Vol. I*, 674.

CHAPTER EIGHT SUICIDE

1 Sylvia Plath, *The Letters of Sylvia Plath, Vol. II: 1956–1963*, ed. Peter K. Steinberg and Karen V. Kukil (London: Faber & Faber, 2018), 968.

2 Anne Sexton, *A Self-Portrait in Letters* (New York: Mariner Books, 2004), 424.

3 Anne Sexton, *The Barfly Ought to Sing* in *The Art of Sylvia Plath: A Symposium*, ed. Charles Newman (London: Faber & Faber, 1970), 177.

4 Al Alvarez, *The Savage God: A Study of Suicide* (London: Penguin, 1971), 299.

5 Ibid., 35.

6 Interview with John Horder, Harriet Rosenstein Papers, Box 2, Folder 2, Rose Library, Emory University.

7 Ted Hughes to Olwyn Hughes, undated, Olwyn Hughes Papers, Add MS 88948/1/1, the British Library.

8 Plath, *The Letters of Sylvia Plath, Vol. II*, 968.

9 Ibid.

10 Interview with Elizabeth Sigmund, Harriet Rosenstein Papers, Box 4, Folder 10, Rose Library, Emory University.

11 Alvarez, *The Savage God*, 33.

12 Email correspondence between the author and Marian Foster, May 2015.

13 Linda Gray Sexton, *Searching for Mercy Street: My Journey Back to My Mother, Anne Sexton* (Boston: Little, Brown, 1994), 168.

14 Sexton, *A Self-Portrait in Letters*, 378.

15 Gray Sexton, *Searching for Mercy Street*, 114.

16 Ibid., 123.

17 Sexton interview with Marjorie Fellow, May 22–23, 1970, Sound Recording C0159, Harry Ransom Center, University of Texas.

18 Trevor Thomas, *Last Encounters: A Memoir of Sylvia Plath* (Bedford, UK: privately published, 1989), 10.

19 Alvarez, *The Savage God*, 48.

20 Interview with Catherine Frankfort, Harriet Rosenstein Papers, Box 1, Folder 27, Rose Library, Emory University.

21 Interview with Lorna Secker-Walker, Harriet Rosenstein Papers, Box 4, Folder 7, Rose Library, Emory University.

22 Sylvia Plath, *Collected Poems* (London: Faber & Faber, 1988), 271.

23 Interview with Lorna Secker-Walker, Harriet Rosenstein Papers, Box 4, Folder 7, Rose Library, Emory University.

24 Assia Wevill had an abortion in March 1963.

25 Interview with Anthony Thwaite, Harriet Rosenstein Papers, Box 4, Folder 17, Rose Library, Emory University.

26 Edward Butscher, *Sylvia Plath: The Woman and the Work* (New York: Dodd, Mead and Company, 1977), 107.

27 Dawn Skorczewski, *An Accident of Hope: The Therapy Tapes of Anne Sexton* (New York: Routledge, 2012), 192.

28 Sexton, *A Self-Portrait in Letters*, 261.

29 Anne Sexton, *The Complete Poems* (New York: Mariner Books, 1999), 126.

30 Sexton, *A Self-Portrait in Letters*, 262.

31 Gray Sexton, *Searching for Mercy Street*, 222.

32 Sexton, *A Self-Portrait in Letters*, 261.

33 Anne Sexton to Al Alvarez, June 6, 1963, Box 17, Folder 2, Harry Ransom Center, University of Texas.

34 Al Alvarez to Anne Sexton, August 4, 1963, Box 17, Folder 2, Harry Ransom Center, University of Texas.

35 Anne Sexton to George MacBeth, June 4, 1973, Box 22, Folder 4, Harry Ransom Center, University of Texas.

36 Gray Sexton, *Searching for Mercy Street*, 174.

37 Ibid., 179.

38 Linda Gray Sexton, notes to author, May 20, 2020.

39 J. D. McClatchy, *Anne Sexton: The Artist and Her Critics* (Bloomington: Indiana University Press, 1978), 101.

40 Gray Sexton, *Searching for Mercy Street*, 295.

41 Sylvia Plath, *Johnny Panic and the Bible of Dreams* (London: Faber & Faber, 1977), 93.

42 Sexton, *A Self-Portrait in Letters*, 415.

EPILOGUE

1 Sylvia Plath interviewed by Peter Orr, October 30, 1962. "A 1962 Sylvia Plath Interview with Peter Orr," *Modern American Poetry*, February 3, 2014, https://www.modern americanpoetry.org/content/1962-sylvia-plath-interview -peter-orr.

2 Sylvia Plath, *The Letters of Sylvia Plath, Vol. II: 1956–1963*, ed. Peter K. Steinberg and Karen V. Kukil (London: Faber & Faber, 2017), 913.

3 Ibid., 859.

4 Sylvia Plath, *Johnny Panic and the Bible of Dreams* (London: Faber & Faber, 1977), 11.

5 Conversations and emails between Al Alvarez and the author.

6 Nicholas Hughes died by suicide at his home in Fairbanks, Alaska, on March 16, 2009.

7 Plath, *The Letters of Sylvia Plath, Vol. II*, xv.

8 Ibid., 844.

9 Ibid., xxv.

10   Diane Middlebrook, *Anne Sexton: A Biography* (London: Virago, 1991), xvi.

11   Sexton interview with Marjorie Fellow, May 22–23, 1970, Sound Recording C0159, Harry Ransom Center, University of Texas.

12   Anne Sexton, *The Complete Poems* (New York: Mariner Books, 1999), 6.

13   Plath, *The Letters of Sylvia Plath, Vol. II*, xxiv.

14   Linda Gray Sexton, *Half in Love: Surviving the Legacy of Suicide* (Berkeley: Counterpoint, 2011), 18.

Bibliography

PRIMARY SOURCES

Plath, Sylvia. *Johnny Panic and the Bible of Dreams.* London: Faber & Faber, 1977.

Plath, Sylvia. *The Journals of Sylvia Plath.* Edited by Ted Hughes and Frances McCullough. New York: Ballantine Books, 1982.

Plath, Sylvia. *The Bell Jar.* London: Faber & Faber, 1986. First published 1963.

Plath, Sylvia. *Collected Poems.* London: Faber & Faber, 1988.

Plath, Sylvia. *Letters Home.* Edited by Aurelia Schober Plath. London: Faber & Faber, 1988.

Plath, Sylvia. *The Journals of Sylvia Plath.* Edited by Karen V. Kukil. London: Faber & Faber, 2000.

Plath, Sylvia. *Ariel: The Restored Edition.* London: Faber & Faber, 2004.

Plath, Sylvia. *The Letters of Sylvia Plath, Volume I: 1940–1956.* Edited by Peter K. Steinberg and Karen V. Kukil. London: Faber & Faber, 2017.

Plath, Sylvia. *The Letters of Sylvia Plath, Volume II: 1956–1963.* Edited by Peter K. Steinberg and Karen V. Kukil. London: Faber & Faber, 2018.

Sexton, Anne. *No Evil Star: Selected Essays, Interviews, and Prose.* Ann Arbor: University of Michigan Press, 1985.

Sexton, Anne. *The Complete Poems of Anne Sexton.* New York: Mariner Books, 1999.

Sexton, Anne. *A Self-Portrait in Letters.* New York: Mariner Books, 2004.

BIOGRAPHICAL SOURCES

Alexander, Paul. *Rough Magic: A Biography of Sylvia Plath.* New York: Penguin, 1991.

Becker, Jillian. *Giving Up: The Last Days of Sylvia Plath.* London: Ferrington, 2003.

Bronfen, Elisabeth. *Sylvia Plath.* Plymouth: Northcote House Publishers, 1998.

Bundtzen, Lynda K. *The Other Ariel.* Stroud: Sutton Publishing, 2005. First published 2001.

Butscher, Edward. *Sylvia Plath: The Woman and the Work.* New York: Dodd, Mead and Company, 1977.

Davison, Peter. *The Fading Smile: Poets in Boston, from Robert Frost to Robert Lowell to Sylvia Plath, 1955–1960.* New York: Knopf, 1994.

Hayman, Ronald. *The Death and Life of Sylvia Plath.* London: Heinemann, 1991.

Middlebrook, Diane. *Anne Sexton: A Biography*. London: Virago, 1991.

Middlebrook, Diane. *Her Husband: Hughes and Plath, A Marriage*. London: Viking, 2003.

Orr, Peter, et al. *The Poet Speaks: Interviews with Contemporary Poets Conducted by Hilary Morrish, Peter Orr, John Press and Ian Scott-Kilvert*. London: Routledge & Kegan Paul, 1966.

Rollyson, Carl. *American Isis: The Life and Art of Sylvia Plath*. New York: St. Martin's Press, 2013.

Sexton, Linda Gray. *Searching for Mercy Street: My Journey Back to My Mother, Anne Sexton*. Boston: Little, Brown, 1994.

Sexton, Linda Gray. *Half in Love: Surviving the Legacy of Suicide*. Berkeley: Counterpoint, 2011.

Sigmund, Elizabeth, and Gail Crowther. *Sylvia Plath in Devon: A Year's Turning*. Stroud, UK: Fonthill Media, 2014.

Skorczewski, Dawn M. *An Accident of Hope: The Therapy Tapes of Anne Sexton*. New York: Routledge, 2012.

Spivack, Kathleen. "Poets and Friends." *Boston Globe Magazine*, August 9, 1981.

Spivack, Kathleen. *With Robert Lowell and His Circle: Sylvia Plath, Anne Sexton, Elizabeth Bishop, Stanley Kunitz, & Others*. Boston: Northeastern University Press, 2012.

Steinberg, Peter K. *Sylvia Plath* (Great Writers). Philadelphia: Chelsea House, 2004.

Steiner, Nancy Hunter. *A Closer Look at Ariel: A Memory of Sylvia Plath*. New York: Harper's Magazine Press, 1973.

Stevenson, Anne. *Bitter Fame: A Life of Sylvia Plath.* London: Viking, 1989.

Thomas, Trevor. *Last Encounters: A Memoir of Sylvia Plath.* Privately published. Bedford, UK, 1989. (My own copy numbered 131 and signed.)

Wagner-Martin, Linda. *Sylvia Plath: A Biography.* London: Chatto & Windus, 1988.

Wilson, Andrew. *Mad Girl's Love Song: Sylvia Plath and Life Before Ted.* London: Simon & Schuster, 2013.

GENERAL BIBLIOGRAPHY

Alvarez, Al. *The Savage God: A Study of Suicide.* London: Weidenfeld & Nicolson, 1971.

Badia, Janet. *Sylvia Plath and the Mythology of Women Readers.* Amherst and Boston: University of Massachusetts Press, 2011.

Banita, Georgiana. "The Same, Identical Woman: Sylvia Plath in the Media." *Journal of the Midwest Modern Language Association* 40, no. 2 (Fall 2007): 38–60.

Bate, Jonathan. *Ted Hughes: The Unauthorised Life.* New York: HarperCollins, 2015.

Beam, Alex. *Gracefully Insane: Life and Death Inside America's Premier Mental Hospital.* New York: PublicAffairs, 2001.

Berman, Eliza. "Life Before Equal Pay Day: Portrait of a Working Mother in the 1950s," *Time,* April 13, 2015. https://time.com/3759822/working-mothe/.

Boyne, John. "Women Are Better Writers Than Men." *Guardian*, December 12, 2017. https://www.theguardian.com /books/2017/dec/12/double-x-factor-why-women-are -better-writers-than-men.

Bronfen, Elisabeth. *Over Her Dead Body: Death, Femininity and the Aesthetic.* Manchester, UK: Manchester University Press, 1992.

Colburn, Stephen, ed. *Anne Sexton: Telling the Tale.* Ann Arbor: University of Michigan Press, 1988.

Contreras, Crystal. "It's Time We Had A Talk About 'The Bell Jar,' The White Feminist, Racist Literary Icon." *Willamette Week*, October 4, 2017, https://www.wweek.com/arts/books /2017/10/04/its-time-we-had-a-talk-about-the-bell-jar-the -white-feminist-racist-literary-icon/.

Crowther, Gail, *The Haunted Reader and Sylvia Plath.* Stroud, UK: Fonthill Media, 2017.

Crowther, Gail, and Peter K. Steinberg. *These Ghostly Archives: The Unearthing of Sylvia Plath.* Stroud, UK: Fonthill Media, 2017.

Doherty, Maggie. *The Equivalents. A Story of Art, Female Friendship, and Liberation in the 1960s.* New York: Knopf, 2020.

Feinstein, Elaine. *Ted Hughes: The Life of a Poet.* London: Weidenfeld & Nicolson, 2001.

Furst, Arthur. *Anne Sexton: The Last Summer.* New York: St. Martin's Press, 2000.

George, Diana Hume, ed. *Sexton: Selected Criticism.* Chicago: University of Chicago Press, 1988.

Goh, Katie. "'I Made Lemonade': The Female Confessional in the Twenty-First Century." *Inciting Sparks*, October 31, 2016. https://incitingsparks.org/2016/10/31/i-made -lemonade-the-female-confessional-in-the-twenty-first -century/.

Golden, Amanda, ed. *This Business of Words: Reassessing Anne Sexton*. Florida: University Press of Florida, 2016.

Helle, Anita, ed. *The Unraveling Archive: Essays on Sylvia Plath*. Ann Arbor: University of Michigan, 2007.

Hillman, James. *Suicide and the Soul*. Dallas, TX: Spring Publications, 1976.

Hockey, Jenny, Jeanne Katz, and Neil Small, eds. *Grief, Mourning and Death Ritual*. Buckingham, UK: Open University Press, 2001.

Hoffman, Nancy Jo. "Reading Women's Poetry: The Meaning and Our Lives." *College English* 34, no. 1 (October 1972): 48–62.

Holbrook, David. *Sylvia Plath: Poetry and Existence*. London: Athlone Press, 1991. First published 1976.

Hu, Jane C. "The Overwhelming Gender Bias in *New York Times* Book Reviews." *Pacific Standard*, August 28, 2017. https://psmag.com/social-justice/gender-bias-in-book -reviews.

Hughes, Olwyn. "The Plath Myth and the Reviewing of *Bitter Fame*." *Poetry Review* 80, no 3. (Fall 1990): 61–63.

Hughes, Ted. *Birthday Letters*. London: Faber & Faber, 1998.

Hughes, Ted. *The Letters of Ted Hughes*. Edited by Christopher Reid. London: Faber & Faber, 2007.

Kane, Julie. "Julie Kane on Anne Sexton." *The Dark Horse.* https://www.thedarkhorsemagazine.com/Featured/Julie-Kane-on-Anne-Sexton.

Kendall, Tim. *Sylvia Plath: A Critical Study.* London: Faber & Faber, 2001.

Krone, Mark Thomas. "Boston Queer History." https://markthomaskrone.wordpress.com/tag/the-punch-bowl/. Originally published in *Boston Spirit* magazine, September/October 2014.

Lawler, Steph. *Mothering the Self: Mothers, Daughters, Subjects.* London and New York: Routledge, 2000.

Lloyd, Annie. "When the Sexually Abusive Artist Is a Woman." *The Establishment,* February 28, 2018. https://medium.com/the-establishment/when-the-sexually-abusive-artist-is-a-woman-b12f6fd49ece.

Lowe, Bridget Anna. "Burning Free: Sylvia Plath's Summer 1962 Bonfires and the Strange Case of the Surviving Christmas Card." *Plath Profiles* 5 (Summer 2012): 57–82.

Malcolm, Janet. *The Silent Woman: Sylvia Plath and Ted Hughes.* New York: Knopf, 1994.

Meyerowitz, Joanne. "The Liberal 1950s? Reinterpreting Postwar American Sexual Culture." In *Gender and the Long Postwar: Reconsiderations of the United States and the Two Germanys, 1945–1989,* edited by Karen Hagemann and Sonya Michel, 295–317. Washington, D.C.: Johns Hopkins University Press and Woodrow Wilson Center Press, 2014.

Moses, Kate. *Wintering: A Novel of Sylvia Plath.* New York: St. Martin's Press, 2003.

Mucci, Clara. "Trauma, Healing and the Reconstruction of Truth." *American Journal of Psychoanalysis* 74, no. 1 (March 2014): 31–47.

Neville, Jill. *Last Ferry to Manly.* Victoria, Australia: Penguin, 1984.

Newman, Charles, ed. *The Art of Sylvia Plath: A Symposium.* London: Faber & Faber, 1970.

Peel, Robin. *Writing Back: Sylvia Plath and Cold War Politics.* London: Associated University Presses, 2002.

Rose, Jacqueline. *The Haunting of Sylvia Plath.* London: Virago, 1991.

Steedman, Carolyn. *Dust.* Manchester, UK: Manchester University Press, 2001.

Timms, Robert J., and Patrick Connors. "Adult Promiscuity Following Childhood Sexual Abuse." *Psychotherapy Patient* 8, no. 1–2 (1992): 19–27.

Trinidad, David. "'Two Sweet Ladies': Sexton and Plath's Friendship and Mutual Influence." *American Poetry Review*, November 1, 2006.

Wagner, Erica. *Ariel's Gift: Ted Hughes, Sylvia Plath, and the Story of* Birthday Letters. London: Faber & Faber, 2000.

Wagner-Martin, Linda, ed. *Sylvia Plath: The Critical Heritage.* London: Routledge, 1988.

Willoughby, Vanessa. "Black Girls Don't Read Sylvia Plath." *Medium*, November 12, 2014, https://medium.com/the -hairpin/black-girls-dont-read-sylvia-plath-1a8034c986b6.